P9-CIV-028

BORDER PATROL EXAM

BORDER PATROL EXAM

4th Edition

LEARNINGEXPRESS ®

NEW YORK

Library of Congress Cataloging-in-Publication Data:
Border patrol exam.—4th ed. / [contributor, Joseph N. Dassaro].
        p. cm.
   In English, Spanish, or an undetermined artificial language.
   ISBN 1-57685-672-0 (978-1-57685-672-7)
   1. United States. Immigration Border Patrol—Examinations—Study guides.   2. Civil service—United
States—Examinations—Study guides.   I. Dassaro, Joseph N.   II. LearningExpress (Organization)
   JV6483.B66   2008
   363.28'5076—dc22

                                                                                          2008037008

Printed in the United States of America

9 8 7 6 5 4 3 2 1

Regarding the Information in this Book

We attempt to verify the information presented in our books prior to publication. It is always a good idea,
however, to double-check such important information as minimum requirements, application, and testing
procedures and deadlines with the Department of Homeland Security (DHS).

For information or to place an order, contact LearningExpress at:
   LearningExpress
   2 Rector Street
   26th Floor
   New York, NY 10006

Or visit us at:
   www.learnatest.com

About the Contributor ▶

Joseph N. Dassaro entered on duty with the U.S. Border Patrol in 1992 and served 13 years as a Senior Border Patrol Agent in Imperial Beach, CA. During his career, he worked as a field agent and an intelligence agent and was a member of the Border Patrol Criminal Alien Program (BORCAP). He holds a master's degree in legal and ethical studies and is currently a labor relations consultant.

Contents

BORDER PATROL EXAM

1 ▶ Becoming a Border Patrol Agent

CHAPTER SUMMARY

If you think you might like to pursue a career as a U.S. Border Patrol Agent, this chapter is the starting point for your journey. It provides a glimpse into the exciting and dangerous world of federal law enforcement with the U.S. Border Patrol. You'll also find out how to locate and apply for job openings, what the job requirements are, and what training you will need.

THE U.S. BORDER PATROL is a highly trained and extremely mobile uniformed federal law enforcement organization that relies on the latest law enforcement training techniques and operational technologies to prevent terrorists and illegal aliens from entering the country. It also prevents smuggling activities and handles the deportation of criminal aliens. The organization is statutorily authorized to enforce myriad federal laws anywhere in the United States and its possessions, which makes it the premier uniformed federal law enforcement agency. Border Patrol Agents operate in all types of environments—from remote areas of the southern border to the highly urbanized downtown areas of cities such as San Diego, CA. Today more than ever, the men and women of the U.S. Border Patrol are relied on to protect the borders of the United States. Today's Border Patrol Agent represents the convergence of tradition, modern technology, advanced training, and unique skills.

▶ A Short History of the U.S. Border Patrol

In order to fully understand all aspects of the Border Patrol Agent position, it is necessary to briefly review its proud tradition. As early as 1904, the U.S. Immigration Service assigned a token force of mounted inspectors to patrol the southern border of the United States to prevent illegal crossings. The officers were untrained and few in number, and authorities were unable to stem the rising tide of illegal aliens. In March 1915, Congress authorized a separate group of inspectors called mounted guards, or mounted inspectors, who operated from El Paso, TX. These guards, who never numbered more than 75, rode on horseback and patrolled as far west as California.

On May 28, 1924, Congress established the U.S. Border Patrol as part of the Immigration Bureau, a division of the Department of Labor. In 1925, patrol areas were expanded to include over 2,000 miles of seacoast extending along the Gulf and Florida coasts.

Initially, the Border Patrol recruited many of the early force of 450 officers from the Texas Rangers and local sheriffs and their deputies. These officers knew the land and the dangers it presented. Appointees from the Civil Service Register of Railroad Mail Clerks supplemented this rough-and-ready crew. The U.S. government initially provided the Border Patrol Agents a badge, a revolver, and an annual salary of $1,680.

Since its inception, the Border Patrol has achieved an almost legendary status in the law enforcement community. As in the past, Border Patrol Agents today continue to provide a critical service as their duties have evolved to encompass much more than preventing illegal entry into the United States.

▶ What the Work of a Border Patrol Agent Is Really About

Even today, the work of a Border Patrol Agent is difficult, diverse, and, more often than not, extremely hazardous. This position is best suited to the rugged individualist who is self-assured, well educated, and well trained. The important task of protecting our sovereign borders in a humane and compassionate way, consistent with American ideals and security needs, has assumed an entirely new dynamic in a post-9/11 environment. So if you think this type of occupation is for you and you are prepared for the challenge of your life, read on!

Important Website Addresses

To find the latest information on all available federal law enforcement positions, including U.S. Border Patrol Agent, visit www.usa jobs.gov.

To determine whether you are veterans' preference eligible, visit www.dol.gov/elaws/ vets/vetpref/mservice.htm.

▶ Salary and Benefits

As a Border Patrol Agent, you will receive all the benefits of federal employment. The generous benefits package includes vacation and sick leave, health and life insurance, and a special law enforcement retirement plan (also referred to as 6c) that offers retirement at age 50 after at least 20 years of service or retirement at any age after 25 years of service. Although not as generous as many law enforcement packages (which provide retirement pay of 3% multiplied by the number of years of service), this retirement plan is generally competitive with the private sector and includes pension and savings plans to form a multitiered, diversified retirement portfolio.

New Border Patrol Agents are always recruited at the GL-5, GL-7, or GL-9 level unless they are transferring from another federal agency. Where you start on the pay scale will depend on your previous education and experience in law enforcement. Salaries are significantly higher in certain metropolitan areas (like San Diego, CA). However, in general, annual starting salaries begin at around $35,000 and rapidly increase. Senior Patrol Agents routinely earn in excess of $70,000 per year, while Supervisory Patrol Agents routinely earn in excess of $80,000 per year. Keep in mind that special overtime provisions known as Administratively Uncontrollable Overtime (AUO) increase the pay of Border Patrol Agents by 25%. Additionally, Border Patrol Agents, like many other law enforcement positions, receive Fair Labor Standards Act (FLSA) pay, which also increases pay depending on the number of hours by which you exceed the normal workweek.

▶ Education and Experience Requirements for Border Patrol Agent Positions

The following table shows the amounts of education and/or experience required to qualify for Border Patrol Agent positions.

	EDUCATION	OR EXPERIENCE	
GRADE		GENERAL	SPECIALIZED
GL-5	four-year course of study above high school leading to a bachelor's degree	one year equivalent to at least GL-4	none
GL-7	one full academic year of graduate education or law school *or* superior academic achievement	none	one year equivalent to at least GL-5
GL-9	none	none	one year equivalent to at least GL-7
GL-11	none	none	one year equivalent to at least GL-9
GL-12 and above	none	none	one year equivalent to at least next lower grade level

Equivalent combinations of education and experience are qualifying for grade levels for which both education and experience are acceptable. Note that academic study may be prorated to allow combinations of education and experience that total one year for GL-5 (e.g., one year of college study is equivalent to three months of general experience, two years of study to six months of general experience, and three years of study to nine months of general experience).

Source: Office of Personnel Management, www.opm.gov/qualifications/SEC-IV/B/GS1800/1896.htm.

Under the accelerated promotion program, after six and a half months at the GL-5 entry level, you will be eligible for promotion to GL-7; individuals hired at the GL-7 level are eligible for promotion to GL-9. Thanks to a legislative lobbying effort by their union, Border Patrol Agents are now promoted noncompetitively to the GL-11 Journeyman level grade. However, these promotions are contingent upon new agents successfully completing their six- and ten-month probationary exams as well as the field training segment of the training program.

Where the Jobs Are

Due to overwhelming illegal immigration originating from our southern border, first duty stations of new Border Patrol Agents are almost always along the Southwest United States/Mexico border in California, Arizona, New Mexico, and Texas. Many initial assignments are located in small, isolated communities, and transfers from initial duty assignments are limited and normally at your own expense.

It is important that prospective agents consider the impact on their families of moving to an isolated community along the border where healthcare access, educational resources, entertainment, and housing may be extremely limited. This cultural shift is most prevalent in families relocating from highly urbanized areas such as New York City to remote locations like Eagle Pass, TX. In cases in which agents are first assigned to large metropolitan areas such as San Diego or Riverside County, CA, prospective agents should consider the cost of housing in local markets to avoid sticker shock. It is always a good idea to first visit the location where you may be assigned prior to formally accepting a position.

Trainee agents are not routinely assigned to their hometowns or within commuting distance of their hometowns. Accordingly, when considering a position, be prepared for a complete household move. This move will be at your own cost (certain expenses may be tax deductible; check with your accountant).

What Makes a Good Candidate?

The task of a Border Patrol Agent is vital to the security of our country, inherently interesting, and exciting for the adventurous among us. If you are disciplined, physically fit, and up for a challenge, this position may be for you. Men and women leaving the military, recent college graduates, and current law enforcement officers are particularly good candidates for this position. Finally, because many local and federal law enforcement agencies seek the traits and training inherent in a Border Patrol Agent position and actively recruit agents, the U.S. Border Patrol often serves as an entry-level law enforcement position. Many Border Patrol Agents routinely move on to other positions throughout the federal government, including U.S. marshal, federal air marshal, drug enforcement agent, special agent, Naval Criminal Investigative Service, Federal Bureau of Investigation, U.S. Secret Service, and even the Central Intelligence Agency.

Duties of a Border Patrol Agent

Border Patrol Agents are employed by the Department of Homeland Security (DHS)'s Bureau of Customs and Border Protection (CBP). Agents predominantly work to deter terrorism and prevent smuggling and illegal entry of aliens into the country. The duties of an agent include the following: patrolling urban and remote areas to apprehend persons seen or suspected of crossing the border illegally, conducting train checks, examining vehicles both at the border and at interior checkpoints, conducting surveillance of areas of the border, preparing intelligence reports and assessments, and conducting drug interdiction efforts. Agents also serve on Joint Terrorism Task Forces, joint operations with other law enforcement agencies, surveillance teams, extradition teams, and various intelligence operations. Many Border Patrol sectors utilize watercraft for patrol activities, particularly in California and Florida.

Although most people normally associate a Border Patrol Agent's duties with the external boundaries of the continental United States, Border Patrol Agents are authorized to engage in federal law enforcement activities anywhere in the United States, including Hawaii, Guam, Alaska, and Puerto Rico. Consequently, Border Patrol Agents can be found in many interior locations of the United States at permanent and temporary checkpoints, major cities, airports, and even attached to some local law enforcement agencies. Following the tragic events of September 11, 2001, Border Patrol Agents were deployed nationwide at U.S. airports as well as aboard commercial flights. Finally, Border Patrol Agents are one of the few law enforcement positions authorized to carry firearms anywhere in the United States and aboard commercial aircraft in flight. Border Patrol Agents are also considered a quasi-national police force capable of rapid full-scale deployment anywhere in the country to represent the interests of the U.S. government. Agents have been deployed in desegregation efforts during the Civil Rights era, in Los Angeles during the riots that followed the Rodney King trial, and even in the Elian Gonzalez reunification operation.

An example of one of the most routine daily activities of a Border Patrol Agent is linewatch. This activity involves the detection, prevention, and apprehension of undocumented aliens and smugglers of aliens at or near the land border by maintaining strict surveillance from predominantly covert positions; following up on intelligence; responding to electronic sensor alarms; using infrared scopes during night operations; operating low-light level television systems; responding to aircraft sightings; and interpreting and following tracks, marks, and other physical evidence. Some of the other major responsibilities are farm and ranch check, traffic check, traffic observation, city patrol, and transportation check. Duties may be administrative, intelligence related, undercover operations, or antismuggling activities.

An agent's job normally involves significant physical exertion under harsh environmental conditions, often requiring exposure to extreme weather for extended periods of time. Border Patrol Agents are well known for their ability to engage suspects in protracted foot chases as well as their ability to track suspects over extended terrain. In recent years, agents have apprehended a million or more illegal aliens per year with as few as 5,200 agents nationwide. Most agents rarely work in pairs, and it is not uncommon for a single agent to arrest 20 or more illegal aliens without assistance at one time. It is routinely noted that Border Patrol Agents singlehandedly operate in an environment that most law enforcement agencies consider a riot situation. Agents may routinely encounter an illegal alien looking for work or criminal aliens evading arrest warrants. In recent years, Border Patrol Agents have begun encountering extreme foreign criminal elements, including terrorists and violent gang members. Most recently, Border Patrol Agents have even engaged in running gun battles with elements of the Mexican military suspected of conducting screen operations for drug cartels.

There are a great many unofficial sources of information for those considering the position of Border Patrol Agent. These sources of information are primarily Internet based and managed by current or former Border Patrol Agents. There is even a moderated Internet message board where you can talk to real Border Patrol Agents and ask questions. Here are a few sources recommended by Border Patrol Agents:

- **www.nbpc1613.org.** This is the official website of the largest Border Patrol Agents association. It provides information on the latest workplace issues affecting Border Patrol Agents, pay, legislation, and general inside information regarding the work of agents.
- **www.honorfirst.com.** This unofficial Border Patrol website is managed by a highly regarded former Border Patrol Agent. Current and former Border Patrol Agents recommend this site because it consolidates real-world information regarding testing, positions, academy schedules, and pay and benefits, and even includes an online message board (moderated by active Border Patrol Agents) to talk to real agents or with other applicants.

Border Patrol Agents make critical decisions—often in split seconds—that require excellent reasoning and critical decision-making skills. As with any law enforcement officer, decisions made by Border Patrol Agents in split seconds are subject to years of scrutiny and legal analysis. On occasion, Border Patrol Agents find themselves working in a highly politicized environment that brings even harsher scrutiny. Therefore, as an agent, you will be required to study and demonstrate comprehension of various types of laws and regulations as well as legal commentary. You will be trained to apply those laws and regulations in dynamic and confrontational situations and to later testify in court proceedings in defense of your decisions. It is critical that Border Patrol Agents are able to articulate and justify their actions in criminal, civil, and administrative proceedings. Prospective agents must have the ability to project a positive and confident image in the field as well as in the courtroom. Public speaking courses are highly recommended for Border Patrol Agent candidates.

▶ Requirements and Qualifications

Preemployment requirements consist of a thorough background investigation, medical examination, fitness test, and drug test. You may also be subject to a polygraph examination. If your background includes past or present arrests, convictions, dismissals from previous jobs, debts and financial issues, excessive use of alcohol, use of illegal drugs, or the sale or distribution of illegal drugs, you most probably will be rated unsuitable for this position.

Job requirements: Border Patrol Agents must wear a uniform, carry a weapon, work overtime and shift work (sometimes under arduous conditions), and be subject to random drug testing. Agents undergo extensive background checks every three to five years.

► General Qualifications

- **Must be a U.S. citizen.** The U.S. Bureau of Customs and Border Protection (CBP) also has a residency requirement that applies to all applicants other than current CBP employees. If you are not a current CBP employee, CBP requires that for the three years prior to filing an application for employment, individuals must meet one or more of the following primary residence criteria:

  1. Applicant resided in the United States or its protectorates or territories (short trips abroad, such as vacations, will not necessarily disqualify an applicant).
  2. Applicant worked for the U.S. government as an employee overseas in a federal or military capacity.
  3. Applicant was a dependent of a U.S. federal or military employee serving overseas.

- **Must possess a valid state driver's license at the time of appointment.**
- **Must be under age 40 to apply.** This position is covered under law enforcement retirement provisions. Therefore, candidates must be referred for selection prior to their 40th birthdays unless they presently serve or have previously served in a position covered by federal civilian law enforcement retirement. (Note: In April 2006, the 40-year limit was raised from the former 37-year limit.)

Disqualifying Misdemeanor

If you have ever been convicted of a misdemeanor crime of domestic violence, it is a felony for you to possess any firearm or ammunition. A misdemeanor crime of domestic violence is defined as any offense that has, as an element, the use or attempted use of physical force or the threatened use of a deadly weapon, committed by a current or former domestic partner, parent, or guardian of the victim. The term *convicted* does not include anyone whose conviction has been expunged or set aside or who has received a pardon. As a condition of employment, individuals selected for Border Patrol Agent positions are required to carry weapons and ammunition as part of their official duties. Therefore, an individual with a conviction of a misdemeanor crime of domestic violence may not be employed in a Border Patrol Agent position.

► General Conditions of Employment

In addition to the qualifications previously mentioned, you must be willing to:

- undergo an extensive background investigation
- accept appointments at any location on or near the Mexican border
- work rotating shifts, primarily at night
- work long and irregular hours, including weekends and holidays
- work alone

- learn the Spanish language
- adhere to strict grooming and dress standards
- carry, maintain, and use a firearm in compliance with applicable laws and regulations
- work under hazardous conditions such as inclement weather, rough terrain, heights, moving trains, high-speed chases, physical assaults, and armed encounters
- operate a wide variety of motor vehicles including SUVs, Police Crown Victorias, and Hummers
- submit to a thorough physical examination
- fly as a passenger/observer in various types of aircraft, including helicopters
- maintain composure and self-control under stressful conditions
- bear initial travel costs to your duty location
- undergo intensive physical and academic training, including a 55- or 95-day course of study at the Border Patrol Academy and subsequent probationary exams
- work on operational details away from home for extended periods (35 days or more; some details may last up to a year)

▶ A Word about the Federal Career Intern Program

Border Patrol Agent positions are full-time positions filled under the Federal Career Intern Program (FCIP). This hiring program helps federal agencies recruit talented individuals for entry-level government positions. FCIP appointments are designed with a two-year internship, during which time you will be learning about the job and the organization, attending formal training programs, and developing job-related skills. If your performance and conduct are satisfactory, your appointment will be made permanent after the two-year internship. However, since the FCIP is an "excepted service" appointing authority, you may be removed from your position anytime during this two-year period for any reason. This is a significant departure from past hiring practices, which provided only a one-year probationary period. The probationary period is extended to two years under this FCIP program.

▶ How to Apply
USAJOBS (Office of Personnel Management Online)

Applications for Border Patrol Agent (trainee) positions are primarily submitted through the Internet. This departure from traditional paper-based methods provides the applicant with a speedier and more reliable application process. To apply online, visit the Office of Personnel Management (OPM)'s website at www.usajobs.gov to check for open positions, or go directly to https://cbpmhc.hr-services.org/BPA. Additionally, many Border Patrol sectors maintain recruiters you can personally talk with to guide you through the process. Here is a current list of contact numbers for Border Patrol sectors that conduct hiring. Additional sector information can be found on the U.S. Customs and Border Protection website at www.cbp.gov/xp/cgov/border_security/border_patrol/border_patrol_sectors/.

SECTOR OFFICE	CONTACT NUMBER
Blaine Sector	360-332-9200
Buffalo Sector	716-774-7200
Del Rio Sector	830-778-7000
Detroit Sector	586-307-2160
El Centro Sector	760-335-5700
El Paso Sector	915-834-8350
Grand Forks Sector	701-775-6259
Harve Sector	406-265-6781
Houlton Sector	207-532-6521
Laredo Sector	956-764-3200
Marfa Sector	432-729-5200
Miami Sector	954-965-6300
New Orleans Sector	504-376-2800
Ramey Sector	787-882-3560
Rio Grand Valley Sector	956-289-4800
San Diego Sector	619-216-4000
Spokane Sector	509-353-2747
Swanton Sector	800-247-2434
Tucson Sector	520-748-3000
Yuma Sector	928-341-6500

▶ A Word about Truthfulness in the Application Process

Throughout this chapter, we will continually mention the importance of truthfulness and full disclosure. Applicants who gain federal employment through material falsification in the application process or through simple omission of key facts are subject to administrative, civil, and/or criminal penalty. If you fail to disclose all your speeding and parking tickets or lie about a credit card payment you did not make, you will be subject to immediate removal from fed-

eral employment and could possibly be barred from future federal employment for a period of five years or more. In addition, if your falsification or omission is discovered even five years after you are hired, you will most likely be removed from your position. When in doubt, always disclose the information. In many instances, waivers may be attainable to overcome what appears to be an obstacle to employment.

Both U.S.-born and foreign-born applicants will be required to disclose all foreign family ties and business interests, no matter how insignificant they may seem. Disclosing this information will actually protect you should your integrity ever be questioned. Be sure to have the most recent contact and financial information available in this regard.

▶ The Next Steps in the Application Process

Following are the next important steps you must take in order to be considered for a Border Patrol Agent position.

The Written Exam

Each year, tens of thousands of people nationwide take the Border Patrol Exam, which is offered when current lists of eligible applicants are depleted and Congress authorizes additional hiring. Fewer than 800 of these candidates will be selected. Tests are normally scheduled at the nearest location to your home and could be administered in a federal building, civic hall, or library. You will be notified where to report for your written exam. When you receive the test notification packet, be sure to read all the material carefully!

You must pass a written exam like the exams contained in this book. The exam consists of the following sections: Logical Reasoning and a language test consisting of *either* the Spanish Language Proficiency Test *or* (if you don't speak Spanish) the Artificial Language Test (which tests your ability to learn languages). There is also an assessment of job-related activities and achievements.

The test takes about four and a half hours. You can practice taking the exam with sample questions in Chapters 10 and 11. Once you have taken the Border Patrol Agent test, you should receive a Notice of Results in the mail within four weeks following the test.

Compressed Testing

For candidates who register to take the written test at a compressed testing location, the CBP, in cooperation with the Office of Personnel Management (OPM), utilizes a compressed testing process that requires approximately eight hours on the day of your test. Compressed testing is normally conducted in Buffalo, NY; San Diego, CA; San Antonio and El Paso, TX; and Tucson, AZ. The initial step in the process is the test itself. After completing the test, a Border Patrol Agent will present an orientation session about the agent position. You will be given a copy of your test results (Notice of Results). If you successfully pass the written exam, you will be given a packet of forms to complete and mail to the Minneapolis Hiring Center, as well as a date (within two weeks of the examination date) for an oral board interview.

If you are unable to attend your scheduled test and you are unable to reschedule your test date with OPM, you will need to reregister during the next Border Patrol Agent open application period.

Logical Reasoning Test

The Logical Reasoning section of the test measures your vocabulary, reading comprehension, and critical thinking skills, which are necessary to prepare and perform the duties required of a Border Patrol Agent.

You should know that Border Patrol Agents are often called upon to testify in legal proceedings, and it is imperative to understand the legal reasoning process. The logical reasoning questions were designed with this application in mind. They are also designed to test your ability to understand complicated written material and derive conclusions. You will be required to make logical conclusions based on various facts in the written material.

Language Testing

If you speak Spanish, you may take a proficiency test that measures that ability. However, if you do not speak Spanish, then you will take an Artificial Language Test that measures your ability to learn the Spanish language. Whether you are a native or near-native speaker of Spanish, you learned Spanish in school, or you don't speak Spanish at all, you'll benefit from the test-preparation materials in this book. The official sample questions for language will show you what the language section of the test will be like. (Even if you're a native speaker, the Spanish section might surprise you. It focuses on grammar, which may not be your strongest suit.) Then you can decide to use either Chapter 8, "Using the Artificial Language Manual," or Chapter 9, "Checking Your Spanish Proficiency" to help you improve your performance.

The Structured Oral Interview

After you pass the written exam, your name is added to a register of eligible persons. As an eligible candidate, you will be called for an oral interview where you must demonstrate the abilities and characteristics important to a Border Patrol Agent. The oral interview is a panel of at least three experienced Border Patrol Agents who will present scenarios that test your ability to think quickly and respond to stressful situations. The oral interview tests your judgment, emotional maturity, and problem-solving skills. You will receive advance notice of the date and place of your interview, and you must appear at your own expense. Business dress is appropriate (i.e., suit and tie for men, suit for women).

The Medical Exam

After passing the oral interview, you will immediately be fingerprinted. A preemployment medical examination is also necessary and is provided at no expense. This exam is normally provided within a month of passing the oral interview. Candidates must be medically able to perform the full duties of a Border Patrol Agent efficiently and without hazard to themselves and others. Also, you must be physically able to perform all of the strenuous duties, sometimes under harsh environmental conditions. Duties require:

- physical stamina
- running long distances
- climbing
- jumping
- withstanding exposure to extreme weather conditions for extended periods
- standing/stooping for long periods of time

In addition, irregular and protracted hours of work are required. The medical examination is designed to find out if you are medically suited for these duties. The exam is given by a medical examiner and paid for by the U.S. government. You will have to pay for any travel to the exam. Also, as a Border Patrol Agent, you will have to pass a urinalysis test to screen for illegal drugs prior to final appointment and then again randomly throughout your career. It is important to note that a positive drug test will, without exception, terminate your current application process and prohibit you from future employment with the Border Patrol.

The Fitness Test

Due to the strenuous nature of Border Patrol Agent duties and the associated training programs, fitness tests are required for entry-level Border Patrol Agent positions. Although fitness tests are a separate preemployment requirement, they are conducted at the same time and location as the medical examination. The three preemployment fitness tests are a push-up test, sit-up test, and five-minute cardiovascular endurance step test.

1. **Push-up test** is a timed test that requires you to complete 20 proper-form push-ups in 60 seconds. The depth of the push-up will be measured using a foam block. If needed, rests between push-ups must be taken in the up position. The test administrator will evaluate your form during the test and will instruct you when to start and stop.
2. **Sit-up test** is a timed test that requires you to complete 25 proper-form sit-ups in 60 seconds. The test administrator will hold your feet during this test and instruct you when to start and stop.
3. **Step test** is a timed test that requires you to step up and down on a 12-inch-high step at a rate of 30 steps per minute for a total time of five minutes. To maintain the cadence, an audiotape is used that maintains a constant beat and gives verbal cues. The audiotape also contains instructions to switch your lead leg every minute to avoid local muscle fatigue.

Note: It is *extremely* important that you are well prepared for the fitness test. If you fail any of the three tests, the fitness testing process will be discontinued and you will immediately lose your conditional job offer with the U.S. Border Patrol. Because there is no fitness retesting, you will have to start the entire application process over the next time a vacancy announcement is advertised.

In order to graduate from the required training at the Border Patrol Academy, all trainees must pass a fitness test that includes running 1.5 miles in 13 minutes or less, running a 220-yard dash in 46 seconds or less, and completing the confidence course in 2 minutes and 30 seconds or less. If a trainee fails the test, he or she will be provided only one additional chance to pass.

The Background Investigation

Your appointment is subject to a thorough background investigation to ensure you have the loyalty, honesty, and integrity expected of a Border Patrol Agent. This can take three months or more, and you can be disqualified for evidence of any of the following:

- habitual use of intoxicants
- disloyalty to the U.S. government
- moral turpitude
- disrespect for law (excessive moving violations, prior arrests)
- failure to honor just financial obligations
- unethical dealings
- misstatement of material fact on the application for employment and any related documents

    Note: Misstatement of material fact or material falsification of employment application discovered at any time in your career is justification for immediate termination without appeal. Furthermore, you will be barred from all government service for no less than five years.

During your background investigation, investigators will examine every part of your life, including schools, jobs, military service, civic organizations, and social groups. Just about everyone you ever knew will be contacted for references and, in many cases, interviews. Additionally, your credit and arrest reports will be collected by the investigator, as well as bank records and financial holdings. The investigator

has wide latitude in evaluating your suitability for employment with the U.S. Border Patrol. Even after you are approved by the investigator, your suitability for employment will be further reviewed by agency suitability specialists. Following your acceptance into the Border Patrol, you will undergo periodic background checks no less than every five years and upon each successive promotion.

Once the background investigation is successfully completed and all other phases of the application process are complete, you will receive your first duty station assignment offer (typically six to eight months). Normally, it is not wise to turn down the offer in anticipation of a better location. However, if it is imperative, you may request another duty station assignment in lieu of the one offered.

Once selected, you may have only a short amount of time to report to your station, and Border Patrol practice requires that you relocate at your own expense. You will need funds to cover travel, lodging, and expenses for three to four days. This is commonly referred to as Entrance on Duty (EOD). You should not bring your family or loved ones with you during your EOD, since you will be busy for no less than ten hours a day. Additionally, you will report right to the Border Patrol Academy from your EOD. If, during the EOD process, any significant errors or omissions are discovered, you may be rejected at that time. It is therefore very important that you have been truthful throughout the entire process. When your EOD is completed, you have successfully been accepted as a Border Patrol Agent trainee.

▶ The Border Patrol Academy

Following your EOD process, you will be detailed to the Border Patrol Academy in Artesia, NM. At the academy, trainees undergo 55 days (95 if you do not speak Spanish) of intensive instruction and receive full pay and benefits. The curriculum includes subjects such as the following:

- Immigration and Nationality Law
- Criminal Law and Statutory Authority
- Intensive Spanish
- Physical Training
- Firearms Training
- Border Patrol Operations
- Drivers Training

▶ A Word on Recycles or Retreads

The U.S. Border Patrol Academy has historically had an unusually high washout rate; many trainees wash out for personal reasons or injury, while others simply cannot perform academically or physically. Trainees who drop out of the academy have the opportunity to recycle from the beginning. In other words, if a trainee drops out of the academy in week 20, he or she will have to repeat the entire program to graduate. To accomplish this, trainees will require the approval of the chief of the Border Patrol Academy as well as their instructors.

▶ Probationary Period

After graduation from the academy, you will continue formal training to prepare for probationary examinations at six and a half and ten months. Postacademy training is predominantly conducted by designated classroom instructors and field training officers in a field training unit. The unit will train as a group in the field and attend regular classroom training when not in the field. Trainees are required to attend all training sessions, both classroom and field. The use of sick or annual leave should be severely limited until the probationary period ends. The classroom component of the postacademy training requires the successful completion of numerous exams in addition to the formal six-and-a-half- and ten-month exams.

All Border Patrol Agents must successfully complete a one-year probationary period concurrently with successful completion of the two-year stipulated FCIP. The Border Patrol probationary period expires at the one-year anniversary date of EOD, whereas the FCIP period expires at the two-year anniversary. Probationary exams consist of essentially three components: law, Spanish, and field assessment (ratings by experienced agents). Failing any of the three exams will result in immediate removal from your position as a Border Patrol Agent. During the FCIP period, you may also be removed from your position for virtually any reason prescribed by your supervisor. Removal from your position under either of these circumstances is generally unappealable.

Information for a Border Patrol Agent's Spouse

If you have a spouse who would like to talk to spouses of current Border Patrol Agents, he or she should visit www.bp spouses.com. This free site, managed by the spouse of a current Border Patrol Agent, provides just about all information any spouse would need regarding life as a spouse of a Border Patrol Agent.

▶ A Special Word on Postacademy Training

Formal training and evaluation and their inherent stresses continue well after the academy graduation ceremony. These stresses, combined with the stress of relocating oneself and one's family, coupled with the ongoing possibility of failing a critical exam, can be burdensome not only for the new agent, but also for the entire family. Many trainees succumb to this stress and fail to prioritize adequately. It is extremely important that new agents continue studying and preparing for their new jobs and the continuing assessments without neglecting their family obligations.

Expenses

Living quarters and meals are provided free at the Border Patrol Academy. In addition, towels, linens, and physical training clothing (except athletic shoes) are provided and are laundered free of charge. As a trainee, you are paid a small per diem for incidental expenses in addition to your salary. The government pays costs to and from the training academy and the first duty station. However, the first year of service with the Border Patrol can be costly, so you should have adequate resources before entering.

Uniforms

On arrival at the academy, trainees must buy official Border Patrol uniforms. A $1,500 allowance offsets this cost; however, you are encouraged to have an additional $100 on hand for the purchase of additional uniform items required while attending the academy. Thereafter, an annual uniform allowance of $500 is provided toward additional or replacement uniforms, but a complete set of official and rough duty uniforms costs approximately $1,275. Border Patrol Agents, particularly trainee agents, wear out a lot of uniforms due to harsh environmental conditions.

Other Tips

The Border Patrol recommends that trainees *not* move households and families to permanent posts of duty until completion of training. Trainees are required to live on campus at the academy, which has no facilities for family members. It is recommended that you not bring your car, as parking is at a premium at the academy. Also, because you must fly from the academy to your first duty station, having a car could prove problematic. While at the academy, you will receive breaks on occasion. These could prove a good opportunity for you to receive visitors. Visitors will not be allowed to stay on campus. Therefore, hotel reservations should be made early. Additionally, there are a number of rental car companies available near the academy.

2 ▶ Other Opportunities with the DHS

CHAPTER SUMMARY

This chapter describes the requirements and hiring procedures for immigration-related entry-level jobs with the Department of Homeland Security (DHS) for positions other than Border Patrol Agent. You will learn the advantages offered by these jobs, how to find the jobs, and what to expect in the application and selection process. Let's take a closer look at what it means to work for the immigration-related component of the DHS.

FOLLOWING THE ESTABLISHMENT of the Department of Homeland Security (DHS) in 2003, several agencies were consolidated. Among them, the U.S. Customs Service and large parts of the former Immigration and Naturalization Service (INS) were combined into the newly formed Bureau of Customs and Border Protection (CBP) within the DHS. As a result, many former positions have been and still are being restructured. Many nonenforcement positions (primarily adjudicatory, asylum, and informational) of the former INS were transferred to a newly formed component of the DHS called U.S. Citizenship and Immigration Services (USCIS). Most enforcement positions such as U.S. Border Patrol Agent were combined into Customs and Border Protection (CBP) or Immigration and Customs Enforcement (ICE). This section focuses on entry-level immigration enforcement–related positions in CBP and ICE.

The DHS expends significant effort ensuring that immigration to the United States is done legally and that prospective immigrants are treated fairly. The DHS has over 22,000 employees to handle these important tasks. Besides Border Patrol Agents, entry-level jobs include:

- Criminal investigator (special agent), ICE
- Deportation officer

- Immigration inspector
- Immigration agent
- Detention enforcement officer
- Adjudications officer

▶ Why Work for the DHS?

Your work will be absorbing and diverse as a member of the DHS team. You'll also enjoy a competitive salary, advancement opportunities, and good benefits. Even at the entry level, you'll earn a respectable income. It's hard to beat the advantages of working for the federal government. Although the benefits may vary slightly from job to job, most career employees are entitled to:

- ten paid holidays per year
- 13–26 days of paid vacation per year
- 13 days of sick leave per year
- regular cost of living adjustments
- death and disability insurance
- group life insurance
- healthcare (medical and dental benefits)
- a government pension
- special employee programs available only to government workers

One of the greatest advantages of working for the federal government is job security. Once you've completed the three-year probationary period, you become a career employee who is not only eligible for full benefits, but also protected from layoffs by several layers of employees. This, in addition to the pride of doing a job that is intrinsically important to the nation, makes working for the DHS an excellent career choice.

Jobs other than Border Patrol Agent require different exams. However, once a candidate becomes a U.S. Border Patrol Agent, it is possible to transfer without further testing, although most Border Patrol Agents choose to take the specific agency tests anyway, as it is sometimes a faster route to getting hired by the other agency.

▶ DHS Programs

As part of the Department of Justice, DHS has both law enforcement and service-oriented positions. Responsibilities include admitting, excluding, investigating, and deporting aliens as well as guiding and assisting them in gaining entry to the United States. Employers may be fined if they knowingly hire aliens not authorized to work in the United States; however, aliens may temporarily reside in the country to meet agricultural labor needs.

The CBP patrols more than 6,000 miles of border with Canada and Mexico, as well as the Gulf of Mexico and the coastline of Florida. Along with ICE, the CBP conducts in-depth criminal investigations dealing with illegal aliens and alien-smuggling rings. In addition, the CBP and ICE work with the Department of State, Department of Health and Human Services, FBI, CIA, DHS, and United Nations, in the admission and resettlement of refugees.

Law Enforcement Positions

The primary immigration enforcement missions of the DHS are to prevent aliens from entering the country illegally and to find and remove those who are living or working here illegally. These functions are performed by the following enforcement programs:

- Border Patrol
- Inspections
- Investigations
- Intelligence
- Detention and Deportation (D&D)

Inspections

The Inspections program is responsible for screening all travelers arriving in the United States by air, land, or sea through some 250 ports of entry. This screening includes the examination and verification of travel documents for every alien seeking to enter the country. Last year, hundreds of millions of travelers passed through immigration inspection.

Investigations

The Investigations program focuses on enforcement of immigration laws within the United States and in territorial possessions. Plainclothes special agents investigate violations, and agents often participate in multiagency task forces against narcotics trafficking, violent crime, document fraud, terrorism, and organized crime. They also identify incarcerated aliens who are deportable because of criminal convictions. Agents monitor and inspect places of employment to apprehend unauthorized alien workers and to impose sanctions against employers who knowingly employ them. The antismuggling branch of Investigations is responsible for detecting sophisticated alien-smuggling operations and apprehending and prosecuting those responsible.

Intelligence

Intelligence collects, evaluates, analyzes, and disseminates information relating to all DHS missions, both enforcement and examinations. Intelligence also directs the Headquarters Command Center, which maintains communications with other offices and agencies 24 hours a day.

Detention and Deportation

Detention and Deportation (D&D) is charged with taking criminals and illegal aliens into custody pending proceedings to determine their status or to expedite their removal from the United States after they have exhausted all relief available to them under due process. D&D operates DHS detention facilities, known as Service Processing Centers, and when necessary, places detainees in Bureau of Prisons institutions, approved contract facilities, or state and local jails.

▶ Jobs Available

The DHS expects to increase and expand its hiring over the next several years as the federal government expands its efforts to curtail illegal immigration and guard against terrorism. In one year, the DHS hired 4,100 employees. The following section details certain key immigration law enforcement positions available within DHS. Other law enforcement and non–law enforcement jobs also exist. (For further information on such positions, follow the instructions in "Finding Job Openings" on page 19.)

Law Enforcement Jobs

Salaries and benefits for the jobs listed in this section are based on the federal government's special rates for law enforcement officers at the GL-5 through GL-7 levels. Entry-level salary ranges change with time, of course, but those listed here can be used as a rough guide. Exact pay information, including special pay for high cost of living areas, can be found in specific vacancy announcements.

GL-5: $32,389–$40,264
GL-7: $36,870–$46,626

The benefits are as outlined in the beginning of this chapter and may also include dependent care, employee support programs, and cost of living/ geographic locality pay for some jobs. Please note that for enforcement jobs, you must not have passed your 40th birthday, although exceptions to the maximum entry age requirement may be granted for persons who have prior federal civilian law enforcement experience or pending legislative change. You must be in qualifying physical condition based on a special medical examination. It should also be noted that education may be substituted for all or part of the experience required. The following are a few of the jobs you might consider.

Criminal Investigator (Special Agent)

These positions start at the GL-5 or GL-7 level, with promotion potential to GL-13. Special agents conduct investigations under the criminal and statutory provisions of the immigration and nationality laws.

Deportation Officer

Like special agents, deportation officers start at GL-5 or GL-7, with potential promotion to GL-12. Deportation officers provide for the control and removal of persons who have been ordered deported or otherwise required to depart from the United States.

Immigrations Inspector

Immigrations inspectors start at GL-5 and can progress to GL-9. The primary function of immigrations inspectors is to determine whether an applicant for admission to the United States may enter. Immigrations inspectors are required to detect false claims or fraudulent documents. Inspectors must have extensive knowledge of laws, regulations, and policies.

Detention Enforcement Officer

Detention enforcement officers start at GL-4 through GL-7 level, with the potential of progressing to GL-7. Detention enforcement officers perform duties related to the custody and care of aliens who have been detained in Service Processing Centers for violations of U.S. immigration laws. Duties include maintaining surveillance over aliens, escorting detained aliens to hearings, and performing administrative duties.

Non-Law Enforcement Jobs

These jobs are primarily found in USCIS. For these jobs, you must be in qualifying physical condition based on a medical examination. Education may be substituted for all or part of the experience required. Adjudications officers, asylum officers, and immigration information officers generally start at the GL-5 through GL-7 levels, with varying potential for promotion.

Adjudications Officer

Adjudications officers review and make determinations regarding the eligibility of aliens requesting benefits, including permanent residence and citizenship, provided under the immigration and nationality laws of the United States. District adjudications officers are located in District Offices nationwide. Center adjudications officers are located in one of the four Service Centers.

Asylum Officer

Asylum officers decide if applicants for asylum meet the requirements of the Immigration and Nationality Act. These officers interview applicants and therefore must have insight into human behavior to determine an applicant's credibility. They work in Asylum Offices throughout the United States.

Immigration Information Officer

Immigration information officers administer the many benefits available under the Immigration and Nationality Act. They provide information about immigration and nationality law, assist in completing forms, and answer questions. Immigration information officers work in District Offices, Sub-Offices, and Service Centers throughout the United States.

Finding Job Openings

In order to qualify for an appointment to most positions in any of the components of DHS, applicants must have current eligibility on an appropriate Office of Personnel Management (OPM) register or have been previously appointed to a federal job on a career or career-conditional basis. If you do not meet these requirements, you should contact your nearest OPM office regarding the application procedures. Phone numbers for OPM offices can be found in the telephone directory or at www.opm.gov.

Job Vacancy Announcements

When a civil service job opens within the DHS, that department will normally issue a *Competition Notice, Exam Announcement, Vacancy Announcement,* or *Civil Service Announcement.* These are four names for essentially the same thing, with the predominant name being *Vacancy Announcement.* Application procedures and eligibility requirements for each vacancy are outlined in the respective announcement. It is important for applicants to study carefully and understand the vacancy announcement, since any deviation from the published instructions will automatically render an applicant ineligible.

Employee Registers/ Eligibility Lists

If the position is one in which there are often regular openings or in which several vacancies are expected before the next job announcement, the agency will keep a list of eligible candidates called a *register* or an *eligibility list.* With such a register, the agency doesn't have to look for new applicants but

can call on a list of candidates it already knows are qualified. This makes it all the more important that you be aware of application windows, as it may be some time before there is another filing period. Generally, however, registers are considered old after three years, and most registers have an average life span of one year.

Job Listings through the OPM

The OPM updates a list of federal job vacancies daily. You can access the list 24 hours a day, seven days a week by visiting the OPM job vacancy website at www.usajobs.gov. Using the USAJOBS website will enable applicants to search the entire database of available jobs by occupation type, geographic location, salary, grade level, and agency or department.

Contacting the DHS Directly

Because the OPM is no longer responsible for overseeing hiring in most agencies, you can also get detailed job information directly from the DHS. The DHS has its own personnel offices that publish their own job lists through the USAJOBS website (www.usajobs.gov). You can also look in your local blue pages for names and addresses to contact. A list of available positions and job descriptions within DHS can be obtained by visiting the DHS website at www.dhs.gov.

How to Apply

The federal government has recently simplified the general application process considerably, and the streamlined process is detailed in this section.

Filing Period

Again, keep in mind that all openings have a *filing period* or *application window,* a specific period during which applications will be accepted. Be sure to find out the dates, because there are no exceptions.

Application Forms and Resume

You may fill out the rather lengthy Standard Form (SF 171) or the Optional Application for Federal Employment (OF 612). These forms are available at any of the websites previously provided. You may also submit a resume instead of an OF 612 or SF 171, but if you do, be sure to include all the information requested on the OF 612 and in the job vacancy announcement or *you will not be considered* for the job. Keep your resume brief, and be sure to include your Social Security number and current federal position (if held).

Test Scheduling Information

For government jobs that require a written exam, you will receive information by mail. It is critical you read, understand, and strictly follow the instructions. Late arrivals at testing centers are not normally permitted. Late arrivals at structured interviews will guarantee ineligibility.

Veterans' Preferences and How to Apply

If you've served on active duty in the military, you may be eligible for veterans' preference, an addition of 5 points—or 10 points, if you are a disabled veteran—to your rating in the job selection process. For information, visit www.usajobs.gov or www.opm.gov/veterans. Veterans can also take an online preference advisor questionnaire that will determine eligibility. To take the questionnaire, go to www.dol.gov/elaws/vets/vetpref/mservice.htm.

▶ Next Steps in the Application Process

If you are selected for further consideration, there are additional steps in the selection process. These may include:

- a written exam (which usually may be retaken after a six-month waiting period if you fail)
- a physical exam
- one or more structured interviews (which will most likely be scheduled only after your agency has determined you are qualified for the job)

Depending on the position, there may be other requirements you might not expect. For instance, you may be asked to fill out a Declaration for Federal Employment (OF 306) to determine your suitability as an employee of the federal government and to authorize the following checks:

- background investigation
- drug screening test
- psychological evaluation or personality test

These checks may significantly lengthen the hiring process, but they're important to ensure the well-being of all the citizens who interact with these employees.

▶ How to Prepare for the Application Process

The best way to prepare for any hiring process is to talk to people who work in the position you desire. They can best tell you about job demands, the hiring process, and on-the-job information. You can learn what qualities are most valued by those departments and what techniques successful candidates have used to get in shape (both physically and mentally) for exams and interviews. You can use the practice exams in this book to help you get ready for the parts of your test that include reading and language skills.

▶ Other Methods of Searching for Jobs

Although most federal job information has been consolidated on www.usajobs.gov, most federal buildings also maintain listings of available jobs. Some locations also maintain job kiosks that provide access to the Internet job databases. Additionally, many agencies and departments utilize internal recruiters to provide information.

3 ▶ The LearningExpress Test Preparation System

CHAPTER SUMMARY

Taking the Border Patrol Exam can be tough. It demands a lot of preparation if you want to achieve a top score and reach the next step of the hiring process. The LearningExpress Test Preparation System, developed by leading test experts, gives you the discipline and attitude you need to be a winner.

FIRST, THE BAD NEWS: Taking the Border Patrol Exam is no picnic, and neither is getting ready for it. Your future as a Border Patrol Agent depends on your getting a passing score, but all sorts of pitfalls can keep you from doing your best on this all-important exam. Here are some of the obstacles that can stand in the way of your success:

- being unfamiliar with the format of the exam
- being paralyzed by test anxiety
- leaving your preparation to the last minute
- not preparing at all
- not knowing vital test-taking skills, such as how to pace yourself through the exam, how to use the process of elimination, and when to guess
- not being in tip-top mental and physical shape
- working through the test on an empty stomach or shivering through the exam because the room is cold

What's the common denominator in all these test-taking pitfalls? One word: *control*. Who's in control, you or the exam?

Now the good news: The LearningExpress Test Preparation System puts you in control. In just nine easy-to-follow steps, you will learn everything you need to know to make sure that you are in charge of your preparation and your performance on the exam. Other test takers may let the test get the better of them; other test takers may be unprepared or out of shape, but not you. You will have taken all the steps you need to take to get a high score on the Border Patrol Exam.

Here's how the LearningExpress Test Preparation System works: Nine easy steps lead you through everything you need to know and do to get ready to master your exam. Each step is part of a plan that takes a mere three hours. It's important to follow each step thoroughly, or you won't be getting the full benefit of the system. The activities in each step take a small amount of time, but they pay off in big benefits to you.

Step 1. Get Information	30 minutes
Step 2. Conquer Test Anxiety	20 minutes
Step 3. Make a Plan	50 minutes
Step 4. Learn to Manage Your Time	10 minutes
Step 5. Learn to Use the Process of Elimination	20 minutes
Step 6. Know When to Guess	20 minutes
Step 7. Reach Your Peak Performance Zone	10 minutes
Step 8. Get Your Act Together	10 minutes
Step 9. Do It!	10 minutes
Total	3 hours

We estimate that working through the entire system will take you approximately three hours, though it's perfectly okay if you work faster or slower than the time estimates assume. If you can take a whole afternoon or evening, you can work through the entire LearningExpress Test Preparation System in one sitting. Otherwise, you can break it up, and do just one or two steps a day for the next several days. It's up to you—remember, *you're* in control.

▶ Step 1: Get Information

Time to complete: 30 minutes
Activities: Read Chapter 1, "Becoming a Border Patrol Agent," Chapter 2, "Other Opportunities with the DHS," Chapter 4, "Logical Reasoning," Chapter 5, "Official Sample Questions for Logical Reasoning," and Chapter 6, "Official Sample Questions for Language."

Knowledge is power. The first step in the LearningExpress Test Preparation System is finding out everything you can about the Border Patrol Exam. Reading the introductory chapters in this book will give you a good overview. Taking advantage of the contact numbers or websites noted in those chapters will be helpful, too. Once you have your information, follow the next steps in the LearningExpress Test Preparation System.

Straight Talk about the Border Patrol Exam

Why do you have to take this exam, anyway? This exam is mandated by the federal government for all applicants for the position of Border Patrol Agent. Border Patrol Agents must speak Spanish at a level rated from good to excellent by the end of their one-year probationary period. Besides including a Spanish test, this exam tests the ability of non-Spanish-speaking applicants to learn a language other than English. The test also emphasizes English-language skills. If an applicant cannot communicate in writing or readily understand written communications, then that applicant simply cannot handle the important duties inherent in positions with the Border Patrol. Fortunately, with the help of this book, you can vastly improve your communication and language skills.

It's important for you to remember that your score on the Border Patrol Exam does not determine how smart you are or even whether you will make a good Border Patrol Agent. There are all kinds of things a written exam like this can't test: whether you are likely to show up late or call in sick a lot, whether you can keep your cool under pressure, whether you can be trusted to enforce the law with integrity. Those kinds of things are hard to evaluate, but the DHS can get a good idea during the oral interview.

This is not to say that filling in the right little circles is not important! The knowledge tested on the written exam is knowledge you will need to do your job. And your opportunity to become a Border Patrol Agent depends on your passing this exam. And that's why you're here—using the LearningExpress Test Preparation System to achieve control over the exam.

What's on the Test

If you haven't already done so, stop here and read Chapters 1 and 2 of this book, which give you an overview of federal government hiring procedures, and take a quick look at Chapters 4, 5, and 6 for an overview of the content of the test.

The Border Patrol Exam consists of two parts.

1. **Logical Reasoning:** You must demonstrate the ability to read, understand, and apply critical thinking skills presented in real-life situations.
2. **Spanish or Artificial Language:** You must demonstrate a good to excellent ability to understand, speak, and write Spanish, *or* if you do not know Spanish at the time you take the exam, you must take the Artificial Language Test, which requires you to demonstrate a good ability to learn a foreign language.

Stop now and read Chapter 4 to unlock the secrets of the Logical Reasoning section. Then decide which part of the language exam you want to take. If you are fluent in Spanish, opt for that section. If you are not, then the Artificial Language section is for you. See Chapters 6 through 9 for language preparation.

▶ Step 2: Conquer Test Anxiety

Time to complete: 20 minutes
Activity: Take the "Test Stress Test."
Having complete information about the exam is the first step in getting control of the exam. Next, you have to overcome one of the biggest obstacles to test success: test anxiety. Test anxiety can not only impair your performance on the exam itself, but it can also even keep you from preparing. In Step 2, you'll learn stress management techniques that will help you succeed on your exam. Learn these strategies now, and practice them as you work through the exams in this book. Then they'll be second nature to you on exam day.

Combating Test Anxiety

The first thing you need to know is that a little test anxiety is a good thing. Everyone gets nervous before a big exam—and if that nervousness motivates you to prepare thoroughly, so much the better. It's said that Sir Laurence Olivier, one of the foremost British actors of the twentieth century, was ill before every performance. His stage fright didn't impair his performance; in fact, it probably gave him a little extra edge—just the kind of edge you need to do well, whether on a stage or in an examination room.

On the next page is the "Test Stress Test." Stop here and answer the questions on that page to find out whether your level of test anxiety is something you should worry about.

Stress Management before the Test

If you feel your level of anxiety getting the best of you in the weeks before the test, here is what you need to do to bring the level down again:

- **Get prepared.** There's nothing like knowing what to expect. Being prepared for the test puts you in control of test anxiety. That's why you're reading this book. Use it faithfully, and remind yourself that you're better prepared than most of the people taking the test.
- **Practice self-confidence.** A positive attitude is a great way to combat test anxiety. This is no time to be humble or shy. Stand in front of the mirror and say to your reflection, "I'm prepared. I'm full of self-confidence. I'm going to ace this test. I know I can do it." Say it into a tape recorder and play it back once a day. If you hear it often enough, you'll believe it.
- **Fight negative messages.** Every time someone starts telling you how hard the exam is or how it's almost impossible to get a high score, start telling them your self-confidence messages. If

the someone with the negative messages is you, telling yourself you don't do well on exams, you just can't do this, don't listen. Turn on your tape recorder and listen to your self-confidence messages.

- **Visualize.** Imagine yourself boarding the plane that will take you to your first duty station. Think of yourself coming home with your first paycheck as a Border Patrol Agent. Visualizing success can help make it happen—and it reminds you of why you're doing all this work preparing for the exam.
- **Exercise.** Physical activity helps calm your body and focus your mind. Besides, being in good physical shape can actually help you do well on the exam and will be essential to your success on the job. Go for a run, lift weights, go swimming—and do so regularly.

Stress Management on Test Day

There are several ways you can bring down your level of test anxiety on test day. Try them out and then practice them in the weeks before the test.

- **Do deep breathing.** Take a deep breath while you count to five. Hold it for a count of one, then let it out on a count of five. Repeat several times.
- **Move your body.** Try rolling your head in a circle. Rotate your shoulders. Shake your hands from the wrist. Many people find these movements very relaxing.
- **Visualize again.** Think of the place where you are most relaxed: lying on the beach in the sun, walking through the park, or whatever. Now close your eyes and imagine you're actually in that place. If you practice in advance, you'll find that you need only a few seconds of this exer-

cise to experience a significant increase in your sense of well-being.

When anxiety threatens to overwhelm you right there during the exam, there are still things you can do to manage the stress level:

- **Repeat your self-confidence messages.** You should have them memorized by now. Say them silently to yourself, and believe them!

- **Visualize one more time.** This time, visualize yourself moving smoothly and quickly through the test, answering every question right and finishing just before time is up. Like most visualization techniques, this one works best if you've practiced it ahead of time.
- **Find an easy question.** Skim over the test until you find an easy question, and answer it. Getting even one circle filled in gets you into the test-taking groove.

Test Stress Test

You need to worry about test anxiety only if it is extreme enough to impair your performance. The following questionnaire will provide a diagnosis of your level of test anxiety. In the blank before each statement, write the number that most accurately describes your experience.

0 = Never   1 = Once or twice   2 = Sometimes   3 = Often

_____ I have gotten so nervous before an exam that I simply put down the books and didn't study for it.

_____ I have experienced disabling physical symptoms such as vomiting and severe headaches because I was nervous about an exam.

_____ I have simply not showed up for an exam because I was scared to take it.

_____ I have experienced dizziness and disorientation while taking an exam.

_____ I have had trouble filling in the little circles because my hands were shaking too hard.

_____ I have failed an exam because I was too nervous to complete it.

_____ **Total: Add up the numbers in the blanks above.**

Your Test Stress Score

Here are the steps you should take, depending on your score.

- **If you scored below 3,** your level of test anxiety is nothing to worry about; it's probably just enough to give you that little extra edge.
- **If you scored between 3 and 6,** your test anxiety may be enough to impair your performance, and you should practice the stress management techniques listed in this chapter to try to bring your test anxiety down to a manageable level.
- **If you scored above 6,** your level of test anxiety is a serious concern. In addition to practicing the stress management techniques listed in this chapter, you may want to seek additional personal help. Call your local high school or community college and ask for the academic counselor. Tell the counselor that you have a level of test anxiety that sometimes keeps you from being able to take an exam. The counselor may be willing to help you or may suggest someone else you should talk to.

- **Take a mental break.** Everyone loses concentration once in a while during a long test. It's normal, so you shouldn't worry about it. Instead, accept what has happened. Say to yourself, "Hey, I lost it there for a minute. My brain is taking a break." Put down your pencil, close your eyes, and do some deep breathing for a few seconds. Then you're ready to go back to work.

Try these techniques ahead of time to find out which ones work best for you.

▶ Step 3: Make a Plan

Time to complete: 50 minutes
Activity: Construct a study plan.
Maybe the most important thing you can do to get control of yourself and your exam is to make a study plan. Too many people fail to prepare simply because they fail to plan. Spending hours on the day before the exam poring over sample test questions not only raises your level of test anxiety, but also is simply no substitute for careful preparation and practice.

Don't fall into the cram trap. Take control of your preparation time by mapping out a study schedule. On the following pages are four sample schedules, based on the amount of time you have before you take the Border Patrol Exam. If you're the kind of person who needs deadlines and assignments to motivate you for a project, here they are. If you're the kind of person who doesn't like to follow other people's plans, you can use the suggested schedules here to construct your own.

Even more important than making a plan is making a commitment. You can't improve your comprehension and language skills in one night. You have to set aside some time every day for study and practice. Try for at least 20 minutes a day. Twenty minutes daily will do you much more good than two hours on Saturday.

Don't put off your study until the day before the exam. Start now. A few minutes a day, with half an hour or more on weekends, can make a big difference in your score.

▶ Step 4: Learn to Manage Your Time

Time to complete: 10 minutes to read, many hours of practice!
Activities: Practice these strategies as you take the sample tests in this book.
Steps 4, 5, and 6 of the LearningExpress Test Preparation System put you in charge of your exam by showing you test-taking strategies that work. Practice these strategies as you take the sample tests in this book, and then you'll be ready to use them on test day.

First, you'll take control of your time on the exam. The Border Patrol Exam has a time limit, which may give you more than enough time to complete all the questions—or may not. It's a terrible feeling to hear the examiner say, "Five minutes left," when you're only three-quarters of the way through the test. Here are some tips to keep that from happening to you.

- **Follow directions.** If the directions are given orally, listen to them. If they're written on the exam booklet, read them carefully. Ask questions *before* the exam begins if there's anything you don't understand. If you're allowed to write in your exam booklet, write down the beginning time and the ending time of the exam.
- **Pace yourself.** Glance at your watch every few minutes, and compare the time to how far you've gotten in the test. When one-quarter of the time has elapsed, you should be a quarter of the way through the test, and so on. If you're falling behind, pick up the pace a bit.

Schedule A: The Leisure Plan

If you have six months or more in which to prepare, you're lucky! Make the most of your time.

Time	Preparation
Exam minus 6 months	Read Chapter 4 for an overview of logical reasoning questions. Practice the official sample questions in Chapter 5.
Exam minus 5 months	Read Chapter 6, and work through the sample questions. Find other people who are preparing for the test and form a study group.
Exam minus 4 months	If you do not speak Spanish, read Chapters 7 and 8, and work through the exercises. Set aside some time every day for some serious reading of books and magazines.
Exam minus 3 months	If you speak and read Spanish, read Chapter 9. If you will be taking the Artificial Language Test, you should review Chapters 6 and 7. In fact, the glossary of grammatical terms in Chapter 7 may help you even if you're taking the Spanish test.
Exam minus 2 months	Take the first practice test in Chapter 10. Review the relevant chapters, and get the help of a friend or teacher.
Exam minus 1 month	Take the second practice test in Chapter 11, and again review the areas that give you the most trouble.
Exam minus 1 week	Review both exams in this book, as well as the sample questions in Chapters 5 and 6. Choose one area to review this week.
Exam minus 1 day	Relax. Do something unrelated to the exam. Eat a good meal and go to bed at your usual time.

Schedule B: The Just-Enough-Time Plan

If you have three to five months before the exam, that should be enough time to prepare for the written test. This schedule assumes four months; stretch it out or compress it if you have more or less time.

Time	Preparation
Exam minus 4 months	Read Chapter 4, and complete the sample logical reasoning questions in Chapter 5.
Exam minus 3 months	Read Chapter 6, and work through the exercises. Start a program of serious reading to improve your vocabulary and reading comprehension.
Exam minus 2 months	Read Chapter 9 if you speak and read Spanish, or Chapter 7 if you do not. If you will be taking the Artificial Language Test, you should also review Chapter 8. In fact, the glossary of grammatical terms in Chapter 7 may help you even if you're taking the Spanish test.
Exam minus 1 month	Take the first practice test in Chapter 10. Review the relevant chapters, and get the help of a friend or teacher.
Exam minus 1 week	Take the second practice test in Chapter 11. See how much you've learned in the past months? Review the chapter on the area that gives you the most trouble.
Exam minus 1 day	Relax. Do something unrelated to the exam. Eat a good meal and go to bed at your usual time.

Schedule C: More Study in Less Time

If you have one to three months before the exam, you still have enough time for some concentrated study that will help you improve your score. This schedule is built around a two-month time frame. If you have only one month, spend an extra couple of hours a week to get all these steps in. If you have three months, take some of the steps from Schedule B and fit them in.

Time	Preparation
Exam minus 8 weeks	Read Chapters 4 and 5. Evaluate your performance to find the area you're weakest in. Choose one chapter from among Chapters 7–9 to read in these two weeks. When you get to that chapter in this plan, review it again.
Exam minus 6 weeks	Read Chapter 6, and work through the exercises.
Exam minus 4 weeks	Read Chapter 9 if you speak and read Spanish, or Chapter 7 if you do not. If you will be taking the Artificial Language Test, you should also review Chapter 8. In fact, the glossary of grammatical terms in Chapter 7 may help you even if you're taking the Spanish test.
Exam minus 2 weeks	Take the first practice test in Chapter 10. Review the areas where your score is lowest.
Exam minus 1 week	Take the second practice test in Chapter 11. Review Chapters 4–9, concentrating on the areas where a little work can help the most.
Exam minus 1 day	Relax. Do something unrelated to the exam. Eat a good meal and go to bed at your usual time.

Schedule D: The Short-Term Plan

If you have three weeks or less before the exam, you really have your work cut out for you. Carve half an hour out of your day, *every day*, for study. This schedule assumes you have the whole three weeks to prepare; if you have less time, you'll have to compress the schedule accordingly.

Time	Preparation
Exam minus 3 weeks	Read Chapters 4 and 5 and complete the sample questions in Chapter 5. Read Chapter 6, and work through the exercises.
Exam minus 2 weeks	Read Chapter 9 if you speak and read Spanish, or Chapter 7 if you do not. If you will be taking the Artificial Language Test, you should also review Chapter 8. Take the first practice test in Chapter 10.
Exam minus 1 week	Take the second practice test in Chapter 11. Evaluate your performance on the practice tests. Review the parts of Chapters 5 and 6 that you had the most trouble with. Get a friend or teacher to help you with the section you had the most difficulty with.
Exam minus 1 day	Relax. Do something unrelated to the exam. Eat a good meal and go to bed at your usual time.

- **Keep moving.** Don't waste too much time on one question. If you don't know the answer, skip the question and move on. Circle the number of the question in your test booklet in case you have time to come back to it later.
- **Keep track of your place on the answer sheet.** If you skip a question, make sure you skip on the answer sheet, too. Check yourself every five to ten questions to make sure the question number and the answer sheet number still match.
- **Don't rush.** Though you should keep moving, rushing won't help. Try to keep calm and work methodically and quickly.

▶ Step 5: Learn to Use the Process of Elimination

Time to complete: 20 minutes
Activity: Complete worksheet on "Using the Process of Elimination."

After time management, your next most important tool for taking control of your exam is using the process of elimination wisely. This standard test-taking wisdom tells you that you should always read all the answer choices before choosing an answer. This helps you find the right answer by eliminating wrong answer choices. And, sure enough, that standard wisdom applies to your exam, too.

Let's say you're facing a reading comprehension question that goes like this:

When a suspect who is merely being questioned incriminates himself, he might later seek to have the case dismissed on the grounds of not having been apprised of his Miranda rights when arrested. So police officers must read suspects their Miranda rights upon taking them into custody.

1. When must police officers read Miranda rights to a suspect?
   a. while questioning the suspect
   b. before taking the suspect to the police station
   c. before releasing the suspect
   d. while placing the suspect under arrest

You should always use the process of elimination on a question like this, even if the right answer jumps out at you. Sometimes, the answer that jumps out isn't right after all.

So you start with answer choice **a**—*while questioning the suspect*. This one is pretty easy to eliminate. The first sentence states that a suspect might incriminate himself while being questioned, so obviously, his Miranda rights should be read to him before questioning begins. Mark an **X** next to choice **a** so you never have to look at it again.

Move to the next choice—*before taking the suspect to the police station*. This looks like a possibility, although you can imagine situations in which a suspect might incriminate himself before being taken to the police station. Still, if no better answer comes along, you might use this one. Put a question mark beside choice **b**, meaning "pretty good answer; this could be the right choice."

Choice **c** has the same problem as choice **a**—*before releasing the suspect* can cover a long time period, certainly long enough for the suspect to incriminate himself. So you place an **X** beside this answer choice, meaning "no good, I won't come back to this one."

Choice **d**—*while placing the suspect under arrest*. Look back at the passage quickly and notice the final sentence, the second half of which reads *upon taking them into custody*. This appears to be restated by choice **d**, the best answer yet, so put a check mark beside it.

Now your question looks like this:

1. When must police officers read Miranda rights to a suspect?
X **a.** while questioning the suspect
? **b.** before taking the suspect to the police station
X **c.** before releasing the suspect
✓ **d.** while placing the suspect under arrest

You've got just one check mark, for a good answer. If you're pressed for time, you should simply mark choice **d** on your answer sheet. If you've got the time to be extra careful, you could compare your check-mark answer to your question-mark answers to make sure that it's better.

It's good to have a system for marking good, bad, and maybe answers. We're recommending this one:

✓ = good
X = bad
? = maybe

If you don't like these marks, devise your own system. Just make sure you do it long before test day—while you're working through the practice exams in this book—so you won't have to worry about it during the test.

Even when you think you're absolutely clueless about a question, you can often use the process of elimination to get rid of an answer choice. If so, you're better prepared to make an educated guess, as you'll see in Step 6. More often, the process of elimination allows you to get down to only *two* possibly right answers. Then you're in a strong position to guess. And sometimes, even though you don't know the right answer, you find it simply by getting rid of all the wrong ones, as you did in this example.

Try using your powers of elimination for the worksheet called "Using the Process of Elimination." The answer explanations for this worksheet show one possible way you might use the process to arrive at the right answer.

The process of elimination is your tool for the next step, which is knowing when to guess.

Using the Process of Elimination

Use the process of elimination to answer the following questions.

1. Ilsa is as old as Meghan will be in five years. The difference between Ed's age and Meghan's age is twice the difference between Ilsa's age and Meghan's age. Ed is 29. How old is Ilsa?
a. 4
b. 10
c. 19
d. 24

2. "All drivers of commercial vehicles must carry a valid commercial driver's license whenever operating a commercial vehicle." According to this sentence, which of the following people need NOT carry a commercial driver's license?
a. a truck driver idling his engine while waiting to be directed to a loading dock
b. a bus operator backing her bus out of the way of another bus in the bus lot
c. a taxi driver driving his personal car to the grocery store
d. a limousine driver taking the limousine to her home after dropping off her last passenger of the evening

3. Smoking tobacco has been linked to
   a. increased risk of stroke and heart attack.
   b. all forms of respiratory disease.
   c. increasing mortality rates over the past ten years.
   d. juvenile delinquency.

4. Which of the following words is spelled correctly?
   a. incorrigible
   b. outragous
   c. domestickated
   d. understandible

Answers

Here are the answers, as well as some suggestions as to how you might have used the process of elimination to find them.

1. d. You should eliminate answer **a** immediately. Ilsa can't be four years old if Meghan is going to be Ilsa's age in five years. The best way to eliminate other answer choices is to try plugging them in to the information given in the problem. For instance, for answer **b**, if Ilsa is 10, then Meghan must be 5. The difference in their ages is 5. The difference between Ed's age, 29, and Meghan's age, 5, is 24. Is 24 two times 5? No. Then answer **b** is wrong. You could eliminate answer **c** in the same way and be left with answer **d**.

2. c. Note the word *not* in the question, and go through the answers one by one. Is the truck driver in choice **a** *operating a commercial vehicle*? Yes, idling counts as operating, so he needs to have a commercial driver's license. Likewise, the bus operator in answer **b** is operating a commercial vehicle; the question doesn't say the operator has to be on the street. The limo driver in **d** is operating a commercial vehicle, even if it doesn't have a passenger in it. However, the cabbie in answer **c** is *not* operating a commercial vehicle, but his own private car.

3. a. You could eliminate answer **b** simply because of the presence of the word *all*. Such absolutes hardly ever appear in correct answer choices. Choice **c** looks attractive until you think a little about what you know—aren't *fewer* people smoking these days, rather than more? So it's unlikely smoking is responsible for a higher mortality rate. (If you didn't know that *mortality rate* means the rate at which people die, you might keep this choice as a possibility, but you'd still be able to eliminate two answers and have only two to choose from.) Choice **d** seems like a stretch, so you could eliminate that one, too. You're left with the correct choice, **a**.

4. a. How you use the process of elimination here depends on which words you recognize as being spelled incorrectly. If you know that the correct spellings are *outrageous*, *domesticated*, and *understandable*, then you are home free.

▶ Step 6: Know When to Guess

Time to complete: 20 minutes
Activity: Complete worksheet on "Your Guessing Ability."

Armed with the process of elimination, you're ready to take control of one of the big questions in test taking: Should I guess? In general, the answer is a resounding yes!

Some exams have what's called a guessing penalty, in which a fraction of your wrong answers is subtracted from your right answers, but the Border Patrol Exam isn't one of them. The number of questions you answer correctly yields your raw score. So you have nothing to lose and everything to gain by guessing.

The more complicated answer to the question "Should I guess?" depends on you—your personality and your guessing intuition. There are two things you need to know about yourself before you go into the exam:

1. Are you a risk taker?
2. Are you a good guesser?

You'll have to decide about your risk-taking quotient on your own. To find out if you're a good guesser, though, complete the worksheet on "Your Guessing Ability," which begins on this page. Even if you're a play-it-safe person with lousy intuition, you're still safe in guessing every time, because there is no penalty. The best thing would be if you could overcome your anxieties and go ahead and mark an answer. But you may want to have a sense of how good your intuition is before you go into the exam.

Your Guessing Ability

The following are ten really hard questions. You're not supposed to know the answers. Rather, this is an assessment of your ability to guess when you don't have a clue. Read each question carefully, just as if you did expect to answer it. If you have any knowledge at all of the subject of the question, use that knowledge to help you eliminate wrong answer choices. Use this answer grid to fill in your answers to the questions.

ANSWER GRID

1. ⓐ ⓑ ⓒ ⓓ
2. ⓐ ⓑ ⓒ ⓓ
3. ⓐ ⓑ ⓒ ⓓ
4. ⓐ ⓑ ⓒ ⓓ
5. ⓐ ⓑ ⓒ ⓓ
6. ⓐ ⓑ ⓒ ⓓ
7. ⓐ ⓑ ⓒ ⓓ
8. ⓐ ⓑ ⓒ ⓓ
9. ⓐ ⓑ ⓒ ⓓ
10. ⓐ ⓑ ⓒ ⓓ

1. September 7 is Independence Day in
   a. India.
   b. Costa Rica.
   c. Brazil.
   d. Australia.

2. Which of the following is the formula for determining the momentum of an object?
   a. $p = mv$
   b. $F = ma$
   c. $P = IV$
   d. $E = mc^2$

3. Because of the expansion of the universe, the stars and other celestial bodies are all moving away from each other. This phenomenon is known as
   a. Newton's first law.
   b. the big bang.
   c. gravitational collapse.
   d. Hubble flow.

4. In what year was American author Gertrude Stein born?
   a. 1713
   b. 1830
   c. 1874
   d. 1901

5. Which of the following is NOT one of the Five Classics attributed to Confucius?
   a. *I Ching*
   b. *Book of Holiness*
   c. *Spring and Autumn Annals*
   d. *Book of History*

6. The religious and philosophical doctrine that holds that the universe is constantly in a struggle between good and evil is known as
   a. Pelagianism.
   b. Manichaeanism.
   c. neo-Hegelianism.
   d. Epicureanism.

7. The third chief justice of the U.S. Supreme Court was
   a. John Blair.
   b. William Cushing.
   c. James Wilson.
   d. John Jay.

8. Which of the following is the poisonous portion of a daffodil?
   a. the bulb
   b. the leaves
   c. the stem
   d. the flowers

9. The winner of the Masters golf tournament in 1953 was
   a. Sam Snead.
   b. Cary Middlecoff.
   c. Arnold Palmer.
   d. Ben Hogan.

10. The state with the highest per capita personal income in 1980 was
   a. Alaska.
   b. Connecticut.
   c. New York.
   d. Texas.

Answers

Check your answers against the correct answers that follow.

1. c.	**6.** b.
2. a.	**7.** b.
3. d.	**8.** a.
4. c.	**9.** d.
5. b.	**10.** a.

How Did You Do?

You may have simply gotten lucky and actually known the answers to one or two questions. In addition, your guessing was more successful if you were able to use the process of elimination on any of the questions. Maybe you didn't know who the third chief justice was (question 7), but you knew that John Jay was the first. In that case, you would have eliminated answer **d** and therefore improved your odds of guessing right from one in four to one in three.

According to probability, you should get two and a half answers correct, so getting either two or three right would be average. If you got four or more right, you may be a really terrific guesser. If you got one or none right, you may be a really bad guesser.

Keep in mind, though, that this is only a small sample. You should continue to keep track of your guessing ability as you work through the sample questions in this book. Circle the numbers of questions you guess on when you make a guess; or, if you don't have time during the practice tests, go back afterward and try to identify the questions you guessed on. Remember, on a test with four answer choices, your chances of getting a right answer are one in four. So keep a separate "guessing" score for each exam. How many questions did you guess on? How many did you get right? If the number you got right is at least one-fourth of the number of questions you guessed on, you are at least an average guesser, maybe better—and you should always go ahead and guess on the real exam. If the number you got right is significantly lower than one-fourth of the number you guessed on, you would be safe in guessing anyway, but maybe you'd feel more comfortable if you guessed only selectively, when you can eliminate a wrong answer or at least have a good feeling about one of the answer choices.

▶ Step 7: Reach Your Peak Performance Zone

Time to complete: 10 minutes to read; weeks to complete!

Activity: Complete the "Physical Preparation Checklist."

To get ready for a challenge like a big exam, you have to take control of your physical, as well as your mental, state. Exercise, proper diet, and rest will ensure that your body works with, rather than against, your mind during your test preparation and on exam day.

Exercise

If you don't already have a regular exercise program going, the time during which you're preparing for an exam is actually an excellent time to start one. And if you're already keeping fit—or trying to get that way—don't let the pressure of preparing for an exam force you to quit. Exercise helps reduce stress by pumping wonderful good-feeling hormones called endorphins into your system. It also increases the oxygen supply throughout your body and your brain, so you'll be at peak performance on test day.

A half hour of vigorous activity—enough to raise a sweat—every day should be your aim. If you're really pressed for time, every other day is okay. Choose an activity you like and get out there and do it. Jogging with a friend always makes the time go faster, or take a radio.

But don't overdo it. You don't want to exhaust yourself. Moderation is the key.

Diet

First of all, cut out the junk. Go easy on caffeine and nicotine, and eliminate alcohol from your system at least two weeks before the exam.

What your body needs for peak performance is simply a balanced diet. Eat plenty of fruits and vegetables, along with protein and carbohydrates. Foods high in lecithin (an amino acid), such as fish and beans, are especially good for your brain.

The night before the exam, you might carbo-load the way athletes do before a contest. Eat a big plate of spaghetti, rice and beans, or whatever your favorite carbohydrate is.

Rest

You probably know how much sleep you need every night to be at your best, even if you don't always get it. Make sure you do get that much sleep, though, for at least a week before the exam. Moderation is important here, too. Extra sleep will just make you groggy.

If you're not a morning person and your exam will be given in the morning, you should reset your internal clock so that your body doesn't think you're taking an exam at 3 A.M. You have to start this process well before the exam. The way it works is to get up half an hour earlier each morning, and then go to bed half an hour earlier that night. Don't try it the other way around; you'll just toss and turn if you go to bed early without having gotten up early. The next morning, get up another half hour earlier, and so on. How long you will have to do this depends on how late you're used to getting up. Use the "Physical Preparation Checklist" on page 38 to make sure you're in tip-top form.

▶ Step 8: Get Your Act Together

Time to complete: 10 minutes to read (time to complete will vary)
Activity: Complete the "Final Preparations" worksheet.

You're in control of your mind and body; you're in charge of test anxiety, your preparation, and your test-taking strategies. Now it's time to take charge of external factors, like the testing site and the materials you need to take to the exam.

Find Out Where the Test Is and Make a Trial Run

The testing agency or OPM will notify you when and where your exam is being held. Do you know how to get to the testing site? Do you know how long it will take to get there? If not, make a trial run, preferably on the same day of the week at the same time of day. Make note, on the "Final Preparations" worksheet on page 39, of the amount of time it will take you to get to the exam site. Plan on arriving 10–15 minutes early so you can get the lay of the land, use the bathroom, and calm down. Then figure out how early you will have to get up that morning, and make sure you get up that early every day for a week before the exam.

Gather Your Materials

The night before the exam, lay out the clothes you will wear and the materials you have to bring with you to the exam. Plan on dressing in layers; you won't have any control over the temperature of the examination room. Have a sweater or jacket you can take off if it's warm. Use the checklist on the "Final Preparations" worksheet on page 39 to help you pull together what you'll need.

Don't Skip Breakfast

Even if you don't usually eat breakfast, do so on exam morning. A cup of coffee doesn't count. Don't have doughnuts or other sweet foods, either. A sugar high will leave you with a sugar low in the middle of the exam. A mix of protein and carbohydrates is best: Cereal with milk, or eggs with toast, will do your body a world of good.

Physical Preparation Checklist

For the week before the test, write down (1) what physical exercise you engaged in and for how long, and (2) what you ate for each meal. Remember, you're trying for at least half an hour of exercise every other day (preferably every day) and a balanced diet that's light on junk food.

Exam minus seven days

Exercise: _____ for _____ minutes

Breakfast: _____

Lunch: _____

Dinner: _____

Snacks: _____

Exam minus six days

Exercise: _____ for _____ minutes

Breakfast: _____

Lunch: _____

Dinner: _____

Snacks: _____

Exam minus five days

Exercise: _____ for _____ minutes

Breakfast: _____

Lunch: _____

Dinner: _____

Snacks: _____

Exam minus four days

Exercise: _____ for _____ minutes

Breakfast: _____

Lunch: _____

Dinner: _____

Snacks: _____

Physical Preparation Checklist (continued)

Exam minus three days

Exercise: _____ for _____ minutes

Breakfast: _____

Lunch: _____

Dinner: _____

Snacks: _____

Exam minus two days

Exercise: _____ for _____ minutes

Breakfast: _____

Lunch: _____

Dinner: _____

Snacks: _____

Exam minus one day

Exercise: _____ for _____ minutes

Breakfast: _____

Lunch: _____

Dinner: _____

Snacks: _____

Final Preparations

Getting to the Exam Site

Location of exam site: _____

Date of exam: _____

Time of exam: _____

Do I know how to get to the exam site?   Yes ___   No ___

(If no, make a trial run.)

Time it will take to get to exam site: _____

Things to Lay Out the Night Before

Clothes I will wear   ____

Sweater/jacket   ____

Watch   ____

Photo ID   ____

Proof of citizenship, etc.   ____

Four #2 pencils   ____

_____   ____

_____   ____

▶ Step 9: Do It!

Time to complete: 10 minutes, plus test-taking time
Activity: Ace the Border Patrol Exam!
Fast-forward to exam day. You're ready. You made a study plan and followed through. You practiced your test-taking strategies while working through this book. You're in control of your physical, mental, and emotional states. You know when and where to show up and what to bring with you. In other words, you're better prepared than most of the other people taking the Border Patrol Exam with you.

Just one more thing: When you're done with the exam, you will have earned a reward. Plan a celebration. Call up your friends and plan a party, or have a nice dinner for two—whatever your heart desires. Give yourself something to look forward to.

And then do it. Go into the exam, full of confidence and armed with test-taking strategies you've practiced till they're second nature. You're in control of yourself, your environment, and your performance on the exam. You're ready to succeed. So do it. Go in there and ace the exam. And look forward to your future career as a Border Patrol Agent!

4 ▶ Logical Reasoning

CHAPTER SUMMARY

The Border Patrol Exam includes a Logical Reasoning section that tests your ability to read, understand, and apply critical thinking skills presented in real-life situations. While on the job, Border Patrol Agents make many decisions using logical reasoning skills. It is important to understand how logical reasoning is used in legal situations, because as a Border Patrol Agent, you may be called on to testify in court. This section of the test is very important in determining whether you'll secure a job as a Border Patrol Agent. The tips and examples in this chapter are designed to help you develop your ability to reason logically and then boost your score on the exam.

THE LOGICAL REASONING SECTION of the exam is a series of scenarios followed by multiple-choice questions. The questions will test your ability to understand complex written information and draw some type of conclusion. You will be asked to make your conclusion based on only the stated facts, so you will need to read carefully and concentrate on what is being asked. You will not need to know any extra information other than what is in the paragraph.

► Logical Reasoning Skills

The most important part of being a successful Border Patrol Agent is your ability to reason competently. Logical reasoning is used in decision-making and problem solving, both on the job and in everyday life.

The questions in this test are different from regular reading comprehension questions that ask you to understand the meaning of a passage. Specifically, this is the kind of reading that will test your ability to draw conclusions and take action. Often, the situations presented in the questions can be quite complex. Careful reading and focused thinking are required to determine what *is* being asked and what *is not* being asked. The logical reading questions vary in level of difficulty from average to difficult.

► Read Carefully

The paragraphs are related to some aspect of Border Patrol or government work. It is important to read very carefully. You are being tested on your ability to read and draw conclusions based only on the facts given, so assume that the facts are correct as given even if they differ from information you know to be true. Remember, you are not being tested on your own knowledge of facts.

There may be different types of information in the paragraph. Take the time to study carefully what information is being given. Sometimes, there may be facts about two or more situations or subjects that can be linked. Some of the information may be positive or negative.

► Identify the Key Lead-In Question

The paragraphs in this test will be followed by a key lead-in phrase that asks you to complete a sentence by selecting choice **a**, **b**, **c**, **d**, or **e**. The lead-in phrase will be either positive or negative: *From the information given above, it can be validly concluded that* or *From the information given above, it CANNOT be validly concluded that*. Take time to carefully consider what is being asked by the lead-in question and whether it is positive or negative. This is the key to answering the question correctly.

For the positive lead-in phrases, you are given a choice of four incorrect conclusions and one correct conclusion. Negative lead-in phrases, in contrast, have four correct conclusions and one incorrect conclusion; the trick is to identify what CANNOT be concluded from the facts given in the paragraph.

In some of the paragraphs, the lead-in phrase may be limiting in some way. The lead-in phrase *From the information given above, it can be validly concluded that, in 2006 in the state of Arizona,* is an example of this. There may be answers that concern other states in other years. However, for the test question, only information from the paragraph dealing with the state of Arizona in 2006 would be valid.

► Avoid Hasty Conclusions

Everyday speech habits can encourage us to come to hasty, and often faulty, conclusions. Ordinarily, you wouldn't hear someone say, "Some of the sandwich has no mustard," unless they are also suggesting that some of the sandwich has mustard. This is not the case when reasoning logically, however, so beware of this type of hasty conclusion. For instance, if a law enforcement officer says, "Some of the tracks were not made by animals," it would be incorrect to conclude that some of the tracks *were* made by animals. That may be the case, but you have not been given enough information to reach this conclusion validly.

Be careful not to reach conclusions too quickly in the practice tests. Think each question through and remember to base your answer on the information given in the statement. You are interested only in the facts.

The following sections will familiarize you with the different types of questions on the exam and hone your reasoning skills.

▶ Reasoning about Groups or Categories

Some of the information in the Logical Reasoning test is about events or situations, and some information is about individuals or groups (categories). We'll be talking about groups or categories in this section.

All Statements

When a test question about two different groups begins with the word *all* or *every*, you are being given an important clue to help draw the right conclusion. When the word *all* or *every* begins a phrase, you now know that the two groups are connected in some way: Everything that is true about one group is also true about the other group. For example, the statement "All the agents at the station are Border Patrol Agents" means that the first group, the agents at the station, are included in the second group, Border Patrol Agents. The *all* statement does not provide enough information to determine whether all members of the second group, Border Patrol Agents, are included in the first group, agents at the station.

This may sound complicated, but it is actually an easy concept once you get the hang of it. Here's

another example: A teacher at the academy tells you that all of the Border Patrol uniforms are at the supply office. You might conclude from this information that all of the uniforms at the supply office are Border Patrol uniforms. It is incorrect, however, to come to this conclusion, because the supply office (the second group) may also have uniforms other than Border Patrol uniforms (the first group). The statement does not let you know whether or not there are other uniforms at the supply office.

Here are some other examples of *all* statements (all of Group A are Group B) followed by an invalid *all* statement (all of Group B are Group A).

True: All Border Patrol Agents are law enforcement officers.

Invalid: Therefore, all law enforcement officers are Border Patrol Agents.

True: Every Border Patrol Agent is a graduate of the Border Patrol Academy.

Invalid: Therefore, every graduate of the Border Patrol Academy is a Border Patrol Agent.

True: All U.S. senators are elected.

Invalid: Therefore, all elected officials are U.S. senators.

True: Every Border Patrol Agent knows Spanish.

Invalid: Therefore, everyone who knows Spanish is a Border Patrol Agent.

To help reinforce this concept, try creating some statements yourself. Remember, you don't have to know about the subject matter. You are only concerned about the logical order of the facts given in the sentence.

Some Statements

All statements give enough information to conclude that at least *some* of the second group are contained in the first group. Following are more examples of true *all* statements (all of Group A are Group B) and a *some* statement (some of Group B are Group A).

True: All Border Patrol Agents are law enforcement officers.

Valid: Therefore, some law enforcement officers are Border Patrol Agents.

True: Every Border Patrol Agent is a graduate of the Border Patrol Academy.

Valid: Therefore, some graduates of the Border Patrol Academy are Border Patrol Agents.

True: All U.S. senators are elected.

Valid: Therefore, some elected officials are U.S. senators.

True: Every Border Patrol Agent knows Spanish.

Valid: Therefore, some individuals who know Spanish are Border Patrol Agents.

Practice creating statements on your own to gain proficiency with questions that involve reasoning about groups or categories.

None and *Not* Statements

When something is NOT true, this is your key to another type of statement where two groups of things are not related. In this type of statement, you can be sure that the two groups have nothing in common. If you can say that no vegetables are sweet, then you also can say that no sweet-tasting food is a vegetable, because the two groups do not overlap. In the test, a word that begins with the prefix *non-*, or a phrase such as *not all of* or *it is not the case that*, establishes a negative fact.

Reasoning about Parts of a Group

When you see the term *some* on the exam, this refers to a part of a larger group. In the example *some trainees are learning Spanish*, the term *some trainees* means a part of a larger group of trainees. Remember, because you know that *some trainees are learning Spanish* does not mean that all trainees are learning Spanish and does not suggest this. A good rule of thumb is that unless information is provided to the contrary, *some* means *at least some*.

Sometimes, statements will use phrases that refer to part of a set. Some of these key phrases are *most*, *a few*, and *almost all*. Some of these statements may also be negative, such as *most trainees do not know Spanish*. While you may be tempted to conclude that there are some trainees who do know Spanish, this would be an incorrect conclusion, because you do not have enough information to know if anyone in the entire group of trainees knows Spanish.

Read very carefully when you see a statement about part of a group. Ask yourself if the statement is talking about part of a group or about the entire group. This will help you reason soundly and avoid errors on the exam.

▶ Reasoning about Events or Situations

Up to this point, we have discussed statements that deal with information about groups or categories. Now let's discuss relationships between events or situations.

The idea of a *chain of events* is important when reasoning about events or situations. This is a line of logical reasoning where one thing leads to another, which in turn leads to another, and so on. An example of a chain of events is *If a driver is convicted of speeding in Orleans County, the driver is guilty of a traffic violation, and drivers found guilty of a traffic violation in Orleans County have points deducted from their driver's licenses.* With this line of reasoning, you can go backward or forward along the chain of events.

You can think forward, meaning that when the first thing happens, then the other events follow. Suppose a friend tells you she has just been convicted of speeding in Orleans County. From the chain of events just described, you also know that your friend is guilty of a traffic violation and that points are deducted from her driver's license.

You can also think backward, meaning that if the later events don't happen, then the earlier events can't have happened, either. If your friend mentions to you, instead, that she has not had any points deducted from her driver's license, you will know that she has not been found guilty of a traffic violation in Orleans County and that she has not been convicted of speeding in Orleans County.

If-Then Statements

The phrase typically used to connect a chain of events is *if-then*. The first event is marked by the word *if* and the second event is marked by the work *then*. An example of this is *If Dick is sent to linewatch duty tonight, then the linewatch duty unit will need an extra vehicle. If-then* can also be used to connect two events that have already happened. *If there are leaves on the ground, then it is fall.*

Another way to express the same connection is to use the words *whenever, each time,* or *every time.*

When you see a sentence that begins with one of these words, two events are being connected: *Whenever I go home, I feel happy,* or *Each time I go home, there is a storm.*

An important point to remember is that the order of the two statements cannot be validly switched. In other words, if you switch the order of the two statements, the wrong conclusion may be reached. Consider the statement *If the tire goes flat, the car will come to a stop.* It cannot be validly concluded that *If the car comes to a stop, the tire has gone flat.*

Here are more examples of this line of reasoning. The first example is a true *if-then* statement and is followed by an invalid *if-then* statement with the statements reversed.

True: If an individual is a Border Patrol Agent, the individual works for the DHS.

Invalid: Therefore, if an individual works for the DHS, then the individual is a Border Patrol Agent.

True: If a person resides in Canada, then the person resides in North America.

Invalid: Therefore, if a person resides in North America, then the person resides in Canada.

True: If a car crosses the border into California, then the car is in the United States.

Invalid: Therefore, if a car is in the United States, then the car has crossed the border into California.

True: If a criminal receives the death sentence, then the criminal has been found guilty.

Invalid: Therefore, if a criminal has been found guilty, then the criminal receives the death sentence.

True: If a plane has no fuel, the plane will not fly.

Invalid: Therefore, if the plane will not fly, the plane has no fuel.

However, the order of these statements can be validly reversed if the statements are negated, or made opposite. Use our example, *If the tire goes flat* (the first statement), *the car will come to a stop* (the second statement). Based on this information, you can validly conclude that *If the car does not stop* (the second statement), *then the tire has not gone flat* (the first statement).

Here are some examples of a true *if-then* statement with a true (or valid) *if-then* statement following where the first and second statements have been reversed and made opposite.

True: If an individual is a Border Patrol Agent, the individual works for the DHS.

True: Therefore, if an individual does not work for the DHS, then the individual is not a Border Patrol Agent.

True: If a person resides in Canada, then the person resides in North America.

True: Therefore, if a person does not reside in North America, then the person does not reside in Canada.

True: If a car crosses the border into California, then the car is in the United States.

True: Therefore, if a car is not in the United States, then the car has not crossed the border into California.

True: If a criminal receives the death sentence, then the criminal has been found guilty.

True: Therefore, if a criminal has not been found guilty, then the criminal has not received the death sentence.

True: If a plane has no fuel, the plane will not fly.

True: Therefore, if the plane is flying, the plane has fuel.

It is important to note that the opposite of the second statement cannot be validly concluded from the opposite of the first statement. Let's use our earlier example: *If the tire goes flat, the car will come to a stop*. It cannot be concluded that *If the tire does not go flat* (the opposite of the first statement), *then the car will not stop* (the opposite of the second statement).

Here are more examples of a true *if-then* statement followed by an invalid conclusion statement.

True: If an individual is a Border Patrol Agent, the individual works for the DHS.

Invalid: Therefore, if an individual is not a Border Patrol Agent, the individual does not work for the DHS.

True: If a person resides in Canada, then the person resides in North America.

Invalid: Therefore, if a person does not reside in Canada, then the person does not reside in North America.

True: If a car crosses the border into California, the car is in the United States.

Invalid: Therefore, if a car does not cross the border into California, the car is not in the United States.

True: If a criminal receives the death sentence, then the criminal has been found guilty.

Invalid: Therefore, if a criminal does not receive the death sentence, then the criminal has not been found guilty.

True: If a plane has no fuel, the plane will not fly.

Invalid: Therefore, if the plane has fuel, the plane will fly.

▶ Warnings about Words

All and *None*

If you have ever had test-preparation training, you may have been advised to avoid answers in reasoning tests that start with the words *all* or *none*. This is not true for the Logical Reasoning Exam. There is a common belief that these two words represent extremes and that correct answers fall somewhere in the midrange between *all* or *none*. This is absolutely untrue for this exam. In both the reading paragraphs as well as the correct and incorrect responses, there will be *all* statements and *none* statements that are correct. The Logical Reasoning Exam will test you with real-life scenarios where *all* and *none* situations do actually exist.

Positive and Negative Words, Prefixes, and Connectors

As a rule, pay careful attention to words that give you clues about information on groups or linked events. These include positive words such as

> all
>
> some
>
> most
>
> always

Negative words and prefixes that should throw up a red flag are

> seldom   non-
>
> never   un-
>
> illegal   dis-
>
> prohibited

Carefully read for connectors that have the key information about the relationship among the facts given in the paragraph. Some common connectors are

> whenever
>
> unless
>
> except

Double Negatives

Single negatives are used commonly in the English language. When the word *not* is used in a sentence, it makes the sentence negative, as in the sentence *That flower is not a sunflower.* The Logical Reasoning Exam may also contain double negatives. On the test, there may be sentences such as *The door is not unlocked,* which means the door IS locked. Double negatives in English make a statement positive. The statement *This question is not unfair* means that the question IS fair. *The gun was fired* might be stated on the test as *It is NOT the case that the gun was not fired.*

Use of the Word *Only*

It is very important to pay careful attention to the word *only* in a statement. Use of the word *only* restricts the meaning of a sentence. For example, *The computer is on only when both buttons are pushed* means very clearly that it is necessary to push both buttons to turn on the computer. Now consider the sentence *The computer is on when both buttons are pushed*. This sentence is less restrictive because, although the computer can be turned on by pushing both buttons, it is possible there are other, unstated, ways to turn it on as well.

The phrase *if and only if* restricts the meaning even further. *The computer is on if and only if both buttons are pushed* means it MUST be the case that both buttons were pushed if the computer is on.

▶ Summary of Logical Reasoning Test Tips

1. When choosing a conclusion, always look for one that can be made based only on the information in the paragraph.
2. Assume all information in the paragraph is true. Do not use other factual information you may already know to reach your conclusion.
3. Focus on the key lead-in sentence and read the paragraph carefully. Consider all of the answer choices carefully before making your final answer selection.
4. Pay special attention to words such as *all, some, none, unless, except,* and *only.* These qualifying words help define the facts in the statement.

5. Keep in mind that negative prefixes such as *non-* or negative words such as *disorganized* or *unfasten* can be critical to an understanding of the information in the statement.
6. If for other tests you have been told to avoid answers that contain the word *all* or *none,* disregard that advice for the Logical Reasoning Exam. These words do not indicate an incorrect answer in this test. *All* and *none* can be in both the incorrect and the correct answers.
7. Answer every question on the test. Guess at an answer only after eliminating answers that you know to be false. While you are not penalized for guessing, your chances of picking a correct answer are greatly improved by using the process of elimination. You have a one in five chance of picking a right answer by blindly guessing. Your chances improve with every choice that is eliminated.
8. Do not pay attention to patterns made by **a, b, c, d,** or **e** on the answer sheet. Correct answer positions are selected randomly. You cannot improve your chances of guessing based on a pattern on the answer sheet. Trying to figure out a pattern is a poor test strategy.
9. The best way to improve your chances on the exam is through practice. Take the tests found in this book and study their answer explanations. This will hone your logical reasoning ability. Remember that the time you put into preparing for the Logical Reasoning Exam is time well spent and will increase your chances of doing well on the test.

5 ▶ Official Sample Questions for Logical Reasoning

CHAPTER SUMMARY

This chapter consists of the official Logical Reasoning Sample Test provided by the U.S. Department of Homeland Security Bureau of Customs and Border Protection and the U.S. Border Patrol. These sample questions are similar to the questions you will find in the actual test in terms of difficulty and format. In general, the test questions deal with situations you might encounter in law enforcement positions. Remember, knowledge of any job-specific subject matter is not required to answer the questions correctly.

▶ Sample Logical Reasoning Test

These questions consist of a paragraph followed by five response options. Some questions will ask you to select the only answer that can be validly concluded from the paragraph; preceding the five response options will be the phrase *From the information given above, it can be validly concluded that*. In other questions, you may be asked to select the only answer that *cannot* be validly concluded from the paragraph; preceding the five response options will be the phrase *From the information given above, it CANNOT be validly concluded that*.

You must use *only* the information provided in the paragraph, without using any outside information whatever.

It is suggested that you take no more than 32 minutes to complete questions 1 through 16. The questions on this test will not be on the real test, but the real questions will be similar to these in form and difficulty. The explanations for the correct and incorrect responses are found at the end of the chapter.

1. Agent Smith is in charge of all of the canine teams in his sector. Fifteen canine teams are stationed in his sector. Most of the canine teams are located at stations along the border. Several canine teams are located away from the border in large urban areas. All of the teams must be available to travel to any duty station within the sector.

    From the information given above, it can be validly concluded that, in Agent Smith's sector,

    a. most of the canine teams are located away from the border in large urban areas.

    b. only teams located along the border must be available to travel to any duty station within the sector.

    c. teams in urban areas do not need to be available to travel to other duty stations within the sector.

    d. none of the teams are exempt from traveling to any duty location within the sector.

    e. few of the canine teams are located at stations along the border.

2. The chief of police strives to provide quality service to the community while using resources efficiently. Accordingly, the chief must take into account several factors when allocating resources. For example, if it is a holiday weekend, additional staff are assigned to duty. However, if additional staff are assigned to duty, special funding is needed from the city council.

    From the information given above, it can be validly concluded that

    a. if it is a holiday weekend, then special funding is not needed from the city council.

    b. if it is not a holiday weekend, then special funding is needed from the city council.

    c. if special funding is not needed from the city council, then it is not a holiday weekend.

    d. if special funding is needed from the city council, then it is a holiday weekend.

    e. if special funding is not needed from the city council, then it is a holiday weekend.

3. Several different means of smuggling, such as cross-border tunnels, are used to bring narcotics, individuals, and contraband into the United States. Cross-border tunnels can be found all along the land border of the United States. They vary significantly in size and complexity of construction, although most are crudely constructed. Further, most cross-border tunnels are used for smuggling narcotics, although illegal aliens and other contraband have also been smuggled using tunnels.

From the information given above, it CANNOT be validly concluded that

a. most cross-border tunnels are not skillfully constructed.

b. all cross-border tunnels are used for narcotics smuggling.

c. at least some cross-border tunnels are not free from narcotics smuggling.

d. at least some of the means used for narcotics smuggling are cross-border tunnels.

e. at least some means used for narcotics smuggling involve crudely constructed tunnels.

4. Naturalized U.S. citizens can lose their U.S. citizenship if and only if they expatriate or are denaturalized. Misrepresentation on a legal permanent residence application, certain crimes, and leaving the United States within one year of naturalization to establish permanent residence elsewhere are all grounds for denaturalization. P.C. is a naturalized U.S. citizen.

From the information given above, it can be validly concluded that

a. if P.C. loses her U.S. citizenship without being denaturalized, then she must have expatriated.

b. if P.C. does not expatriate, then she cannot lose her U.S. citizenship.

c. if P.C. is denaturalized, then she must have made a misrepresentation on her legal permanent residence application.

d. if P.C. has committed no crimes, then she cannot be denaturalized.

e. P.C. cannot lose her U.S. citizenship without being denaturalized.

5. Following the Vietnam War, many people from Southeast Asia were paroled into the United States with an indefinite immigration status. In 2003, a new rule was developed to allow for adjustment of immigration status for some of these people. According to the new rule, all nationals of Vietnam (and some others—for example, nationals of Cambodia) who were paroled into the United States through the Orderly Departure Program were eligible to apply for permanent resident status.

From the information given above, it can be validly concluded that, based on the new rule of 2003,

a. everyone eligible to apply for permanent resident status is a national of Vietnam who was paroled into the United States through the Orderly Departure Program.

b. no one ineligible to apply for permanent resident status was a national of Vietnam who was paroled into the United States through the Orderly Departure Program.

c. only nationals of Vietnam who were paroled into the United States through the Orderly Departure Program were eligible to apply for permanent resident status.

d. some nationals of Vietnam who were paroled into the United States through the Orderly Departure Program were ineligible to apply for permanent resident status.

e. some of those who were ineligible to apply for permanent resident status were nationals of Vietnam who were paroled into the United States through the Orderly Departure Program.

6. An employer is permitted to hire a new employee only if the employer is able to verify that the applicant's employment documentation establishes both of the following: (1) the applicant is authorized to work in the United States and (2) the applicant who presents the employment authorization document is the person to whom the documentation was issued. An employer cannot request that an applicant provide more or different documents than required. If the documentation appears false or unrelated, employers must refuse acceptance and ask for other documentation from the government's list of acceptable documents.

From the information given above, it CANNOT be validly concluded that

a. no employer is permitted to limit which documents it will accept for verification of employment authorization.

b. if an employer cannot verify that an applicant is authorized to work, then the employer is not permitted to hire the applicant.

c. if an applicant's documentation appears to be true and relevant to an employer, the employer must refuse acceptance and ask for other documentation from the government's list of acceptable documents.

d. an employer may request different employment documentation if the provided documentation appears to be altered.

e. if an applicant is permitted to be hired, then the applicant has verifiable employment authorization.

7. Although the owner of a certain farm said that all her Central American (for example, Salvadoran and Honduran) workers were working legally, Border Patrol Agents discovered that many of the farm's employees were not authorized to work in the United States. After checking the employees' documentation, Border Patrol Agents discovered that all of the female employees were working in the United States legally and none of the illegal workers were from Honduras.

From the information given above, it can be validly concluded that, concerning the employees on this farm,

a. all of the employees from Honduras were working legally.

b. some of the women were illegal workers.

c. none of the employees from Honduras were female.

d. some of the female employees were from Honduras.

e. all of the Salvadoran employees were women.

8. The two ways of acquiring U.S. citizenship at birth are by place of birth and inheritance from U.S. citizen parents. Any child born in the United States while under American jurisdiction is a U.S. citizen at birth. Because foreign ambassadors are not subject to American jurisdiction, children born in the United States to foreign ambassadors do not obtain U.S. citizenship at birth. Children born overseas to U.S. citizen parents derive U.S. citizenship at birth, as long as the parents previously lived in the United States for a sufficient period of time. All others must naturalize to become citizens. J.B. was not a U.S. citizen at birth.

From the information given above, it can be validly concluded that

a. J.B. was born in the United States.

b. J.B. was born overseas to U.S. citizen parents.

c. J.B. was not born in the United States to U.S. citizen parents.

d. J.B. was not born overseas to U.S. citizen parents.

e. J.B. was born to U.S. citizen parents.

9. In a certain border state, all state peace officers have the authority to issue state citations for misdemeanor marijuana and paraphernalia offenses committed in their presence. Early last year, a certain Border Patrol sector in the state began a new operation with state police. Under this operation, all sector canine handlers were cross-designated as state peace officers.

From the information given above, it CANNOT be validly concluded that, in the border state discussed,

a. at least some law enforcement officers who can issue citations for misdemeanor marijuana and paraphernalia offenses committed in their presence are state peace officers.

b. all sector canine handlers have the authority to issue state citations for misdemeanor marijuana and paraphernalia offenses committed in their presence.

c. at least some individuals who have the authority to issue citations for misdemeanor marijuana and paraphernalia offenses committed in their presence are sector canine handlers.

d. no sector canine handlers lack the authority to issue state citations for misdemeanor marijuana and paraphernalia offenses committed in their presence.

e. only sector canine handlers have the authority to issue citations for misdemeanor marijuana and paraphernalia offenses committed in their presence.

10. Reinstatement allows a former federal employee to reenter the federal competitive service workforce without competing with the public in a civil service examination. If an applicant has reinstatement eligibility, the applicant is eligible to apply for any open civil service examination, as well as for federal jobs open only to federal employees. There is no time limit on reinstatement eligibility in certain cases. For example, if an applicant has veterans' preference or has acquired federal career tenure by completing three years of substantially continuous creditable service, the applicant has permanent reinstatement eligibility. C.P. formerly worked in the federal competitive service workforce.

From the information given above, it can be validly concluded that

a. if C.P. has neither three years of continuous creditable service nor veterans' preference, then C.P. cannot apply for a job open only to status candidates.

b. if C.P. has permanent reinstatement eligibility, then C.P. must have veterans' preference or three years of continuous creditable service.

c. if C.P. is not reinstatement eligible, then C.P. is not eligible to apply for any open civil service examination or job open only to status candidates.

d. if C.P. is eligible to apply for any open civil service examination or job open only to status candidates, then C.P. must have veterans' preference or three years of continuous creditable service.

e. if C.P. has veterans' preference, then C.P. is eligible to apply for any open civil service examination.

11. When officers must physically force entry into a home, they are required to ensure that the home is in a secure condition when they leave. Failure to secure the home leaves the officers liable for loss of items from the home and/or damage to the home that results from leaving the property unsecured. It is legal to break down doors in order to gain entry, if that degree of force is determined by an officer to be necessary. If an officer forces entry, the officer is required to take measures to minimize damage to the property. Officer Stoler needs to gain entry into a suspect's home.

From the information given above, it CANNOT be validly concluded that

a. Officer Stoler is required to minimize damage to the home if Officer Stoler forces entry.

b. if Officer Stoler is not required to ensure that the home is secure upon leaving, then Officer Stoler did not force entry into the home.

c. if Officer Stoler forces entry and fails to secure the home, Officer Stoler may be liable for loss of items resulting from leaving the home unsecured.

d. if Officer Stoler must physically force entry into the home, then Officer Stoler is not required to ensure that the home is secure upon leaving.

e. Officer Stoler will be required to secure the home unless Officer Stoler does not force entry.

12. Recently, Border Patrol Agents received leads from informants about possible illegal activity at La Rosita Park. When agents arrived at the park, they drove through the parking lots, looking for individuals and vehicles matching their leads. They examined several suspicious vehicles, including many unregistered vehicles. All of the unregistered vehicles contained bundles of marijuana. No arrests have been made in connection with this incident.

From the information given above, it can be validly concluded that

a. several arrests have been made in connection with this incident.

b. some of the vehicles that did not contain bundles of marijuana were unregistered.

c. all of the vehicles that contained bundles of marijuana were unregistered.

d. all of the vehicles that did not contain bundles of marijuana were registered.

e. some of the vehicles that contained bundles of marijuana were registered.

13. Green cards authorize aliens to work in the United States. The cards have a ten-year expiration period. Application for a renewal of a green card can be made beginning six months in advance of expiration. In order to apply for renewal of a green card, the applicant is required to apply in person and bring his or her current green card, application, fee, and new photos. It may take one year for applicants to receive new green cards, but temporary documents are provided.

From the information given above, it CANNOT be validly concluded that

a. an application that does not require the applicant to apply in person cannot be a renewal application for a green card.

b. application for a replacement green card cannot be made more than six months in advance of expiration.

c. green cards are the only work authorization documents that expire after ten years.

d. it is not the case that some green cards never expire.

e. some renewed green cards are not available in less than one year.

14. If a nonimmigrant alien (for example, a tourist) enters the United States illegally or enters legally but violates his or her nonimmigrant status, the alien is considered to be an undocumented alien. If an alien accepts unauthorized employment, remains longer than permitted, or commits one of several other violations, the alien has violated his or her nonimmigrant status. Some of these undocumented aliens purchase counterfeit documents or assume another person's identity by using fraudulently obtained genuine documents. R.G. is a nonimmigrant alien who is living in the United States.

From the information given above, it can be validly concluded that

a. if R.G. is an undocumented alien, then R.G. must have entered the United States illegally.

b. if R.G. has violated nonimmigrant status but has not remained in the United States longer than permitted, then R.G. has accepted unauthorized employment.

c. if R.G. has not remained in the United States longer than permitted, R.G. is not an undocumented alien.

d. if R.G. is an undocumented alien, then R.G. entered the United States legally.

e. if R.G. is not an undocumented alien, then R.G. has not accepted unauthorized employment.

15. When an illegal alien is being removed, the alien's passport in U.S. government possession is returned to the issuing government, not to the illegal alien. If the illegal alien's departure is voluntary, the passport is allowed to be returned to the alien. The U.S. government holds the passport of H.B., an illegal alien who must leave the country.

From the information given above, it CANNOT be validly concluded that

a. H.B.'s departure is not voluntary if H.B.'s passport is allowed to be returned to H.B.

b. if H.B.'s passport is not returned to the issuing government upon H.B.'s departure, then H.B. is not being removed.

c. H.B.'s departure is not voluntary unless the passport is allowed to be returned to H.B.

d. if H.B.'s passport is not allowed to be returned to H.B., then H.B.'s departure is not voluntary.

e. if H.B. is being removed, then H.B.'s passport is to be returned to the issuing government.

16. Oleoresin capsicum (OC), or pepper spray, is an effective law enforcement tool for incapacitating violent or threatening arrestees without using deadly force. Pepper spray causes a burning sensation of the eyes and skin and tearing and swelling of the eyes. Almost all arrestees are unable to see after being sprayed with OC. Some law enforcement agencies that have adopted OC sprays have fewer allegations of use of excessive force. Many law enforcement agencies have reported a reduction in officer and arrestee injuries as a result of the introduction of OC sprays.

From the information given above, it can be validly concluded that

a. any use of a law enforcement tool that causes a burning sensation of the eyes is considered to be the use of deadly force.

b. few arrestees are able to see after being sprayed with OC.

c. all law enforcement agencies that have reduced officer and arrestee injuries have also reduced allegations of use of excessive force.

d. no agencies that have adopted OC sprays have fewer allegations of use of excessive force.

e. only pepper spray is an effective law enforcement tool for incapacitating violent or threatening arrestees without using deadly force.

▶ Answer Explanations

1. d. None of the teams are exempt from traveling to any duty location within the sector.

This question is about the canine teams in Agent Smith's sector. According to the last sentence in the paragraph, all of the canine teams must be available to travel to any duty station within the sector. This is equivalent to saying that none of the teams are exempt from traveling to any duty location within the sector, choice **d**. Choices **b** and **c** contradict the information in the last sentence.

The third sentence in the paragraph informs us that most teams are stationed along the border. Choices **a** and **e** contradict this information.

2. c. If special funding is not needed from the city council, then it is not a holiday weekend.

Combining the information in the last two sentences, we know that if it is a holiday weekend, then special funding is needed from the city council due to assigning additional staff to duty. Accordingly, if special funding is not needed, then it must not be a holiday weekend; otherwise, special funding would be needed.

Choices **a** and **e** are false because they contradict the information in the paragraph. Choices **b** and **d** might be true, but they are not fully supported by the paragraph.

3. b. All cross-border tunnels are used for narcotics smuggling.

This is an example of a test question with a negative lead statement. It asks for the conclusion that is NOT supported by the paragraph. That means that four of the statements are valid conclusions based on the paragraph while one is not. In this case, choice **b** is invalid. The paragraph says that *most* cross-border tunnels are used for smuggling narcotics, but choice **b** says that *all* cross-border tunnels are used for smuggling narcotics.

Choice **a** is based on the information that most cross-border tunnels are crudely constructed. Choices **c** and **d** are based on the information that most cross-border tunnels are used to smuggle narcotics. Finally, choice **e** combines all information about the tunnels being crudely constructed and used for smuggling narcotics.

4. a. If P.C. loses her U.S. citizenship without being denaturalized, then she must have expatriated.

This question concerns a situation where there are two ways for naturalized U.S. citizens to lose U.S. citizenship, either by expatriation or by denaturalization. In choice **a**, the situation is considered in which P.C. has lost her U.S. citizenship without being denaturalized. Expatriation is the only option remaining to explain the loss of U.S. citizenship.

Choices **b** and **e** are invalid because they fail to consider that there is more than one way for P.C. to lose U.S. citizenship. Choices **c** and **d** are about situations in which P.C. may or may not be denaturalized. These two choices are invalid because they fail to consider that there are several possible reasons for denaturalization.

5. **b.** No one ineligible to apply for permanent resident status was a national of Vietnam who was paroled into the United States through the Orderly Departure Program.

This paragraph is mainly about the group of Vietnamese nationals who were paroled into the United States under the Orderly Departure Program with indefinite immigration status. In 2003, a new rule made everyone in this group of Vietnamese nationals (and some others) eligible to apply for permanent resident status. Accordingly, anyone who is not eligible to apply for permanent resident status must not be part of this group of Vietnamese nationals, which is equivalent to choice **b**.

Choices **a** and **c** fail to recognize that others, such as nationals of Cambodia, were also eligible to apply for permanent resident status. Choices **d** and **e** contradict the information that everyone in the group of Vietnamese nationals who were paroled into the United States under the Orderly Departure Program was eligible to apply for permanent resident status.

6. **c.** If an applicant's documentation appears to be true and relevant to an employer, the employer must refuse acceptance and ask for other documentation from the government's list of acceptable documents.

This question asks for the response option that CANNOT be validly concluded from the information in the paragraph. The only response option that cannot be validly concluded is choice **c**. Choice **c** is invalid because the paragraph does not say that employers must refuse acceptance of documentation that appears to be true and relevant.

Choices **b** and **e** are valid based on the information in the first sentence. Choice **a** is valid based on the information in the second sentence that employers cannot change documentation requirements. Choice **d** is valid based on the information in the last sentence stating that employers may request different documentation when they believe the documentation submitted appears to be altered.

7. a. All of the employees from Honduras were working legally.

The correct answer is **a.** The last sentence of the paragraph states that none of the illegal workers were from Honduras, which is equivalent to saying that none of the employees from Honduras were working illegally. Given that none were working illegally, it must be the case that all were working legally.

From the information in the paragraph, we know that all of the female employees were working legally and that all of the employees from Honduras were working legally. However, there is insufficient information to determine if any of the female employees were from Honduras. Therefore, choices **c**, **d**, and **e** cannot be validly concluded. Choice **b** contradicts the information that all of the female employees were working legally.

8. c. J.B. was not born in the United States to U.S. citizen parents.

According to the paragraph, there are two ways of acquiring U.S. citizenship at birth. Also, the paragraph states that J.B. did not acquire U.S. citizenship at birth. Therefore, the only conclusion that can be validly drawn is that J.B. did not meet either of the two conditions for acquiring U.S. citizenship at birth. Specifically, J.B. was not born in the United States to U.S. citizen parents, and J.B. was not born overseas to U.S. citizen parents who previously lived in the United States for the required period of time. Any other conclusion is not supported by the information in the paragraph.

9. e. Only sector canine handlers have the authority to issue citations for misdemeanor marijuana and paraphernalia offenses committed in their presence.

This question is a negative lead item, so the correct response is the only response option that CANNOT be validly concluded. The first sentence states that all state peace officers have authority to issue certain drug-related citations. Choice **e** is invalid because it says that only sector canine handlers have such authority.

The first sentence states that all state peace officers have authority to issue certain drug-related citations; therefore, at least some who have authority to issue certain drug-related citations must be peace officers, choice **a**. The last sentence states that all sector canine handlers are state peace officers; therefore, all sector canine handlers have authority to issue certain drug-related citations because the handlers are state peace officers, choice **b**. Moreover, given that all sector canine handlers have authority to issue certain drug-related citations, it must be the case that at least some individuals who have authority to issue certain drug-related citations are sector canine handlers, choice **c**. Finally, given that all sector canine handlers have authority to issue certain drug-related citations, it must be the case that no sector canine handlers lack authority to issue certain drug-related citations, choice **d**.

10. e. If C.P. has veterans' preference, then C.P. is eligible to apply for any open civil service examination.

The fourth sentence in the paragraph states that when an applicant has veterans' preference, the applicant has permanent reinstatement eligibility. The second sentence states that an applicant with reinstatement eligibility is eligible to apply for any civil service examination. Therefore, if an applicant has veterans' preference, the applicant is eligible to apply for any civil service examination due to having reinstatement eligibility. Accordingly, choice **e** is valid because C.P. will be eligible to apply for any open civil service examination if C.P. has veterans' preference.

Choices **a**, **b**, **c**, and **d** are invalid because they make assumptions that cannot be supported by the information in the paragraph. Choice **b** assumes that the only two ways of attaining reinstatement eligibility is to have veterans' preference or three years of creditable service. Choice **c** assumes that applicants are allowed to apply for open civil service examinations and jobs open only to status candidates only when applicants have reinstatement eligibility. Choices **a** and **d** assume that applicants are allowed to apply for open civil service examinations and jobs open only to status candidates when and only when applicants have veterans' preference or three years of creditable service.

11. d. If Officer Stoler must physically force entry into the home, then Officer Stoler is not required to ensure that the home is secure upon leaving.

This is a negative lead question, so the correct response is the only response option that CANNOT be validly concluded. The first sentence in the paragraph states that when officers must physically force entry into a home, the officers are required to ensure that the home is in a secure condition when they leave. Choice **d** contradicts this information in saying that Officer Stoler is not required to leave the home in a secure condition. Thus, choice **d** is the correct response.

Choice **a** is valid and follows from the information in the fourth sentence. Choices **b** and **e** are valid and follow from the information in the first sentence. Choice **c** follows from the information in the second sentence and is valid.

12. d. All of the vehicles that did not contain bundles of marijuana were registered.

The fourth sentence contains the information that all of the unregistered vehicles contained bundles of marijuana. Accordingly, if a vehicle did not contain bundles of marijuana, it could not be one of the unregistered vehicles since all unregistered vehicles contained marijuana. Therefore, it can be deduced that all of the vehicles that did not contain bundles of marijuana were registered.

Choice **a** contradicts the information in the last sentence. Choice **b** contradicts the information in the fourth sentence. Choice **c** assumes that only unregistered vehicles contained bundles of marijuana, but there is insufficient information to make that conclusion. Choice **e** assumes that some of the registered vehicles also contained bundles of marijuana, but there is insufficient information to make that conclusion.

13. c. Green cards are the only work authorization documents that expire after ten years.

This is a negative lead question, so the correct response is the only response option that CANNOT be validly concluded. Choice **c** is invalid because it assumes from the information that green cards are the *only* work authorization documents that expire after ten years.

The fourth sentence states that all green card applicants must apply in person; therefore, an application that does not require applicants to apply in person cannot be a green card application, choice **a**. Choice **b** is valid and is based on the information in the third sentence. The second sentence establishes that green cards have an expiration date, so choice **d** is valid. The last sentence says that sometimes it takes a year to receive a new green card, so choice **e** is valid.

14. **e.** If R.G. is not an undocumented alien, then R.G. has not accepted unauthorized employment.

Based on the information in the first sentence, if R.G. is not an undocumented alien, then R.G. has not violated his nonimmigrant status. Based on the information in the second sentence, if R.G. has not violated his nonimmigrant status, then R.G. has not accepted unauthorized employment. Therefore, if R.G. is not an undocumented alien, then R.G. has not accepted unauthorized employment, choice **e.**

Choices **a** and **d** are invalid because it cannot be determined whether R.G. entered the United States illegally based only on the information that R.G. is an undocumented alien, because R.G. may have violated his nonimmigrant status. Choice **c** is invalid because R.G. may be an undocumented alien for several different reasons even if he did not remain in the United States longer than permitted. Likewise, choice **b** is invalid because R.G. could have committed a violation other than accepting unauthorized employment that resulted in violation of nonimmigrant status.

15. **a.** H.B.'s departure is not voluntary if H.B.'s passport is allowed to be returned to H.B.

This is a negative lead question, so the correct response is the only response option that CANNOT be validly concluded. According to the second sentence, if the alien's departure is voluntary, then the passport is allowed to be returned to the alien. Based on this information, choice **a** is invalid.

Choices **c** and **d** are both valid and are supported by the information in the second sentence that the passport is allowed to be returned to H.B. if his departure is voluntary. Choices **b** and **e** are valid and are supported by the information in the first sentence that H.B.'s passport will be returned to the issuing government if H.B. is being removed.

16. b. Few arrestees are able to see after being sprayed with OC.

The third sentence says that almost all arrestees are unable to see after being sprayed with OC. Accordingly, few arrestees are able to see after being sprayed with OC, choice **b**.

Choice **a** is false because, according to the first sentence, OC is an example of a tool that causes a burning sensation of the eyes but is not deadly force. Sentences four and five do not say that the agencies that have experienced fewer allegations of use of excessive force are the same agencies that have reported a reduction in officer and arrestee injuries; thus choice **c** is invalid.

Choice **d** is false because it contradicts the information in the fourth sentence that some agencies using OC have experienced fewer allegations. Finally, the first sentence states that OC is an effective, non-lethal tool for violent or threatening arrestees, but it does not state that OC is the only tool (choice **e**).

Official Sample Questions for Language

CHAPTER SUMMARY

This chapter consists of the official explanations and sample questions, provided by the Border Patrol, for the Spanish Language and Artificial Language tests. The official explanation for the Spanish Language test begins on this page. Sample questions for the Artificial Language Test (ALT) begin on page 69.

▶ Sample Questions for the Spanish Language Test

You will soon take the Spanish Language Proficiency Test. This part of the chapter provides samples of the types of questions found in that test. The test is divided into two parts. Part I consists entirely of vocabulary items; Part II is divided into three sections, each section dealing with a different type of grammar item. These sample questions are similar to the questions you will find in the actual test in terms of difficulty and form.

▶ Part I

Read the sentence and then choose the most appropriate synonym for the italicized word.

1. Es muy *complicado* pilotar mi avión.
   a. fácil
   b. difícil
   c. divertido
   d. compilado
   e. comparado

The word *complicado* means complicated. In the context of the sentence, it refers to something that is hard to do. Hence, choice **b**, *difícil* (difficult), is the best synonym. Choice **a**, *fácil* (easy), is opposite to the meaning of *complicado*. Choice **c**, *divertido*, has the same beginning syllable (*di-*) as the correct answer, but its meaning (amusing) is completely different. The basic meanings of choices **d** and **e** (compiled and compared, respectively) are completely different from the meaning of *complicado*, although both *compilado* and *comparado* are phonetically similar to it.

2. Es fácil *comprender* lo que el agente está diciendo.
   a. responder
   b. comprobar
   c. entender
   d. pretender
   e. desentender

The word *comprender* means to understand something after watching, listening to, or reading it. Hence, choice **c**, *entender* (to understand), is the best synonym. Choice **e**, *desentender*, is the exact opposite of the correct answer; in fact, it is *entender*, but with a negative prefix added to it, thus giving it the meaning of to misunderstand. Choices **a**, **b**, and **d** (to respond, to verify, and to pretend) are completely unrelated to the meaning of *comprender*.

▶ Part II

Section I
Read each sentence carefully. Select the appropriate word or phrase to fill each blank space.

1. Me gusta entrar _____ la puerta que está _____ de la oficina.
   a. a, sobre
   b. en, desde
   c. con, bajo
   d. en, al lado
   e. por, detrás

The correct answer is choice **e**, *por, detrás*. Choices **a**, **b**, **c**, and **d** all use incorrect prepositions.

2. La agente me _____ la correspondencia cuando yo no _____ en casa.
   a. traido, estoy
   b. traer, estuviera
   c. trajo, estaba
   d. traerá, habré estado
   e. habrá traido, estar

The correct answer is choice **c**, *trajo, estaba*, because both verbs represent the correct past tense in the indicative mood (preterite indefinite *trajo* and preterite imperfect *estaba*). In choices **a**, **b**, **d**, and **e**, the wrong forms of the verb have been used.

Section II

Read each sentence carefully. Select the one sentence that is correct.

1. a. Todos los agentes coincidieron del sospechoso cuando entrarían por la puerta.
   b. El sospechoso que entró fue señalado en la puerta con los agentes coincidiendo.
   c. Todos los agentes señalaron al mismo sospechoso cuando entró por la puerta.
   d. Todos los agentes coincidió en señalar al sospechoso cuando entrarán por la puerta.

The correct answer is choice **c**, because it has the proper sentence structure (subject, verb, direct object) and contains no errors. Choices **a**, **b**, and **d** contain various errors, including incorrect prepositions, illogical structures, or incorrect verb forms; hence, none of them can be the correct answer.

2. a. La inmigración ilegal y el contrabando suponen un gran problema para muchos paises.
   b. La inmigración ilegal y el contrabando supongo un problema grande para muchos paises.
   c. Muchos paises con gran problemas suponían la inmigración ilegal y el contrabando.
   d. La inmigración ilegales y el contrabando suponen un gran problema para muchos paises.

The correct answer is choice **a**, because it has the proper sentence structure (subject, verb, direct object, indirect object) and contains no errors. Choices **b**, **c**, and **d** contain various errors, including incorrect subjects, illogical structures, or incorrect verb forms; hence, none of these choices can be the correct answer.

Section III

Read each sentence carefully. Select the correct word or phrase to replace the italicized portion of the sentence. In those cases in which the sentence needs no correction, select choice **e**.

1. Los agentes detectaron el contrabando antes de *abrir* la maleta.
   a. abriendo
   b. abrirá
   c. abriremos
   d. abrió
   e. No es necesario hacer ninguna corrección.

The correct answer is choice **e**, because after the preposition, *de*, the infinitive form of the verb, *abrir*, must be used. Incorrect forms of the verb have been used in choice **a** (gerund), choices **b** and **c** (future imperfect), and choice **d** (preterite indefinite).

2. Es necesario tener *todo las* documentos de identificación en regla.
   a. todos las
   b. todo el
   c. todas las
   d. todos los
   e. No es necessario hacer ninguna corrección.

The correct answer is choice **d**, because *todos los* is plural in number and masculine in gender, and thus in agreement with *documentos*. Choices **a**, **b**, and **c** have either the wrong gender or the wrong number.

▶ Sample Questions for the Artificial Language Test

The questions selected as sample questions for the ALT are similar to the questions you will find in the actual test in terms of difficulty and form. In general, the test questions deal with an Artificial Language created to measure your ability to learn a language. Remember that *knowledge of a specific language other than English is not required to answer the questions correctly.*

In the actual test, you will be given a Supplemental Booklet containing all the vocabulary for this language, all the rules of the language, and a glossary of grammatical terms. It is in this Supplemental Booklet that you will find information necessary to answer the questions in the test.

The following rules and vocabulary provide the information needed to answer the sample questions. However, this information is not the same as you will see on the actual test.

Grammar Rules

1. To form the feminine singular of a noun, a pronoun, or an adjective, add the suffix *-exc* to the masculine singular form. In the artificial language, there are only masculine and feminine forms for words. There are no neuter forms. When gender is not specified, the masculine form is used.

Example

If a male baby is a *belkoy*, then a female baby is a *belkoyexc*.

2. To form the plural of nouns, pronouns, or adjectives, add the suffix *-am* to the correct singular form.

Examples

If one male baby is a *belkoy*, then two or more male babies are *belkoyam*.

If an ambitious woman is a *tosleexc* woman, several ambitious women are *tosleexcam* women.

3. Adjectives modifying nouns and pronouns with feminine and/or plural endings must have endings that agree with the words they modify.

Example

If an active male baby is a *sojle belkoy*, an active female baby is a *sojleexc belkoyexc*, and several active female babies are *sojleexcam belkoyexcam*.

4. The stem of a verb is obtained by omitting the suffix *-gar* from the infinitive form of the verb.

Example

The stem of the verb *tilgar* is *til-*.

5. All subjects and their verbs must agree in number; that is, singular subjects require singular verbs and plural subjects require plural verbs. (See Rules 6 and 7.)

6. To form the present tense of a verb, add the suffix *-il* to the stem for the singular or the suffix *-al* to the stem for the plural.

Example

If *nalgar* means to bark, then *nalil* is the present tense for the singular (the dog barks), and *nalal* is the present tense for the plural (the dogs bark).

7. To form the past tense of a verb, first add the suffix *-con* to the stem; then add either the suffix *-il* if the verb is singular or *-al* if it is plural.

Example

If *nalgar* means to bark, then *nalconil* is the past tense of the singular (the dog barked). *Nalconal* is the past tense of the plural (the dogs barked).

Word List

yev	he, him
bex	a, an (all genders)
avekoy	enemy (masculine form)
syngar	to be
wir	the (all genders and numbers)
deggar	to fire
fo	at
daqkoy	jeep

Sample Questions

Translate the following sentences:

1. She was an enemy.

   Yevexc synconil bex avekoyexc.

In the first word, *Yevexc*, the suffix *-exc* was added to the masculine singular form of the pronoun *he*, making it the feminine singular form.

Two suffixes were added to the stem of the verb *syngar*: *-con* because the verb is in the past tense, and *-il* because it is the singular form.

In the word *avekoyexc*, the suffix *-exc* was added to the masculine singular form, making it the feminine singular form.

2. The enemies fired at the jeep.

   Wir avekoyam degconal fo wir daqkoy.

In the word *avekoyam*, the suffix *-am* was added to the masculine singular form to make it the plural form.

Two suffixes were added to the stem of the verb *degconal*: *-con* because the verb is in the past tense, and *-al* because it is the plural form.

7 ▶ Artificial Language Manual

CHAPTER SUMMARY

This chapter presents the official Preparation Manual for the U.S. Border Patrol Artificial Language Test, as provided by the Department of Homeland Security. This manual will help you prepare for the test you have to take if you don't speak Spanish. Luckily, you don't have to memorize the information here; most of it will be available to you as you take the test. See Chapter 8 for tips on using this manual to your best advantage.

THE PURPOSE OF THIS MANUAL is to prepare you for the Artificial Language Test (ALT). This test is part of the examination battery used in the selection of Border Patrol Agent trainees.

The ALT is intended to assess an applicant's ability to learn neo-Latin languages such as Spanish. Therefore, the test is based on an Artificial Language, the rules of which are based on some of the grammatical structures of neo-Latin languages. (The term *neo-Latin languages*, which is a synonym of the expression *Romance languages*, is used to refer to languages such as Spanish or French that are derived directly from Latin.)

All Border Patrol Agents are required to know the Spanish language, so it is important to assess language-learning abilities of all applicants to the Border Patrol. All applicants who successfully pass the entry-level examination battery for Border Patrol Agent are eligible to become agent trainees at the U.S. Border Patrol Academy. Applicants selected to become agent trainees will receive extensive training in many areas, including the Spanish language.

A validation study conducted by the U.S. Office of Personnel Management in 1991, and an attrition study conducted at the Border Patrol Academy in 1993, demonstrate that the Artificial Language Test (ALT) is an extremely effective predictor of success in learning Spanish at the academy. Accordingly, you are encouraged to study this manual with special care and attention.

As you progress through the Artificial Language Manual practice questions and the exams, you will see variations in suffixes, vocabulary, and rules, as well as how these three critical components interact with one another. Please note slight variations for sets of rules in Chapters 10 and 11, for instance. However, you will always be provided the relevant information you need to arrive at the correct answer. These deviations—some minor and some major—are intentional and, when combined, provide multiple variations of the ALT. You must not depend on memorization, but instead rely on your understanding of the rules, suffixes, and vocabulary words that are provided at the time you take the test.

▶ The Preparation Manual

Purpose of the Manual

The purpose of the manual is to help you prepare well for the ALT. The ALT can be a challenging test, especially for applicants who have never studied a foreign language.

The present manual was designed to allow you every opportunity to study the grammatical rules of the Artificial Language prior to taking the ALT. In this way, you can spend concentrated time learning to use grammatical rules that you will need to apply not only in the test, but also in the process of learning Spanish if you are selected for a Border Patrol Agent trainee position.

Organization of the Manual

The manual contains four parts: vocabulary lists (or dictionary) for the Artificial Language; a set of grammatical rules; a glossary of grammatical terms (for applicants who do not remember the meaning of some of these terms); and directions and sample questions. The official manual contains a full-length ALT and answer explanations, but this chapter does not.

The parts of the manual are organized in the following sequence.

First: The Vocabulary Lists

The lists of words need not be memorized, because during the actual test they will be available to you for consultation.

Second: Grammatical Rules for the Artificial Language

These rules are the backbone of the Artificial Language, because they are its connection to the structures of the Spanish language. There is no need to memorize the rules, though, because they will be available to you during the test. Also, you should note that some details of the rules will be different in the actual test. For example, if the feminine form of a noun takes the suffix -*nef* in the rules presented in this manual, in the actual test the feminine form of a noun may take a different ending. Other than these minor variations, the rules are identical in the sense that they deal with the same grammatical structures as the actual test.

Third: Glossary of Grammatical Terms

This glossary will provide a refresher mini-course in grammatical terms (such as *verb*, *noun*, *adjective*, and *adverb*) for applicants who have forgotten the meanings of these terms. The glossary will also be available for consultation during the actual test. In this manual, however, the meaning of the terms will be discussed in greater depth, and it is therefore advisable for you to study the discussion in this manual with special attention and concentration.

Fourth: Directions and Sample Questions

The official manual contains a full-length ALT and answer explanations, but this chapter contains only the directions and sample questions.

▶ Part One: The Vocabulary Lists

The words on the following two lists are the same; they are merely arranged differently, as they would be in a bilingual dictionary. In the first list, you can look up words in English to find their equivalent words in the Artificial Language. In the second list, you can look up words in the Artificial Language to find their equivalents in English. During the test, you will have the vocabulary lists with you for consultation at all times. You should note that some of the following words are not the same as those given in the actual test. Therefore, it is best not to try to memorize them before taking the actual test.

▶ Word List

Arranged Alphabetically by the English Word

ENGLISH	ARTIFICIAL LANGUAGE	ENGLISH	ARTIFICIAL LANGUAGE
a, an	bex	skillful	janle
alien	huslek	that	velle
and	loa	the	wir
boy	ekaplek	this	volle
country	failek	to be	synker
difficult	glasle	to border	regker
enemy	avelek	to cross	chonker
friend	kometlek	to drive	arker
from	mor	to escape	pirker
government	almanlek	to guard	bonker
he, him	yev	to have	tulker
jeep	daqlek	to identify	kalenker
legal	colle	to injure	liaker
loyal	inle	to inspect	zelker
man	kaplek	to shoot	degker
of	quea	to spy	tatker
paper	trenedlek	to station	lexker
river	browlek	to work	frigker

► Word List

Arranged Alphabetically by the Artificial Language Word

ARTIFICIAL LANGUAGE	ENGLISH	ARTIFICIAL LANGUAGE	ENGLISH
almanlek	government	kaplek	man
arker	to drive	kometlek	friend
avelek	enemy	lexker	to station
bex	a, an	liaker	to injure
bonker	to guard	loa	and
browlek	river	mor	from
chonker	to cross	pirker	to escape
colle	legal	quea	of
daqlek	jeep	regker	to border
degker	to shoot	synker	to be
ekaplek	boy	tatker	to spy
failek	country	trenedlek	paper
frigker	to work	tulker	to have
glasle	difficult	velle	that
huslek	alien	volle	this
inle	loyal	wir	the
janle	skillful	yev	he, him
kalenker	to identify	zelker	to inspect

▶ Part Two: Grammatical Rules for the Artificial Language

The grammatical rules given in this part of the manual are exactly the same as those used in the ALT, except that the prefixes (word beginnings) and suffixes (word endings) used in the test differ from those used in this manual.

During the test, you will have access to the rules at all times. Consequently, it is important that you understand these rules, but it is not necessary that you memorize them. In fact, memorizing them will hinder rather than help you, because the beginnings and endings of words are different in the version of the Artificial Language that appears in the actual test.

You should note that Part Three of this manual contains a glossary of grammatical terms to assist you if you are not thoroughly familiar with their meanings.

Rule 1

To form the feminine singular of a noun, a pronoun, an adjective, or an article, add the suffix *-nef* to the masculine singular form. Only nouns, pronouns, adjectives, and articles take feminine endings in the Artificial Language. When gender is not specified, the masculine form is used.

Examples

If a male eagle is a *verlek*, then a female eagle is a *verleknef.*

If an ambitious man is a *tosle* man, an ambitious woman is a *toslenef* woman.

Rule 2

To form the plural of nouns, pronouns, and adjectives, add the suffix *-oz* to the correct singular form.

Examples

If one male eagle is a *verlek*, then several male eagles are *verlekoz.*

If an ambitious woman is a *toslenef* woman, several ambitious women are *toslenefoz* women.

Rule 3

Adjectives modifying nouns and pronouns with feminine and/or plural endings must have endings that agree with the words they modify. In addition, an article (*a*, *an*, and *the*) preceding a noun must also agree with the noun in gender and number.

Examples

If an active male eagle is a *sojle verlek*, an active female eagle is a *sojlenef verleknef* and several active female eagles are *sojlenefoz verleknefoz.*

If this male eagle is *volle verlek*, these female eagles are *vollenefoz verleknefoz.*

If the male eagle is *wir verlek*, the female eagle is *wirnef verleknef* and the female eagles are *wirnefoz verleknefoz.*

If a male eagle is *bex verlek*, several male eagles are *bexoz verlekoz.*

Rule 4

The stem of a verb is obtained by omitting the suffix *-ker* from the infinitive form of the verb.

Example

The stem of the verb *tirker* is *tir.*

Rule 5

All subjects and their verbs must agree in number; that is, singular subjects require singular verbs and plural subjects require plural verbs. (See Rules 6 and 7.)

Rule 6

To form the present tense of a verb, add the suffix *-em* to the stem for the singular form or the suffix *-im* to the stem for the plural.

Example

If to bark is *nalker*, then *nalem* is the present tense for the singular (the dog barks) and *nalim* is the present tense for the plural (the dogs bark).

Rule 7

To form the past tense of a verb, first add the suffix *-zot* to the stem, and then add the suffix *-em* if the verb is singular or the suffix *-im* if it is plural.

Example

If to bark is *nalker*, then *nalzotem* is the past tense for the singular (the dog barked) and *nalzotim* is the past tense for the plural (the dogs barked).

Rule 8

To form the past participle of a verb, add to the stem of the verb the suffix *-to*. It can be used to form compound tenses with the verb *to have*, as a predicate with the verb *to be*, or as an adjective. In the last two cases, it takes masculine, feminine, singular, and plural forms in agreement with the noun to which it refers.

Example of use in a compound tense with the verb *to have*

If to bark is *nalker* and to have is *tulker*, then *tulem nalto* is the present perfect for the singular (the dog has barked) and *tulim nalto* is the present perfect for the plural (the dogs have barked). Similarly, *tulzotem nalto* is the past perfect for the singular (the dog had barked) and *tulzotim nalto* is the past perfect for the plural (the dogs had barked).

Example of use as a predicate with the verb *to be*

If to adopt is *rapker* and to be is *synker*, then a boy was adopted is a *ekaplek synzotem rapto* and many girls were adopted is *ekapleknefoz synzotim raptonefoz*.

Example of use as an adjective

If to delight is *kasker*, then a delighted boy is a *kasto ekaplek* and many delighted girls are *kastonefoz ekapleknefoz*.

Rule 9

To form a noun from a verb, add the suffix *-lek* to the stem of the verb.

Example

If *longker* is to write, then a writer is a *longlek*.

Rule 10

To form an adjective from a noun, substitute the suffix *-le* for the suffix *-lek*.

Example

If *pellek* is beauty, then a beautiful male eagle is a *pelle verlek*, and a beautiful female eagle is a *pellenef verleknef*. (Note the feminine ending *-nef*.)

Rule 11

To form an adverb from an adjective, add the suffix *-ki* to the masculine form of the adjective. (Note that adverbs do not change their form to agree in number or gender with the words they modify.)

> **Example**
> If *pelle* is beautiful, then beautifully is *pelleki*.

Rule 12

To form the possessive of a noun or pronoun, add the suffix *-ae* to the noun or pronoun after any plural or feminine suffixes.

> **Examples**
> If a *boglek* is a dog, then a dog's collar is a *boglekae* collar.
> If he is *yev*, then his book is *yevae* book.
> If she is *yevnef*, then her book is *yevnefae* book.

Rule 13

To make a word negative, add the prefix *fer-* to the correct affirmative form.

> **Examples**
> If an active male eagle is a *sojle verlek*, an inactive male eagle is a *fersojle verlek*.
> If the dog barks is *boglek nalem,* then the dog does not bark is *boglek fernalem.*

▶ Glossary of Grammatical Terms

A glossary will be available to you during the actual test, but it is recommended that you study *this* glossary before taking the test. This glossary contains basic grammatical concepts that apply to English, Spanish, and the Artificial Language. This glossary contains fairly extensive and comprehensive explanations of each grammatical concept. The explanations in the actual test are *not* comprehensive. Consequently, it is particularly important that you study these explanations very carefully.

Article

An article is a word that precedes a noun and determines whether it is a definite or indefinite noun: for instance, *the* book, *an* object.

Adjective

An adjective is a word used to modify a noun or pronoun (for example, *intelligent* women). Generally, an adjective serves to answer questions such as *which, what kind of, how many*. For example, (1) "*this* book" would be the adjectival answer to the question "which book?" (2) "a *beautiful* book" would be the adjectival answer to the question "what kind of book?" and (3) "*several* days" would be the adjectival answer to the question "how many days?"

In English, adjectives have only one form, regardless of the type of noun they modify. More specifically, whether a noun is feminine or masculine, singular or plural, the adjective used to modify it remains the same; for example, the adjective *strong* is exactly the same when it refers to one man, one woman, many women, or many men. By contrast, in both Spanish and the Artificial Language, the ending of the adjective is different if the adjective is modifying a singular masculine noun, a singular feminine noun, a plural feminine noun, or a plural masculine noun.

Adverb

An adverb is a word used to modify a verb. For example, the sentence "It was produced" could be modified to express *where* it was produced by saying "It was produced *locally*."

Generally, an adverb is used to answer the questions *where* (as in the example above), *when* (for example, "he comes *frequently*"), or *how* (for example, "she thinks *logically*").

Adverbs sometimes are used to modify an adjective or another adverb. An example of an adverb modifying an adjective is the sentence "She has a *really* beautiful mind," in which the adverb *really* modifies the adjective *beautiful* to intensify its meaning. An example of an adverb modifying another adverb is the sentence "She thinks *very* logically," in which the adverb *very* modifies the adverb *logically*, again to intensify its meaning.

In the Artificial Language (and hence in the ALT), the only adverbs used are those that modify verbs. In the Spanish language, as well as in the English language, adverbs are used to modify verbs, adjectives, and other adverbs.

Gender

As a grammatical concept, gender refers to the classification of words according to whether they are masculine, feminine, or neuter.

As previously stated, Spanish takes masculine or feminine endings for nouns, adjectives, and articles. The neuter form is used sometimes to express abstraction in a more emphatic manner. The neuter form is *NOT* used in the Artificial Language. Consequently, it is very important for you to remember that in the Artificial Language *all* nouns, adjectives, and articles take either a masculine or a feminine ending according to whether the sentence refers to a male or a female.

Also, all nouns and adjectives in the Artificial Language were conceived (for the sake of simplicity) to be masculine. Thus, unless the feminine gender is specified in the sentence, the masculine gender is used always.

Infinitive

Infinitive is the name given to the general, abstract form of a verb: for example, *to look, to think, to remember, to walk.* Once the action expressed by a verb is attached to a specific subject (a person, an animal, or a thing), then we say the verb is *conjugated*, or linked to that subject: *she thinks, the dog runs,* or *the table broke.*

In contrast to the way that an infinitive in English is preceded by the word *to* (as in *to think*), in the Artificial Language all infinitives have the same ending. In the version of the Artificial Language used in this manual, this ending (or suffix) is *-ker*; in the actual test, the ending will be different.

Noun

A noun is a word that names a person, place, thing, or abstraction: *Lindsay, Chicago, tree, wisdom.* A noun can refer to an individual (as in *Lindsay*, an individual person, or *Chicago*, an individual place) or to a set (as in *stones, trees, cities*).

Prefix

A prefix always occurs at the beginning of a word. It can be a single letter or a sequence of letters: *a*moral, *il*legal, *dys*functional.

A prefix is the opposite of a suffix (which always occurs at the end of a word), but both serve to change the basic word in some way. For example, *polite* is the basic word (in this case an adjective) to express the concept of behavior that conforms to accepted social norms; adding the prefix *im-* and creating the word *impolite* transforms the word *polite* into its contradictory concept.

You should note that in the Artificial Language, a prefix is used to create a negative concept (see Rule 13). This rule mimics both Spanish and English, in which negation is usually expressed by using a negative prefix.

Pronoun

A pronoun is a word used in place of a noun: *she* instead of *Lindsay*, *they* instead of *the guards*, *it* instead of *the stone*, *herself* instead of *the judge*.

In English, as well as in other languages, including Spanish, there is a difference between a pronoun that stands for the subject of an action (as in "*She* threw the stone," meaning that *Lindsay* threw the stone), and a pronoun that stands for the object of an action (as in "The stone was thrown at *her*," meaning that the stone was thrown at *Lindsay*).

By contrast, in the Artificial Language, there is no grammatical difference between *he* and *him*, both being *yev*. You should remember, however, that in the Artificial Language, pronouns take feminine endings when the subject or object of the action is feminine. Accordingly, in the version of the Artificial Language given in this manual, both *she* (subject) and *her* (object) would be *yevnef* (i.e., *yev* plus the feminine suffix *-nef*).

Suffix

A suffix always occurs at the end of a word. It can be a single letter or a sequence of letters—for example, cream*y*, read*able*, nice*ly*. Unlike prefixes, suffixes often change the part of speech (i.e., the type of word). For example, in the case of *creamy*, the suffix *-y* changes the noun *cream* into the adjective *creamy*, and in the case of *nicely*, the suffix *-ly* changes the adjective *nice* into the adverb *nicely*.

In addition, suffixes are used to conjugate verbs (for example, to change the present tense into the past tense: *you walk*, *you walked*) and to create the plural form of nouns (for example, *boy*, *boys*). In Spanish, suffixes are used for the same purposes, but they are used for other purposes too, such as creating plural forms for adjectives and changing the gender of a word.

In the Artificial Language, suffixes are used (1) to change the part of speech (for example, Rule 11 uses a suffix to change an adjective into an adverb), (2) to conjugate verbs (for example, Rules 6 and 7 use suffixes to express the present and past tenses), and (3) to create the plural forms of nouns, pronouns, adjectives, and articles (Rules 2 and 3). In addition, the Artificial Language mimics Spanish in using a suffix to express gender.

You should study all the rules on suffixes in the Artificial Language, and you should practice using these rules, but you should NOT memorize them because (1) you will have them available to you at all times during the actual test, and (2) in the actual test, some of the suffixes and prefixes are different from the ones used in this practice test.

Verb

A verb is used to express either an action or a state of being. For example, "he *prepared* dinner" expresses the action of making the dinner, while "he *is* a citizen" expresses the state or condition of being a citizen.

You should note that a state of being can be permanent or transitory. For example, "the agent's horse *is* a bay mare" expresses a permanent condition for the horse (its being a bay mare), while "George *is* at lunch" expresses a transitory condition for George (that of being at lunch at the present moment).

The Spanish language, unlike English, has two different verbs to express permanent and transitory conditions. The Artificial Language is akin to English, rather than to Spanish, in its use of a single verb to express any state of being.

When a verb is linked to a subject (i.e., conjugated), it changes from the abstract infinitive form to a specific form such as a present tense or a past tense. The Artificial Language primarily uses only two tenses: the simple past tense and the simple present tense in the indicative mood (see Rules 6 and 7). (Verbs in the indicative mood express a *real* action or condition, whereas verbs in the subjunctive mood express *hypothetical* actions or conditions. The subjunctive mood does not exist in the Artificial Language, but it is very important in Spanish.)

You may find that the past participle is used in the test (see Rule 8). In that case, the present perfect tense (they *have crossed*) and the past perfect tense (they *had crossed*) will be used in the Artificial Language.

Be sure to apply the rules as directed in the test material. If no rule governing the past participle is listed in the actual test material, then the past participle is treated as a simple past tense.

▶ Part Four: Directions and Sample Questions

Here, you will find only the directions and sample questions from the official Artificial Language Manual. For more practice, see Chapters 10 and 11.

Directions for Questions 1 through 20

For each sentence, decide which words have been translated correctly. Use scratch paper to list each numbered word that is correctly translated into the Artificial Language. When you have finished listing the words that are correctly translated in sentences

1 through 20, select your answer according to the following instructions:

Mark:

a. if *only* the word numbered 1 is correctly translated.

b. if *only* the word numbered 2 is correctly translated.

c. if *only* the word numbered 3 is correctly translated.

d. if *two or more* of the numbered words are correctly translated.

e. if *none* of the numbered words is correctly translated.

Be sure to list only the *numbered* words that are *correctly* translated.

Study the sample question before going on to the test questions.

Sample Sentence
He identifies the driver.

Sample Translation
Volle kalenim wir arlek.
    1   2   3

The word numbered 1, *volle*, is incorrect because the translation of *volle* is *this*. The word *yev* should have been used.

The word numbered 2, *kalenim*, is also incorrect, because the singular form *kalenem* should have been used.

The word numbered 3 is correct and should be noted. *Arlek* has been correctly formed from the infinitive *arker* (to drive) by applying Rules 4 and 9. Because the word numbered 3 has been noted, the answer to the sample question is **c.**

Directions for Questions 21 through 30

For each question in this group, select the one of the five suggested choices that correctly translates the italicized word or group of words into the Artificial Language.

Sample Question

There is *the boy*.
a. bex kaplek
b. wir kaplek
c. wir ekaplek
d. velle ekaplek
e. bex ekaplek

Choice **c** is the correct translation of the italicized words, *the boy*.

Directions for Questions 31 through 42

For this group of questions, select the one response option that is the correct translation of the English word or words in parentheses. You should translate the entire sentence in order to determine what form should be used.

Sample Question

(The man) synem bex avelek.
a. Bex kaplek
b. Bex ekaplek
c. Loa kaplek
d. Wir kaplek
e. Wirlek kaplek

Because *Wir kaplek* is the only one of these expressions that means *The man*, choice **d** is the correct translation.

Directions for Questions 43 through 50

For the last group of questions, select the one of the five suggested choices that is the correct form of the italicized expression as it is used in the sentence. At the end of the sentence, you will find instructions in parentheses telling you which form to use. In some sentences, you will be asked to supply the correct forms of two or more expressions. In this case, the instructions for these expressions are presented consecutively in the parentheses and are separated by a dash (for example, past tense—adverb). Be sure to translate the entire sentence before selecting your answer.

Sample Question

Yev *bonker* wir browlek. (present tense)
a. bonzotem
b. bonzotim
c. boneim
d. bonim
e. bonem

Choices **a** and **b** are incorrect because they are in the past tense. Choice **c** is misspelled. Choice **d** is in the present tense, but it too is incorrect because the subject of the sentence is singular and therefore takes a verb with a singular rather than a plural ending. Choice **e** is the correct verb form.

8 ▶ Using the Artificial Language Manual

CHAPTER SUMMARY

This chapter provides instructions and suggestions on using all sections of the Artificial Language Manual to help you prepare for the Artificial Language Test (ALT). The chapter also provides you with a short practice test.

T HE ARTIFICIAL LANGUAGE, of course, is of no use by itself—you'll never hear anyone speak it. It was devised to test your ability to learn languages, especially Spanish. The official Artificial Language Manual may look daunting at first. It's several pages long and probably unlike anything else you've encountered, although the Artificial Language rules are very similar to those of Spanish. With study, and especially with practice using the manual and taking the practice tests in this book, this pseudo-language will come to make sense, though, and begin to seem familiar. You may even start dreaming in Artificial Language before you're through!

▶ Purposes of the Artificial Language Manual

The Artificial Language Manual has two main purposes:

1. To help you prepare for the ALT by giving you a chance to study the Artificial Language grammatical rules ahead of time—not to memorize them, just to study them—so that you'll have a leg up when you actually start answering the Artificial Language questions during the test-taking process.
2. To give you a start on mastering the Spanish language, which you will have to do if you become a Border Patrol Agent trainee. As mentioned, the grammatical rules of Artificial Language are very similar to those of Spanish.

▶ Tips on Using the Artificial Language Manual

As with most tasks, approaching the Artificial Language Manual in separate small steps, rather than trying to grasp the whole thing at once, will help immensely. First, let's look at the manual's separate parts.

The Vocabulary Lists

Part One of the manual consists of two word lists. The lists actually contain the same words; they're just arranged differently. One is arranged alphabetically by the English word and one by the Artificial Language word, just as is the case in most bilingual dictionaries.

It is important to note that, for two reasons, it is not to your advantage to memorize the vocabulary lists in the manual:

1. The lists for the actual test will not necessarily contain the same words that appear in the manual.
2. You will have vocabulary lists in front of you during the test, so you can refer to them throughout.

The Grammatical Rules

In Part Two of the manual, you will find the grammatical rules for the Artificial Language. Again, as with the vocabulary lists, it is not to your advantage to memorize them. They will be provided for you during the test. Also, some or all of the prefixes (beginnings) and suffixes (endings) given in the manual are different from those employed on the test. However, because the way the grammatical rules work (that is, the way words are formed) is the same in the manual as on the test, you should learn how the formation of the various grammatical parts of speech works in the Artificial Language. In other words, you do need to understand how to apply the rules.

You may find it helpful to practice forming words from items on the vocabulary lists. For example, you could form the past and present singular tenses of each verb on the vocabulary list.

Glossary of Grammatical Terms

Be sure to thoroughly familiarize yourself with the meaning and use of each grammatical term in Part Three. The manual will be helpful in that it will remind you of definitions of parts of speech in

English, in case you have forgotten. Once you feel sure you are familiar with each grammatical term, work on how the parts of speech function together in actual sentences. For example, you might practice by identifying which grammatical terms apply to each of the words in some simple English sentences.

Another helpful way to practice is to identify which grammatical terms apply to each word on the vocabulary lists for the Artificial Language. *Note:* There may be more than one grammatical term that applies to a single word in both English and the Artificial Language. For example:

- "I will *guard* the door" uses the word *guard* as a verb.
- "The *guard* stood by the door" uses the word *guard* as a noun.

Knowing the grammatical terms and their functions will help you learn and understand the grammar of the Artificial Language efficiently; moreover, it will help you apply the grammar of the Artificial Language more quickly to translations in the exam.

▶ Practice Test

The following is the most important part of this chapter—the practice test items. You can learn much more by doing than by reading about, so these items, as well as those on the tests in Chapters 10 and 11, will help you more than anything else if you apply yourself diligently.

There are four different types of questions on the Artificial Language Exam. This practice test gives you two examples of each type of question. You should refer to the vocabulary lists and grammatical rules for the Artificial Language included in the Artificial Language Manual in Chapter 7 to answer these questions.

Be sure to pay special attention to the answer explanations that follow the questions.

1. ⓐ ⓑ ⓒ ⓓ ⓔ
2. ⓐ ⓑ ⓒ ⓓ ⓔ
3. ⓐ ⓑ ⓒ ⓓ ⓔ

4. ⓐ ⓑ ⓒ ⓓ ⓔ
5. ⓐ ⓑ ⓒ ⓓ ⓔ
6. ⓐ ⓑ ⓒ ⓓ ⓔ

7. ⓐ ⓑ ⓒ ⓓ ⓔ
8. ⓐ ⓑ ⓒ ⓓ ⓔ

For each sentence, decide which words have been translated correctly. Use scratch paper to list each numbered word that is correctly translated into the Artificial Language. When you have finished listing the words that are correctly translated, select your answer according to the following instructions:

Mark:

a. if *only* the word numbered 1 is correctly translated.

b. if *only* the word numbered 2 is correctly translated.

c. if *only* the word numbered 3 is correctly translated.

d. if *two or more* of the numbered words are correctly translated.

e. if *none* of the numbered words is correctly translated.

Be sure to list only the *numbered* words that are *correctly* translated.

1. Those women are illegal aliens.

Translation

Velleoz kapleknefoz synzotim fercollenefoz
1   **2**   **3**
husleknefoz.

2. The inspector shot the enemy spy.

Translation

Wir zellek degem wir avele tatlek.
  1   **2**   **3**

For each question in this group, select the one of the five suggested choices that correctly translates the italicized word or group of words into the Artificial Language.

The men and women who *guard the border loyally*
                                  3
have a complex and difficult job. They have to deal with both friendly and unfriendly aliens, as well as with well-trained and skillful spies. *They have to inspect* and
                                  4
identify complex governmental papers, and they have to make difficult decisions, often alone and away from their stations.

3. a. bonem wir reglek inle
    b. bonim wir reglek inleki
    c. bonim wir regker inleki
    d. bonim wir reglek inle
    e. bonem wir reglek inleki

4. a. Yevoz tulzotim zelker
    b. Yev tulem zelker
    c. Yevoz tulim zelim
    d. Yev tulzotim zelzotim
    e. Yevoz tulim zelker

For this group of questions, select the one response option that is the correct translation of the English word or words in parentheses. You should translate the entire sentence in order to determine what form should be used.

5. Wiroz (papers were skillfully) zeltooz.
   a. trenedlekoz synzotim janleki
   b. trenedleknefoz synzotim janleki
   c. trenedlekoz synim janleki
   d. trenedlekoz synzotem janleki
   e. trenedlekoz synzotim janle

6. Bex zellek synzotem (injured from the shooting).
   a. litato mor bex deglek
   b. liato mor wir degker
   c. liato mor wir deglek
   d. liazotem quea wir deglek
   e. liazotim mor wir deglek

For the last group of questions, select the one of the five suggested choices that is the correct form of the italicized expression as it is used in the sentence. At the end of the sentence, you will find instructions in parentheses telling you which form to use. In some sentences, you will be asked to supply the correct forms of two or more expressions. In this case, the instructions for these expressions are presented consecutively in the parentheses and are separated by a dash (for example, past tense—adverb). Be sure to translate the entire sentence before selecting your answer.

7. Wirnefoz *ekaplek* kometlek synem bex tatlek. (feminine plural possessive noun)
   a. ekapleknefoz
   b. ekaplekozae
   c. ekaplekefozae
   d. ekapleknefozae
   e. ekapleknefae

8. Bex *kometlek* huslek pirzotem janleki mor bexnef reglenef *bonker*. (negative masculine adjective—feminine singular noun)
   a. kometlek—bonleknef
   b. ferkometle—bonleknefoz
   c. ferkometle—bonleknef
   d. kometle—bonleknef
   e. ferkometle—bonlek

▶ Answers

1. c. The word numbered 1, *velleoz* (those), is incorrect. Although this adjective has the plural ending, *-oz*, it must have the feminine plural ending, *-nefoz*, to agree in number and gender with the feminine plural noun it modifies (see Rules 1, 2, and 3). The correct translation would be the feminine plural adjective, *vellenefoz*. The word numbered 2, *synzotim*, is an incorrect translation of the verb *are*. It is incorrect because *synzotim* (were) is the past plural conjugation of the verb; the correct translation is *synim* (are), which is the present plural conjugation of the verb (Rules 4 and 6). The word numbered 3, *fercollenefoz* (illegal), is correctly translated. As an adjective modifying the feminine plural noun *husleknefoz* (aliens), it has the correct feminine plural ending (Rules 1, 2, and 3). Furthermore, it has the correct negative prefix, *fer-*, to change the meaning of the adjective *legal* to illegal (Rule 13). Because only the word numbered 3 should be checked as correct, **c** is the correct choice.

2. d. The word numbered 1, *zellek*, is correct; it is the noun *inspector*, formed from the infinitive *zelker* (to inspect), following Rule 9. The word numbered 2, *degem*, is incorrect because it is the present singular conjugation of *degker* (to shoot); the correct translation is the past singular conjugation, *degzotem* (Rules 4, 5, and 7). The word numbered 3, *avele* (enemy), is in the correct form. In this sentence, the word *enemy* is an adjective modifying the word *spy*; therefore, it takes the adjectival ending, following Rule 10. Because both the words numbered 1 and 3 should be checked as correct, the correct answer is **d**.

3. b. Choice **b** is correct because the verb is in the correct present plural conjugation (Rules 4, 5, and 6); the noun, *reglek*, is correctly formed according to Rule 9; and the adverb, *inleki*, is correctly formed according to Rule 11. Choice **a** is incorrect because the verb, *bonem*, is in the present singular conjugation; it should be in the present plural form, *bonim*, to agree in number with the subject of the sentence, *men and women* (Rules 5 and 6). Also, the word *inle* (loyal) is lacking the suffix needed to make it into the adverb, *inleki* (loyally), following Rule 11. Choice **c** is incorrect because the noun *reglek* (border), formed according to Rule 9, is incorrectly translated as the infinitive *regker* (to border). Choice **d** is incorrect because the word *inle* (loyal) is lacking the suffix needed to make it into the adverb *inleki* (loyally), following Rule 11. Choice **e** is incorrect because the verb, *bonem*, is in the present singular conjugation; it should be in the present plural form, *bonim*, to agree in number with the subject of the sentence, *men and women* (Rules 5 and 6).

4. e. Choice **e** is correct because the pronoun is in the correct masculine plural form, *yevoz* (Rule 2); the verb, *tulim*, is in the correct present plural conjugation (Rules 4, 5, and 6); and the infinitive, *to inspect*, is correctly translated as *zelker*. Choice **a** is incorrect because the verb, *tulzotim*, is in the past plural conjugation; it should be the present plural, *tulim* (Rules 4, 5, and 6). Choice **b** is incorrect because the pronoun, *yev* (he), is in the masculine singular form; it should have the masculine plural ending to form the plural pronoun, *yevoz* (they), according to Rule 2. The verb, *tulem*, is in the present singular form; it should be present plural to agree with the subject, *they* (Rules 5 and 6). Choice **c** is incorrect because the verb, *zelim*, is in the present plural conjugation; it should be in the infinitive form, *zelker,* to correctly translate as *to inspect*. Choice **d** is incorrect because the pronoun, *yev*, should be in the masculine plural form, *yevoz* (they) according to Rule 2. Also, the verb, *tulzotim*, is in the past plural form; it should be the present plural (*tulim*), according to Rules 4, 5, and 6, and the infinitive, *to inspect* (*zelker*), is incorrectly translated as the past plural conjugation, *zelzotim*, of the verb.

5. a. *Wiroz trenedlekoz synzotim janleki zeltooz* means *The papers were skillfully inspected.* Choice **a** is correct because the noun, *trenedlekoz*, is in the proper masculine plural form (Rule 2); the verb, *synzotim*, is in the correct past plural conjugation (Rules 4, 5, and 7); and the adverb, *janleki*, has the correct adverbial suffix (Rule 11). Choice **b** is incorrect because the noun, *trenedleknefoz*, is in the feminine plural form; it should be the masculine plural, *trenedlekoz* (Rules 2 and 3). Choice **c** is incorrect because the verb, *synim*, is in the present plural form; it should be the past plural form, *synzotim* (Rules 4, 5, and 7). Choice **d** is incorrect because the verb, *synzotem*, is in the past singular conjugation; it should be the past plural, *synzotim* (Rules 4, 5, and 7). Choice **e** is incorrect because the word *janle* is in its adjectival form; it should be in the adverbial form, *janleki* (skillfully), formed according to Rule 11.

6. c. *Bex zellek synzotem liato mor wir deglek* means *An inspector was injured from the shooting.* Choice **c** is correct because the verb is a past participle, *liato* (Rule 8); the words *from* (*mor*) and *the* (*wir*) are correctly translated; and the noun *shooting* (*deglek*) is correctly formed from the infinitive, *degker*, following Rule 9. Choice **a** is incorrect because the word *the* (*wir*) is mistranslated as *bex*. Choice **b** is incorrect because the noun *shooting* (*deglek*), formed according to Rule 9, is mistranslated as the infinitive, *degker* (to shoot). Choice **d** is incorrect because the word *from* (*mor*) is mistranslated as *quea* (of). Choice **e** is incorrect because the verb, *liazotim*, is in the past plural form; it should be in the past singular form, *liazotem*, to agree with the singular subject, *zellek* (inspector) (Rules 4, 5, and 7).

7. d. *Wirnefoz ekapleknefozae kometlek synem bex tatlek* means *The girls' friend is a spy*. Choice **d** is correct because it is the feminine plural possessive noun, formed according to Rules 1, 2, and 12. Choice **a** is incorrect because it is the feminine plural noun; it lacks the possessive ending. Choice **b** is incorrect because it is the masculine plural possessive form; it should be feminine plural possessive. Choice **c** is incorrect because it is misspelled. Choice **e** is incorrect because it is the feminine singular possessive.

8. c. *Bex ferkometle huslek pirzotem janleki mor bexnef reglenef bonleknef* means *An unfriendly alien escaped skillfully from a border guard*. Choice **c** is correct because *ferkometle* is the negative masculine adjective, formed according to Rules 10 and 13, and *bonleknef* is the feminine singular noun, formed according to Rules 1 and 9. Choice **a** is incorrect because *kometlek* is the masculine singular noun, not the negative adjective. Choice **b** is incorrect because *bonleknefoz* is the feminine plural noun, not the feminine singular. Choice **d** is incorrect because *kometle* is lacking the negative prefix, *fer-*. Choice **e** is incorrect because *bonlek* is the masculine singular noun, not the feminine singular.

▶ Summary

Focus your study time on learning and recognizing the meanings and the relationships of the various grammatical parts of language as detailed in the glossary of grammatical terms. Understanding the parts of speech and their relationships in sentences will help you understand and use the grammatical rules of the Artificial Language to form various parts of speech. Be careful to learn and understand relationships between words, such as agreement in gender between nouns and their adjectives, that are not used in English but are important features of the Artificial Language.

Remember also that the Artificial Language questions will become clearer and easier as you progress through the practice tests in this book, so approach them with confidence.

Tips for Using the Artificial Language Manual

- **Do not** memorize the vocabulary lists.
- **Do not** memorize the grammatical rules.
- **Do** study and familiarize yourself with the grammatical terms in the glossary.
- **Do** learn thoroughly how to apply the grammatical rules, but **do not** memorize the prefixes and suffixes.
- **Do** practice applying the rules as often as you can before the exam—that is, you should do not only the practice exam questions in this chapter, but the two full-length practice exams in this book, as well.

9 ▶ Checking Your Spanish Proficiency

CHAPTER SUMMARY

This chapter will give you hints and suggestions on how to score well on the Spanish Language portion of the Border Patrol Exam, along with a list of resources to help you study more effectively. This chapter also includes sample Spanish test questions and explanations. Use this chapter only if you speak Spanish. If you don't, review for the Artificial Language Test in Chapters 7 and 8 instead.

TODAY, MORE THAN EVER BEFORE, the ability to speak a second language is in demand. Modern technology has enabled people anywhere on Earth to communicate with each other quickly and easily. For many millions of people, this communication takes place in the Spanish language. Someone who speaks Spanish can function more productively in the modern workplace both at home and abroad. Also, if you know the language, you will have a much richer experience when traveling to Spanish-speaking countries.

As a Border Patrol Agent, you'll find that speaking Spanish well will be an invaluable aid in doing your job. First, the probability of miscommunication is greatly reduced when both parties speak the same language. Second, speaking in another person's native language demonstrates your goodwill and a basic respect for that person. Every Border Patrol Agent is required to know Spanish, so you're ahead of the game if you already have a working knowledge of the language.

This chapter assumes you have that working knowledge. It will give you some tips on how to review your Spanish, if necessary. It reviews some of the essential grammar rules you may have forgotten—this section could be essential if you are a native speaker of Spanish who never really had to learn the rules. In this chapter, you'll also find some sample questions with tips on how to answer them, as well as a list of resources you can use to review.

▶ Some Helpful Hints for Reviewing

Learning or reviewing Spanish effectively is mostly a matter of establishing a set of good habits and then practicing, practicing, practicing. Here are some useful hints to help you get started.

- Schedule study time in small units. If you need to do a lot of studying, study for a half-hour, then do something else, then study for another half-hour, and so on.
- If you know a native Spanish-speaker who speaks the language well, see if you can arrange practice sessions with that person. If that is not possible, the next best thing is to listen to a reading by someone who speaks Spanish well.
- Study out loud. It is important to hear yourself speaking Spanish. Doing this will enable you to speak more comfortably and easily. If possible, try to study with a friend. That way, you can check each other's pronunciation and grammar. You will find that this will enable you to learn the material more quickly, and the learning process will be more interesting.
- Spend extra time memorizing vocabulary. This is very important. There are a number of books available in bookstores and libraries that have vocabulary lists. A good choice would be

Mastering Spanish Vocabulary: A Thematic Approach by José Navarro and Axel Navarro Ramil.

- Spend extra time on pronunciation. Be sure to get it right. This is essential, because, as in English, many Spanish words have different meanings when pronounced differently; for example, *paso* (I am passing by) is very different from *pasó* (he/she/you passed by). Correct pronunciation will help you choose the correct written word on the test.
- Always think of the meaning. When practicing, as you repeat basic sentences, think about their meanings and try to speak with feeling; that is, try to make your expression match the meaning. This will reinforce your learning, and practice won't become mere mechanical repetition.
- Continually review earlier material as you progress through the lessons. When you go back and review earlier, easier lessons, you will reinforce what you have already memorized.
- Use what is called the *pattern sentence technique*. This is a good way to systematically learn or review material. Pattern sentences can be used to practice verb conjugations, pronoun usage, and adjective endings. When practicing, alone or with a friend, try using this technique. Here's how it works:
  - Take a correct sentence that uses a regular -*ar*, -*er*, or -*ir* verb form; then change the subject and repeat the new sentence aloud. For instance, if you say *¿Habla Ud. con él?* (Do you speak with him?), you or another person could respond *Sí, hablo con él* (Yes, I speak with him).
  - Practice correct pronoun and adjective usage this way, too. If you asked the person *¿Ud. le dio el libro a mi hermano?* (Did you give the book to my brother?), the person could answer *Sí, se lo di* (Yes, I gave it to him).

▶ Some Essential Grammatical Rules

Following is a list of grammatical rules you'll need to know. Supplement the information here by finding a good Spanish grammar book and studying it to be sure you understand the terms. A solid understanding of these rules of correct usage is the key to doing well on the Spanish Language portion of the Border Patrol Exam.

Nouns and Gender

A noun is a word that denotes a person, place, or thing. All nouns in Spanish are either masculine or feminine in gender.

- Nouns ending in -*o* are usually masculine, but an important exception is *la mano* (hand). Many nouns ending in consonants are masculine as well.
- Nouns ending in -*e* may be masculine or feminine.
- Feminine nouns require a feminine article, *la* (the) or *una* (a or an). Feminine nouns usually end in -*a*, -*ción*, -*umbre*, -*dad*, -*tad*, or -*tud*.
- Always memorize the noun together with its masculine or feminine article: *el padre*, *la madre*. This is essential. It will also make learning the irregular ones easier. For instance, *el mapa* (the map) is an example of an irregular noun.

Types of Pronouns

A pronoun is a word that takes the place of a noun.

Subject Pronouns

Subject pronouns take the place of the subject of the sentence. The subject pronouns are *yo, tú, usted, él, ella, nosotros, nosotras, ustedes, ellos,* and *ellas. Vosotros* is another plural form of *you,* used in Spain, but we will not discuss it here.

- Subject pronouns may be omitted when the form of the verb identifies the subject. An example is *yo voy. Voy* can only mean *I go,* so *yo* can be omitted.
- However, subject pronouns may be added for greater clarity, emphasis, or contrast, as in the sentence *Ella va, no él* (she is going, not him).
- In the polite form of address, *usted* and *ustedes* (abbreviated *Ud.* or *Vd.* and *Uds.* or *Vds.*) are often kept to avoid confusion with *él, ella, ellos, ellas.* That's why *usted* and *ustedes* are repeated so often.

Direct Object Pronoun

A direct object pronoun takes the place of a person or thing that directly receives the action of the verb. The direct object pronouns are *me, te, nos, la, las, lo,* and *los.* An example is *los veo* (I see them).

Indirect Object Pronoun

The indirect object pronoun takes the place of a person to whom, or for whom, an action is performed. It is the ultimate receiver of the action of a verb. The indirect object pronouns are *me, te, nos, le,* and *les.* An example is *les habla* (he speaks to them).

Prepositional Pronoun

Prepositional pronouns are pronouns that come after a preposition. Prepositional pronouns are the same as regular pronouns, except for *me,* which becomes *mí,* and *te,* which becomes *ti:* for example, *para ti* (for you). When the preposition *con* appears before *mí* or *ti,* the two words are contracted and become *conmigo* and *contigo.*

Reflexive Direct and Indirect Object Pronouns

Reflexive direct and indirect objects are used when the subject performs the action to, or on, itself. The reflexive direct and indirect object pronouns are *me, te, se, nos,* and *se.* An example is *él se sienta* (he sits down, or more literally, he sits himself down).

Correct Position of Object Pronouns

Object pronouns come before conjugated verb forms. They should be placed in the following order: reflexive pronoun first, followed by the indirect object pronoun, then the direct object pronoun, and finally the verb. There is a device that will help you remember this correct order—it goes like this:

Indirect before direct, reflexive first of all.

Although it is quite common to have an indirect object pronoun followed by a direct object pronoun, it is rare to encounter a reflexive, a direct object, and an indirect object pronoun all together. When it does happen, though, this device will help you remember the right order.

Object pronouns are placed after, and attached to, both infinitives and affirmative commands, making all one word. An example is *mándamelo* (order it for me).

Adjectives

Adjectives modify or give specific information about nouns in a sentence. They tell qualities such as size, weight, color, and so forth. Some examples are *la casa es blanca* (the house is white) and *los muchachos son simpáticos* (the boys are nice). Adjectives must agree in number and gender with the nouns they modify.

Verbs

Verbs are words that tell action or state of being in a sentence. For example, *ellos llegan mañana* (they arrive tomorrow) is an example of a verb that tells action, whereas *es su hermano* (he is your brother) tells state of being.

- Spanish verbs have three regular conjugations ending in: -*ar* (e.g., *cantar*), -*er* (e.g., *vender*), or -*ir* (e.g., *recibir*).
- Usually, verbs are formed by dropping the last two letters of the infinitive and adding the endings in their place. However, there are a number of quite common irregular verbs that must be memorized.
- The future and conditional tenses are formed by adding the endings to the entire infinitive.
- Two of the most frequently encountered verbs are *ser* (to be) and *estar* (to be). It will be easier to know which one to use if you remember this:
  - *Ser* is used for a characteristic or essence of something.
  - *Estar* is used for a location or condition.

Adverbs

An adverb is a word that gives additional information about a verb, an adjective, or another adverb. It tells how, when, or where the action or state is taking place.

- Adverbs are formed by adding -*mente* to the feminine form (ending in *a*) of the adjective. An example is when *rápido* becomes *rapidamente* (quickly).
- For adjectives ending in *e* or a consonant, just add -*mente* without changing it to an *a*. An example is when *gentil* becomes *gentilmente* (elegantly).

Conjunctions

Conjunctions are joining words. They link words, or groups of words, into more complex sentences. A few examples are *y* (and), *pero* (but), and *sin embargo* (although*). Que* (that) is a common connecting word that links clauses.

Personal *a*

In Spanish, an *a* must be used after a verb when the direct object is a person. An example would be *conozco a su hermano* (I know your brother).

- The personal *a* may be used when referring to pets that one is especially fond of. *Quiero a Spot* (I love Spot) is an example. But it is mostly used only when people are the direct object of the verb.
- The only verb that the personal *a* is not used after is *tener*. Never use the personal *a* after *tener*: *Tengo un hermano mayor.*

▶ Practice Questions with Tips

The practice questions that follow are like those in the practice exam in this book—and like those in the real exam. There are four different kinds of questions. Study each sample carefully and use the information provided to answer them.

Part I

The best way to prepare for the vocabulary part of the test is to memorize, memorize, memorize. Using flash cards or a book of vocabulary lists, spend time every day drilling your vocabulary. This is an effective way to increase your Spanish comprehension and reinforce what you have already learned.

The surest way to do well on the test is to study your vocabulary as much as possible. However, even then, you may run across a key word or a choice you don't know. How do you proceed? A useful tip is to look not only for the meaning of the word but also for its part of speech. For example, is the word a noun, a pronoun, or a verb? Often, several choices can be eliminated just by observing that they are the wrong number and gender for the noun, the wrong pronoun, or the wrong form of the verb. In the first example that follows, three of the choices are the wrong verb forms to match the sentence. This leaves only two possibilities. Now you can make an educated guess about the right one. However, the best approach is to know your vocabulary.

Read the sentence and then choose the most appropriate synonym for the italicized word or phrase.

1. *Deseamos* oír todo la historia.
   a. Vienen
   b. Le dijo
   c. Robaremos
   d. Queremos
   e. Habló

The correct choice is **d**, *Queremos* (we want), because it is closer in meaning to *Deseamos* (we wish) than the other choices—*Vienen* (they come), *Le dijo* (he said), *Robaremos* (we will steal), and *Habló* (he spoke)—and because it has the correct verb form.

2. *El director* de la organización es nuevo.
   a. El jefe
   b. Los hermanos
   c. La secretaria
   d. Los curas
   e. La madre

The correct choice is **a**, *El jefe* (the boss), because it is closest in meaning to *El director* (the director). In this case, the word in question is a noun. You will observe that incorrect number or gender combinations rule out all possibilities except choice **a**.

In the vocabulary section, if you already know the meaning of the word in question, look at it from a grammatical point of view only to check your work.

3. *La mujer* del presidente es gorda.
   a. Los muebles
   b. El mono
   c. La señora
   d. Las hijas
   e. La jira

Choice **c** is the one that is closest in meaning and has the correct number and gender.

Part II, Section I

For this part of the test, the important thing to focus on is the grammar. Look for the combination of words that not only has an appropriate meaning, but also matches grammatically. Look for obvious errors such as choices using the wrong number and gender or an incorrect verb form.

When evaluating verbs, begin by looking for the one with a form that matches the subject, which may be either a noun or a pronoun. Then look for one that uses the appropriate tense. This will quickly eliminate several possibilities. As in the following examples, it may not even be necessary to know the meaning of the verb to be able to choose the correct answer using this technique.

Read each sentence carefully. Select the appropriate word or phrase to fill each blank space.

1. Ellos _____ en el jardín cuando _____ la música.
   a. está, oyo
   b. estaban, oyeron
   c. estarán, vienen
   d. han estado, oían
   e. estuvieron, oí

Choice **b** is the correct use of the imperfect and the preterite verb tenses. The other choices use a wrong verb form.

2. Las _____ fueron completamente _____ por la bomba.
   a. está, destruida
   b. cartas, encontrados
   c. casas, destruidas
   d. días, perdidos
   e. ventana, nueva

Choice **c** uses the correct verb form. The other possibilities are wrong because of incorrect verb form or gender agreement—not to mention that some of them, such as choice **e**, would simply make no sense in this context no matter what their forms.

3. Mi amigo no _____ el libro de _____ hermano.
   a. quiero a, ni
   b. va, al
   c. habido, nos
   d. tiene, su
   e. ve, que

Choice **d** is correct because the verb form agrees with the subject, and *su* makes sense before *hermano*. The other verb choices are ungrammatical, and many of the choices for the second word make no sense at all.

Part II, Section II

This section requires you to put it all together. It tests your ability to recognize various language elements and incorporate them into a complete picture, the correct sentence. To do well on this portion of the Spanish Language exam, look for errors of grammar, sentence structure, or incorrect word usage.

Read each sentence carefully. Select the one sentence that is correct.

1. a. El señor García nos enviamos los papeles.
   b. Eso no valen la pena.
   c. Hay muchas flores en el jardín.
   d. Hay un gato durmiendo en la ventana.

Choice **c** is the only choice that does not have mistakes in verb form.

2. a. Más tarde la señora Smith y yo van a tomar café en el restaurante.
   b. Ella estaba llorando sin saber por qué.
   c. Me gusto el pollo frito.
   d. Juan nos invité a tomar algo.

The only correct sentence is choice **b**. The other possibilities use incorrect verb forms.

3. a. ¿Vimos Uds. al presidente de México?
   b. Fuimos a un café.
   c. El muchacha es pequeña.
   d. ¿Es aburrido la examen?

The correct answer is **b**. It is the only choice that does not have an error in verb form or gender agreement.

Part II, Section III

This section also tests your overall comprehension. It requires you to decide whether or not a selection is correct. If it is incorrect, you will need to choose an alternative to the italicized word.

First, decide if the italicized word is used correctly in the sentence. Having a strong vocabulary will help you here! If the word seems to have an appropriate meaning, then look for the right grammatical structure. If the italicized word is a noun, look for matching number and gender; if it is a verb, look for correct form and tense. This is where the time you spend studying Spanish grammar will pay off! If the italicized word passes both of these tests, choice **e** is the right one—the sentence does not need any correction.

What if you spot an error, as in the first example? In this case, proceed as you would in the earlier sections and evaluate the choices according to meaning, grammatical correctness, and complete sentence structure.

Read each sentence carefully. Select the correct word or phrase to replace the italicized portion of the sentence. In those cases in which the sentence needs no correction, select choice **e**.

1. El fútbol y el béisbol son dos ejemplos de *montañas.*
   a. alfombras
   b. escuelas
   c. maderas
   d. deportes
   e. No es necesario hacer ninguna corrección.

Choice **d**, *deportes* (sports), is correct. The italicized word, *montañas* (mountains), is an example of wrong usage and incorrect matching of gender. The other choices have no relationship to the subjects of the sentence, *el fútbol y el béisbol,* so choice **d** is the only correct one.

2. Comprendo por qué él *establecen* de los gatos.

   a. tiene miedo

   b. entiendo

   c. niegan

   d. establecemos

   e. No es necesario hacer ninguna corrección.

The correct choice is **a** because it is the only one that will make a grammatically correct sentence. The other options use incorrect verb forms.

3. Esta *flor* es para mi abuela.

   a. regalos

   b. melón

   c. numero

   d. moscas

   e. No es necesario hacer ninguna corrección.

The right answer is **e** because the sentence is correct. The other choices use the wrong number or gender agreement.

▶ Conclusion

Spanish, like any language, is nothing more than a code or set of symbols with a definite organization of meanings. All you have to do is learn the code in order to open up a whole new world of opportunity.

Learning and speaking Spanish is a rewarding experience. When you can speak Spanish fluently, you are better able to understand the culture and perspective of its native speakers. Improved understanding will make your job as a Border Patrol Agent easier and more rewarding. In fact, such understanding can lead to greater cooperation not only between individuals, but also between nations.

Making use of the tips and methods presented in this chapter, along with diligent study and practice, ensures that you will do well on the Spanish Language portion of the Border Patrol Exam.

▶ Resources

There are many resources for you if you want to learn or brush up on the Spanish language. The traditional methods of using a textbook and conversational practice are today augmented by a range of new methods. The widespread use of the computer has created many new opportunities for learning. It is now possible to learn Spanish online, and interactive compact disks (CDs), some of which will even correct your pronunciation, are also available.

What follow are just some of the many widely available resources that will help you to prepare confidently for the Spanish Language portion of the Border Patrol Exam.

Conversation

Most of the following books come with an audio CD that provides essential practice in the sounds and pronunciation of Spanish words and phrases. Check online or at your local bookstore for more information.

Conversational Spanish, 3rd Edition by Juan Kattan-Ibarra (McGraw-Hill, 1997).

Conversational Spanish in Nothing Flat (Language Dynamics, 2002).

Instant Immersion Spanish Audio Deluxe (Topics Entertainment, 2006).

Mastering Spanish: Conversation Basics (Penton Overseas Inc., 2005).

Spanish Conversation Study Cards (Visual Education Association, 1997).

Spanish (Instant Conversation) (Pimsleur, 2002).

Teach Yourself Spanish Conversation by Juan Kattan-Ibarra and Angela Howkins (Teach Yourself, 2005).

Grammar

The Everything Spanish Grammar Book: All the Rules You Need to Master Español by Julie Gutin (Adams Media Corporation, 2005).

Interactive Spanish Grammar Made Easy by Mike Zollo (McGraw-Hill, 2006).

Mastering Spanish Grammar by Pilar Munoz and Mike Thacker (McGraw-Hill, 2006).

Modern Spanish Grammar: A Practical Guide, 2nd Edition by Juan Kattan-Ibarra and Chris Pountain (Routledge, 2003).

Practice Makes Perfect: Complete Spanish Grammar by Gilda Nissenberg (McGraw-Hill, 2004).

Spanish Grammar and Verb Tables, 3rd Edition (HarperCollins, 2005).

Spanish Grammar the Easy Way by Boris Corredor, Ph.D. (Barron's Educational Series, 2003).

10 ▶ Border Patrol Practice Exam 1

CHAPTER SUMMARY

Here is a sample test based on the Border Patrol Exam. After reviewing the sample questions in Chapters 5 and 6, take this test to see how much your abilities have improved.

LIKE THE REAL BORDER PATROL EXAM, the exam that follows tests your logical reasoning abilities and your Spanish-language ability or aptitude. There are three sections, and you must take two: Logical Reasoning, and **either** Spanish Language **or** Artificial Language. Take the Spanish test if you speak and read Spanish; otherwise, take the Artificial Language test.

For this exam, you should simulate the actual test-taking experience as closely as you can. Find a quiet place to work where you won't be disturbed. Tear out the answer sheet on the next page if you own this book, or xerox it if not, and find some number two pencils to fill in the circles. You should give yourself three hours to complete the Logical Reasoning section and the Spanish Language or the Artificial Language test. Set a timer or stopwatch for practice, but do not worry too much if you go over the allotted time on this practice exam. You can work more on timing when you take the second practice exam in Chapter 11.

After the exam, use the answer explanations to see how you did, and to find out why the right answers are right and the wrong ones are wrong.

▶ Logical Reasoning

1. (a) (b) (c) (d) (e)
2. (a) (b) (c) (d) (e)
3. (a) (b) (c) (d) (e)
4. (a) (b) (c) (d) (e)
5. (a) (b) (c) (d) (e)
6. (a) (b) (c) (d) (e)

7. (a) (b) (c) (d) (e)
8. (a) (b) (c) (d) (e)
9. (a) (b) (c) (d) (e)
10. (a) (b) (c) (d) (e)
11. (a) (b) (c) (d) (e)
12. (a) (b) (c) (d) (e)

13. (a) (b) (c) (d) (e)
14. (a) (b) (c) (d) (e)
15. (a) (b) (c) (d) (e)
16. (a) (b) (c) (d) (e)

▶ Spanish Language

1. (a) (b) (c) (d) (e)
2. (a) (b) (c) (d) (e)
3. (a) (b) (c) (d) (e)
4. (a) (b) (c) (d) (e)
5. (a) (b) (c) (d) (e)
6. (a) (b) (c) (d) (e)
7. (a) (b) (c) (d) (e)
8. (a) (b) (c) (d) (e)
9. (a) (b) (c) (d) (e)
10. (a) (b) (c) (d) (e)
11. (a) (b) (c) (d) (e)
12. (a) (b) (c) (d) (e)
13. (a) (b) (c) (d) (e)
14. (a) (b) (c) (d) (e)
15. (a) (b) (c) (d) (e)
16. (a) (b) (c) (d) (e)
17. (a) (b) (c) (d) (e)

18. (a) (b) (c) (d) (e)
19. (a) (b) (c) (d) (e)
20. (a) (b) (c) (d) (e)
21. (a) (b) (c) (d) (e)
22. (a) (b) (c) (d) (e)
23. (a) (b) (c) (d) (e)
24. (a) (b) (c) (d) (e)
25. (a) (b) (c) (d) (e)
26. (a) (b) (c) (d) (e)
27. (a) (b) (c) (d) (e)
28. (a) (b) (c) (d) (e)
29. (a) (b) (c) (d) (e)
30. (a) (b) (c) (d) (e)
31. (a) (b) (c) (d) (e)
32. (a) (b) (c) (d) (e)
33. (a) (b) (c) (d) (e)
34. (a) (b) (c) (d) (e)

35. (a) (b) (c) (d) (e)
36. (a) (b) (c) (d) (e)
37. (a) (b) (c) (d) (e)
38. (a) (b) (c) (d) (e)
39. (a) (b) (c) (d) (e)
40. (a) (b) (c) (d) (e)
41. (a) (b) (c) (d) (e)
42. (a) (b) (c) (d) (e)
43. (a) (b) (c) (d) (e)
44. (a) (b) (c) (d) (e)
45. (a) (b) (c) (d) (e)
46. (a) (b) (c) (d) (e)
47. (a) (b) (c) (d) (e)
48. (a) (b) (c) (d) (e)
49. (a) (b) (c) (d) (e)
50. (a) (b) (c) (d) (e)

▶ Artificial Language

1. (a) (b) (c) (d) (e)
2. (a) (b) (c) (d) (e)
3. (a) (b) (c) (d) (e)
4. (a) (b) (c) (d) (e)
5. (a) (b) (c) (d) (e)
6. (a) (b) (c) (d) (e)
7. (a) (b) (c) (d) (e)
8. (a) (b) (c) (d) (e)
9. (a) (b) (c) (d) (e)
10. (a) (b) (c) (d) (e)
11. (a) (b) (c) (d) (e)
12. (a) (b) (c) (d) (e)
13. (a) (b) (c) (d) (e)
14. (a) (b) (c) (d) (e)
15. (a) (b) (c) (d) (e)
16. (a) (b) (c) (d) (e)
17. (a) (b) (c) (d) (e)

18. (a) (b) (c) (d) (e)
19. (a) (b) (c) (d) (e)
20. (a) (b) (c) (d) (e)
21. (a) (b) (c) (d) (e)
22. (a) (b) (c) (d) (e)
23. (a) (b) (c) (d) (e)
24. (a) (b) (c) (d) (e)
25. (a) (b) (c) (d) (e)
26. (a) (b) (c) (d) (e)
27. (a) (b) (c) (d) (e)
28. (a) (b) (c) (d) (e)
29. (a) (b) (c) (d) (e)
30. (a) (b) (c) (d) (e)
31. (a) (b) (c) (d) (e)
32. (a) (b) (c) (d) (e)
33. (a) (b) (c) (d) (e)
34. (a) (b) (c) (d) (e)

35. (a) (b) (c) (d) (e)
36. (a) (b) (c) (d) (e)
37. (a) (b) (c) (d) (e)
38. (a) (b) (c) (d) (e)
39. (a) (b) (c) (d) (e)
40. (a) (b) (c) (d) (e)
41. (a) (b) (c) (d) (e)
42. (a) (b) (c) (d) (e)
43. (a) (b) (c) (d) (e)
44. (a) (b) (c) (d) (e)
45. (a) (b) (c) (d) (e)
46. (a) (b) (c) (d) (e)
47. (a) (b) (c) (d) (e)
48. (a) (b) (c) (d) (e)
49. (a) (b) (c) (d) (e)
50. (a) (b) (c) (d) (e)

▶ Logical Reasoning

1. Among other requirements, an applicant for citizenship must show that he or she is "attached to the principles of the Constitution of the United States and well-disposed to the good order and happiness of the United States." The courts have defined *attachment to the Constitution* as a belief in representative democracy, a commitment to the ideals embodied in the Bill of Rights, a belief that political change should be effected only in an orderly way, and general satisfaction with life in the United States. These requirements do NOT, however, preclude a belief that it might be desirable to make a change in our form of government as long as the change is made within constitutional limits.

   From the information given above, it can be validly concluded that

   a. all persons who want the U.S. government to change should be denied citizenship.

   b. only persons who believe that it might be desirable to work toward change in the U.S. government should be granted citizenship.

   c. all persons who work within constitutional limits toward change in the U.S. government should be granted citizenship.

   d. a commitment to the ideals embodied in the Bill of Rights is only one aspect of *attachment to the Constitution*.

   e. *attachment to the Constitution* cannot include a belief that it might be desirable to change the form of government of the United States.

2. The United States is a country of immigrants who came to inherit the land neither by divine right nor by open immigration policy. Because the land was taken from indigenous inhabitants, it is wrong for current citizens to exclude future immigrants. However, some people believe that too much immigration may compromise the standard of living in the United States. As a result, jobs and resources may be taken from persons who are already citizens, so that the very reasons immigrants were historically attracted to the United States—that is, all its advantages and opportunities—may be threatened if the country becomes overcrowded.

   From the information given above, it can be validly concluded that

   a. because current citizens did not inherit this land by divine right, too much immigration may compromise the United States' standard of living.

   b. if too much immigration would compromise the United States' standard of living, then its citizens should want an open immigration policy.

   c. if the citizens of the United States want an open immigration policy, then the United States standard of living would not be compromised.

   d. if the United States does not have an open immigration policy, then the land was taken away from its indigenous inhabitants.

   e. some people believe the very reasons immigrants were historically attracted to the United States will be compromised by an open immigration policy.

3. The U.S. immigration laws are designed to protect the health, welfare, and security of the United States. Therefore, these laws prohibit the issuance of visas to applicants who fit within certain categories. Among those who must be refused visas are those with a communicable disease, those with a dangerous physical or mental disorder, those who have committed serious criminal acts, and those who have used illegal means to enter the United States.

From the information given above, it can be validly concluded that, under U.S. immigration laws,

a. everyone who is refused a visa has committed a serious criminal act.

b. no one who is refused a visa has a communicable disease.

c. everyone with a dangerous physical or mental disorder must be refused a visa.

d. using illegal means to enter the United States does not always prohibit issuance of a visa.

e. Only those who meet these criteria will be denied visas.

4. If a state has the final authority to determine citizenship, this can result in some persons having dual nationalities and others being stateless. A child can be born stateless when two situations arise simultaneously—the state in which the child is born only recognizes the child as receiving the nationality of the parents, and the parents' home state only recognizes the nationality of the state where the child is born.

From the information given above, it can be validly concluded that, in the case of a child born in a state other than his parents' home state,

a. the child has dual nationality if the parent's home state recognizes only the nationality of the state where a child is born.

b. the child is considered to have dual nationality if the state in which he is born only recognizes a child as receiving the nationality of the parents.

c. the child is considered stateless if the state in which he is born and the parents' home state each only recognizes a child as receiving the nationality of the parents.

d. the child is considered stateless if his parents' home state only recognizes the child as receiving the nationality of the parents.

e. the child is considered to have dual nationality if the state where he was born recognizes the birthplace of the child and his parents' home state recognizes the nationality of the parents.

5. According to the Fourteenth Amendment to the U.S. Constitution, "No state shall make or enforce any law which shall abridge the privileges or immunities of citizens of the United States, nor shall any state deprive any person of life, liberty, or property, without due process of law; nor deny to any person within its jurisdiction the equal protection of the laws."

From the information given above, it can be validly concluded that

a. no state can abridge the privileges of its citizens under any circumstances.

b. states can abridge the privileges of its citizens without due process.

c. a state can abridge the privileges of its citizens only with due process.

d. the Constitution does not allow citizens and noncitizens to be treated differently.

e. equal protection of the laws is a privilege given to citizens only.

6. Criminals should be held accountable for their behavior. If holding criminals accountable for their behavior requires harsh sentencing, then so be it. However, no person should be held accountable for behavior over which he or she had no control.

From the information given above, it can be validly concluded that

a. criminals should not be held accountable for the behavior of other people.

b. people have control of their own behavior.

c. people cannot control the behavior of other people.

d. behavior that cannot be controlled should not be punished.

e. criminals have control over their own behavior that may subject them to harsh punishment.

7. Under Immigration and Nationality Act (INA) law, any alien who is believed likely to become a public charge is excludable at the time of application. However, in *Matter of Kohama* (1978), it was decided that an immigrating couple who had no means of support other than reliance on their daughter and son-in-law, who were U.S. residents, could not be excluded as likely to become public charges. The daughter and son-in-law gave depositions and submitted affidavits as evidence of their ability and willingness to support the couple. The court held that such evidence was sufficient to overcome the belief that they would become charges of the state.

From the information given above, it can be validly concluded that

a. persons may be permitted to immigrate to the United States if they have relatives in their home country willing to support them.

b. for the court to accept a claim that relatives will support an immigrant to the United States, the relatives must submit evidence supporting their ability to do so.

c. if relatives agree to support a person and can submit evidence supporting their ability to do so, then that person must immigrate to the United States.

d. if a person wishes to immigrate to the United States and has no relative willing and able to financially support him or her, then that person may not immigrate to the United States.

e. if a person immigrates to the United States, he or she has relatives willing and able to support him or her.

8. One strategy to control the nation's borders involves demonstrating the futility of crossing the borders illegally. This sometimes requires Border Patrol Agents to perform activities within the United States, away from the borders. Among the reasons for this are to seek out and arrest aliens living illegally inside the United States, and to find and stop the modes of transportation used to transport illegal aliens across and within U.S. borders.

From the information given above, it can be validly concluded that

a. controlling the nation's borders can occur only at the borders themselves.

b. controlling the nation's borders can never occur at the borders themselves.

c. Border Patrol Agents' activities at the borders are more important than those away from the borders.

d. Border Patrol Agents' activities away from the borders are more important than those at the borders.

e. activities at the borders and away from the borders work together to protect the nation's borders.

9. One concern of law enforcement officials is the risk of terrorists taking advantage of illegal immigration along the southern border and becoming lost in the flow of aliens entering the United States there. Focusing on the entrance of illegal aliens across U.S. borders might have the additional effect of impacting national security in a positive way.

From the information given above, it can be validly concluded that

a. all terrorists are illegal aliens.

b. all illegal aliens are terrorists.

c. efforts to limit illegal immigrations are likely to help deter terrorism.

d. terrorists are entering the United States through the southern border.

e. illegal aliens and terrorists work together to enter the United States illegally.

10. Protecting the United States' northern border presents unique challenges due to its length, geography, and weather. The solutions to protect the northern border include a combination of maintaining sufficient workforce levels, improved communications and other technology, additional air assets, partnerships with state and local authorities, and use of checkpoints and other deterrents.

From the information given above, it can be validly concluded that

a. the challenges involved in protecting the northern border are mostly about maintaining workforce levels.

b. any one solution to protect the northern border will go a long way toward achieving success.

c. checkpoints and other deterrents have not been successful in the past.

d. a combination of solutions to protect the northern border will likely be more successful than any one solution.

e. relationships with Canadian officials are not an important factor in protecting the U.S.'s northern border.

11. The legal authority of a Border Patrol Agent is derived from congressional legislation; this is called *statutory authority*. However, Congress does not have the final word regarding the interpretation and application of legislation, as this power is reserved for the judicial branch of government. Following the codification of statutory authority, written guidance regarding the codified statutory authority is created by federal agencies and published and updated annually in the Federal Register; this is known as the Code of Federal Regulations. However, Border Patrol Agents are ultimately required to operate in accordance with agency regulations or directives that are more restrictive than a plain reading of statutory law. Agency regulations and directives are promulgated by an agency to provide field-level guidance to agents to use when exercising their statutory authority. These regulations comply with the requirements of both statutory legislation and the Code of Federal Regulations. Additionally, the American judicial system is constantly rendering decisions that affect the interpretation and application of legislation enacted by Congress. Border Patrol Agents routinely receive legal updates regarding judicial decisions that ultimately decide how agents exercise their statutory authority in the field.

From the information given, it can be validly concluded that

a. the legal authority of a Border Patrol Agent is derived from agency directives.

b. the legal authority of an agency to publish written guidance in the Federal Register is derived from statutory authority.

c. the courts interpret and apply the Code of Federal Regulations in legal matters.

d. statutory authority is interpreted through field-level agency regulations and directives.

e. the judicial system ultimately interprets and applies congressional legislation, and these decisions affect the method and means by which Border Patrol Agents exercise their statutory authority.

12. Technology can be of great value in protecting U.S. borders. Border Patrol Agents need to know how this technology works and when to use it. Among the tools available are remote video surveillance and sensing (RVSS) cameras, radiation detection equipment, satellite communications, and remote access to national law enforcement databases. These devices can give agents an advantage in keeping illegal immigrants out, and in apprehending them once they've entered the United States illegally.

From the information given above, it can be validly concluded that

a. technology is always an advantage in protecting U.S. borders.
b. protecting U.S. borders would be impossible without technology.
c. Border Patrol Agents need to know how to use radiation detection equipment to be successful at their jobs.
d. technology is only as good as the agents who use it.
e. knowing what technology to use and how to use it is a valuable resource for agents, both in preventing illegal immigration and in apprehending illegal aliens.

13. Maintaining and knowing how to use firearms are important for all law enforcement officials. Many Border Patrol Agents say that they have never had to fire a weapon, even after many years on the job. Others report that they've found themselves in situations requiring that they use their weapon after only days or weeks on the job. Decisions an agent makes in a split second under life-and-death pressure may be analyzed and evaluated over the course of years. Extensive training in the use of firearms is critical to an agent making the best possible decision when called upon to do so.

From the information given above, it can be validly concluded that

a. firearms should never be used unless a superior orders an agent to do so.
b. firearms should never be used unless an agent's life is in immediate danger.
c. there is no way to know in advance if or how often a Border Patrol Agent will need to fire a weapon.
d. decisions made under pressure in a fraction of a second are never good decisions.
e. the best training always results in the best decision when it comes to using firearms.

14. Under INA law, unless an applicant for citizenship is physically unable to do so through blindness or deafness, he or she must be able to speak, understand, read, and write simple English. Before 1978, the act provided an exemption to the literacy requirement for persons who, on the effective date in 1952, were over 50 years of age and had been residing in the United States for periods totaling at least 20 years. In 1978, Congress amended the provision to exempt any person who was over the age of 50 at the time of filing a petition and who had been lawfully admitted for permanent residence for periods totaling 20 years.

From the information given above, it can be validly concluded that, on the effective date in 1952, all people over 50 years of age

a. became exempt from the literacy requirement unless they had lived in the United States for 20 years.

b. could become exempt from the literacy requirement if they had lived in the United States for 20 years.

c. had to meet the literacy requirements if they had lived in the United States for 20 years.

d. met the literacy requirements if they had lived in the United States for 20 years.

e. who had been in the United States at least 20 years met the literacy requirements.

15. Police Sergeant O'Malley reports that all police precincts in the city of Garrison have drug-seeking dogs, and that some police precincts in the same city have search-and-rescue dogs. Sergeant O'Malley professes to know all about dogs. Search-and-rescue dogs, he says, are better at tracking, but are disobedient, whereas drug-seeking dogs are obedient. All the precincts, Sergeant O'Malley maintains, have discontinued the use of attack dogs, because they are too dangerous.

From the information given, it CANNOT be validly concluded that, according to Sergeant O'Malley,

a. all police precincts have disobedient dogs.

b. some police precincts have disobedient dogs.

c. all police precincts have obedient dogs.

d. no police precincts have attack dogs.

e. no police precincts have dangerous dogs.

16. Under immigration law, one way a child under age 16 can receive a visa and be adopted is if that child is an orphan. A child is considered an orphan if both parents have died, disappeared, or abandoned the child, or if the sole or surviving parent is incapable of providing the child with proper care, and if that parent has irrevocably released the child for emigration and adoption. The orphan must be adopted by, or be traveling to the United States to be adopted by, a U.S. citizen and spouse jointly, or by an unmarried U.S. citizen at least 25 years of age.

From the information given above, it can be validly concluded that a child would be considered an orphan only if

a. her parents are unable to care for her but will not release her for emigration and adoption.

b. her parents are dead, or alive but have disappeared or abandoned her, or are unable to care for her and have released the child for emigration and adoption.

c. she is adopted by spouses jointly.

d. she is adopted by an unmarried single person over 25.

e. she is under age 16 and her parents are dead.

▶ Spanish Language

If you are taking the Artificial Language Test, turn to page 126.

Part I

Read the sentence and then choose the most appropriate synonym for the italicized word or phrase.

1. Es muy *sencillo* conducer un coche.
   a. fácil
   b. difícil
   c. divertido
   d. compilado
   e. comparado

2. Es muy difícil *oír* lo que el agente está diciendo.
   a. responder
   b. comprobar
   c. entender
   d. pretender
   e. desentender

3. Estás bajo *detención*.
   a. encontrar
   b. concentrar
   c. aclarar
   d. custodia
   e. aplastar

4. Examinaremos la evidencia *ante* la corte.
   a. frente a
   b. anteriormente
   c. estipendios
   d. cortesías
   e. ofrendas

5. Mi casa está *al lado de* la iglesia.
  a. a caudillo por
  b. lejos de
  c. por aquí
  d. menos de
  e. cerca de

6. ¡Por favor, *siéntense* en el sofá!
  a. piensen
  b. sitúense
  c. váyanse
  d. echen
  e. quítense

7. Está abierta solamente *por la mañana.*
  a. hasta mediodía
  b. dentro de tarde
  c. por la madera
  d. hasta la noche
  e. hoy día

8. Ella está *enferma.*
  a. mentirosa
  b. infeliz
  c. temblorosa
  d. mala
  e. enfadosa

9. *Buscamos* una secretaria que hable inglés.
  a. Necesitamos
  b. Pegamos
  c. Pagamos
  d. Presentamos
  e. Escuchamos

10. Y tu *alcoba*, ¿dónde está?
  a. guayaba
  b. cuchillo
  c. jardín
  d. dormitorio
  e. cuchara

11. Yo soy de Nuevo México, y mi amigo es de Colorado; somos *norteamericanos.*
  a. japonés
  b. noruegos
  c. de españa
  d. espaldas
  e. yanquis

12. *Quiero* presentar a mi hermano.
  a. Deseo
  b. Odio
  c. Quedo
  d. Amo
  e. Necesito

13. En la bandera de México hay un emblema interesante: un *águila* sobre un nopal devorando una serpiente.
  a. gato
  b. zozobra
  c. zorro
  d. tortuga
  e. pájaro

14. La Cruz Roja pidió *donaciones* para las víctimas del terremoto.
  a. piedras
  b. contribuciones
  c. nieves
  d. contrabandos
  e. domicilios

15. En México, el padre Hidalgo, como George Washington en los Estados Unidos, se conoce como el Padre *de la Patria*.
   a. del Patológico
   b. de la Armada
   c. del País
   d. del Pato
   e. del Pavo

16. Hemos trabajado *bastante* hoy.
   a. ilegítimo
   b. harto
   c. batalla
   d. bizcocho
   e. vendaje

17. ¡*Vámonos* ahorita!
   a. Gritemos
   b. Descansemos
   c. Traduzcamos
   d. Salguemos
   e. Vistámonos

18. Ellos se encontraron diez años *después* en la playa.
   a. antes
   b. frecuente
   c. más tarde
   d. despacio
   e. brevemente

19. El jai alai, un juego de pelota de origen español, *se parece* a nuestro juego de handball.
   a. es diferente
   b. es similar
   c. se aburre
   d. se habla
   e. espera

20. Si *la gente* tiene miedo todos los días, el gobierno no estará bién.
   a. el pueblo
   b. la ciudad
   c. el gerente
   d. el conejo
   e. el general

Part II, Section I

Read each sentence carefully. Select the appropriate word or phrase to fill each blank space.

21. Me gusta entrar _____ el edificio _____ través de la oficina.
   a. a, sobre
   b. en, desde
   c. con, bajo
   d. en, al lado
   e. en, a

22. La viuda me _____ que ella _____ los documentos apropiados.
   a. dijo, entregó
   b. dice, entregue
   c. dirá, entrar
   d. traído, entregue
   e. habrá traído, entrar

23. Los oficiales _____ usan la sala de reunions para discutir asuntos _____.
   a. sumariamente, difícil
   b. frecuentemente, variadas
   c. normalmente, diversos
   d. rara vez, personal
   e. ocasionalmente, unilateral

24. _____ a los detendios y _____ al tanto de los resultados.
   a. Visita, ponlos
   b. Visite, ponerlos
   c. Visitaré, ponga
   d. Habré visitado, ponder
   e. Visitando, había puesto

25. Los agentes _____ con cada _____ en el avión.
   a. volando, droga
   b. llegan, espeja
   c. hablaban, persona
   d. harto, especialista
   e. habían, choque

26. _____ piden permiso para _____ una llamada por teléfono.
   a. Ella, hagan
   b. Yo, haga
   c. Nuestro, hacer
   d. Nosotros, hablando
   e. Ellos, hacer

27. Este _____ no _____ entrar legalmente.
   a. niña, podía
   b. muchacho, quiso
   c. niña, quiso
   d. joven, pudieron
   e. muchacha, pudieron

28. ¿Quién _____ ha recibido los paquetes _____ Colombia?
   a. aquí, de
   b. aquel, por
   c. aquella, por
   d. ustedes, de
   e. usted, hasta

29. Yo _____ un hermano menor y _____ hermana menor también.
   a. traigo, mucha
   b. tuvo, una
   c. tengo, una
   d. tenemos, mucha
   e. perdiden, una

30. ¿Van _____ a la iglesia el domingo _____ nosotros?
   a. Ud., el
   b. somos, de
   c. tú, para
   d. tú, de
   e. Uds., con

Part II, Section II

Read each sentence carefully. Select the one sentence that is correct.

31. **a.** Los oficiales entran en la casa el frente y el sospechoso.
   b. Los oficiales convenidos entrarían en la casa del sospechoso delantero.
   c. Los oficiales decidieron entrar en el frente de la casa y rodear al sospechoso.
   d. Los sospechosos acordaron incorporar el frente de la casa y rodearlo.

32. **a.** El contrabando de extranjeros ilegales plantea un gran riesgo a nuestro país.
 b. Contrabando del riesgo a nuestro país.
 c. Nuestro país es a los contrabandistas y al país.
 d. Los contrabandistas del extranjero ilegal podrían ser un riesgo al país.

33. **a.** El juez conviene con veredicto.
 b. El juez no convino con el veredicto del jurado hasta más adelante.
 c. El veredicto del juez convino con más adelante.
 d. El veredicto del jurado no convino con el juez.

34. **a.** El tratado fue firmado por muchos países que rechazaron firmar el país que el tratado fue firmado en ese entonces.
 b. Muchos países firmaron el tratado en efecto a la hora del tratado.
 c. Aunque muchos países firmaron el tratado en efecto hasta tiempo todos los países firmaron.
 d. Aunque muchos países firmaron el tratado, no estará en efecto hasta que todos los países lo hayan firmado.

35. **a.** Asegurar que estar correcta.
 b. Asegúrese de que esté correcta.
 c. No ese es la correcta.
 d. Esto él correcto está.

36. **a.** Tú estoy viviendo en la ciudad durante el verano.
 b. Ellos mienten cuando puedan.
 c. Él está al lado de la oficina.
 d. ¿No sabes que yo somos el jefe?

37. **a.** Sé que María entienda la pregunta.
 b. Después de llegar a casa, diera un paseo en el parque.
 c. Es obvio que no tengas el conocimiento necesario.
 d. Antes de que comience el desfile, mi padre compró unos tacos.

38. **a.** Mi casa es el más impresionante del pueblo.
 b. La perro feo volvió al casa.
 c. Ese hombre que nos visitó era flaco y un poco misterioso.
 d. Soy yo la médico especializada que quieres consultar.

39. **a.** Tú no está la acordar con Ud.
 b. No estoy de acuerdo con Ud.
 c. No ha está en acuerdo contigo.
 d. Tenemos que acuerdo con Ud.

40. **a.** ¿Cómo te llamas el director del departamento?
 b. Me dijiste el jefe que no podía continuar.
 c. Es importante en todo lo casos que me veas.
 d. Quiero que los alumnos hagan el trabajo sin quejar.

Part II, Section III

Read each sentence carefully. Select the correct word or phrase to replace the italicized portion of the sentence. In those cases in which the sentence needs no correction, select choice **e**.

41. No puedo *crear* los problemas que afectan nuestro país.
 a. creer
 b. pensar
 c. manejar
 d. divertir
 e. No es necesario hacer ninguna corrección.

42. El agente no *hablé* con los extranjeros detenidos.
   a. discutí
   b. entiende
   c. habló
   d. hablaste
   e. No es necesario hacer ninguna corrección.

43. Tenemos que dejar que la mujer sospechosa *llame* a su familia.
   a. llamo
   b. llama
   c. calar
   d. hablara
   e. No es necesario hacer ninguna corrección.

44. Varios políticos dicen que los Estados Unidos *hay* la obligación de ayudar a los países que están en desarrollo.
   a. haga
   b. tenga
   c. cuenta
   d. tienen
   e. No es necesario hacer ninguna corrección.

45. En México se *cómo* muchos frijoles.
   a. haber
   b. tiene
   c. comen
   d. servir
   e. No es necesario hacer ninguna corrección.

46. Es mi deber guardar la frontera entre los Estados Unidos y su *vecino* al sur.
   a. vizcaíno
   b. veinte
   c. inversión
   d. vacación
   e. No es necesario hacer ninguna corrección.

47. Hoy, por desgracia, mi hermano *es* enfermo y no nos acompañará a la playa.
   a. puede
   b. tiene
   c. él
   d. está
   e. No es necesario hacer ninguna corrección.

48. ¿Cuántos días *fue* que salió de su trabajo?
   a. era
   b. hace
   c. haz
   d. sé
   e. No es necesario hacer ninguna corrección.

49. Según el presidente de la compañía, no importa dónde *es* la fiesta.
   a. pasar
   b. tendrá
   c. está
   d. esté
   e. No es necesario hacer ninguna corrección.

50. Cuando tenía quince años, empecé a *atender* a este colegio.
   a. mirar
   b. empezar
   c. asistir
   d. lograr
   e. No es necesario hacer ninguna corrección.

▶ Artificial Language Supplemental Booklet

To answer the Artificial Language questions, refer to the sections in this Supplemental Booklet: Vocabulary Lists and Grammatical Rules. (See Chapters 7 and 8 of this book for additional information.)

Some of the words given in the following Vocabulary Lists are not the same as those that will be given in the actual Border Patrol Exam. Therefore, it is best not to memorize them before taking the actual test. The Grammatical Rules are the same as those used in the actual test, except that some of the prefixes (word beginnings) and suffixes (word endings) used in the real test differ from those used in this Supplemental Booklet. You may also need to refer to the glossary of grammatical terms in Chapter 7 as you take the practice exams.

▶ Vocabulary Lists for the Artificial Language

Arranged Alphabetically by the English Word

ENGLISH	ARTIFICIAL LANGUAGE	ENGLISH	ARTIFICIAL LANGUAGE
a, an	bex	skillful	autile
alien	huslek	that	velle
and	cre	the	ric
boy	ekaplek	this	volle
country	failek	to be	synbar
difficult	brale	to border	regbar
enemy	avelek	to cross	chonbar
friend	kometlek	to drive	arbar
from	mor	to escape	pirbar
government	almanlek	to guard	bonbar
he, him	yev	to have	tulbar
jeep	cublek	to identify	kalenbar
legal	colle	to injure	liabar
loyal	inle	to inspect	zelbar
man	kaplek	to shoot	degbar
of	quea	to spy	tatbar
paper	trenedlek	to station	lexbar
river	browlek	to work	frigbar

Arranged Alphabetically by the Artificial Language Word

ARTIFICIAL LANGUAGE	ENGLISH	ARTIFICIAL LANGUAGE	ENGLISH
almanlek	government	kalenbar	to identify
arbar	to drive	kaplek	man
autile	skillful	kometlek	friend
avelek	enemy	lexbar	to station
bex	a, an	liabar	to injure
bonbar	to guard	mor	from
brale	difficult	pirbar	to escape
browlek	river	quea	of
chonbar	to cross	regbar	to border
colle	legal	ric	the
cre	and	synbar	to be
cublek	jeep	tatbar	to spy
degbar	to shoot	trenedlek	paper
ekaplek	boy	tulbar	to have
failek	country	velle	that
frigbar	to work	volle	this
huslek	alien	yev	he, him
inle	loyal	zelbar	to inspect

▶ Grammatical Rules for the Artificial Language

The grammatical rules given here are the same as those used in the Border Patrol Exam, except that the prefixes (word beginnings) and suffixes (word endings) used in the exam differ from those used here.

During the exam, you will have access to the rules at all times. Consequently, it is important that you understand these rules, but it is not necessary that you memorize them. In fact, memorizing them will hinder rather than help you, because the beginnings and endings of words are different in the version of the Artificial Language that appears in this manual than the one that appears in the actual test.

You should note that Part Three of the official Artificial Language Manual contains a glossary of grammatical terms to assist you if you are not thoroughly familiar with the meanings of these grammatical terms. You can review these now by referring back to Chapter 7.

Rule 1

To form the feminine singular of a noun, a pronoun, an adjective, or an article, add the suffix -*zof* to the masculine singular form. Only nouns, pronouns, adjectives, and articles take feminine endings in the Artificial Language. When gender is not specified, the masculine form is used.

Examples

If a male eagle is a *verlek*, then a female eagle is a *verlekzof*.

If an ambitious man is a *tosle* man, an ambitious woman is a *toslezof* woman.

Rule 2

To form the plural of nouns, pronouns, and adjectives, add the suffix *-ax* to the correct singular form.

Examples

If one male eagle is a *verlek*, then several male eagles are *verlekax*.

If an ambitious woman is a *toslezof* woman, several ambitious women are *toslezofax* women.

Rule 3

Adjectives modifying nouns and pronouns with feminine and/or plural endings must have endings that agree with the words they modify. In addition, an article (*a*, *an*, and *the*) preceding a noun must also agree with the noun in gender and number.

Examples

If an active male eagle is a *sojle verlek*, then an active female eagle is a *sojlezof verlekzof* and several active female eagles are *sojlezofax verlekzofax*.

If this male eagle is *volle verlek*, these female eagles are *vollezofax verlekzofax*.

If the male eagle is *ric verlek*, the female eagle is *riczof verlekzof* and the female eagles are *riczofax verlekzofax*.

If a male eagle is *bex verlek*, several male eagles are *bexax verlekax*.

Rule 4

The stem of the verb is obtained by omitting the suffix *-bar* from the infinitive form of the verb.

Example

The stem of the verb *tirbar* is *tir*.

Rule 5

All subjects and their verbs must agree in number; that is, singular subjects require singular verbs and plural subjects require plural verbs. (See Rules 6 and 7.)

Rule 6

To form the present tense of a verb, add the suffix *-ot* to the stem for the singular form or the suffix *-et* to the stem for the plural.

Example

If to bark is *nalbar*, then *nalot* is the present tense for the singular (the dog barks) and *nalet* is the present tense for the plural (the dogs bark).

Rule 7

To form the past tense of a verb, first add the suffix *-rem* to the stem, and then add the suffix *-ot* if the verb is singular or the suffix *-et* if it is plural.

Example

If to bark is *nalbar*, then *nalremot* is the past tense for the singular (the dog barked), and *nalremet* is the past tense for the plural (the dogs barked).

Rule 8

To form the past participle of a verb, add to the stem of the verb the suffix *-to*. It can be used to form compound tenses with the verb *to have*, as a predicate with the verb *to be*, or as an adjective. In the last two cases, it takes masculine, feminine, singular, and plural forms in agreement with the noun to which it refers.

Example of use in a compound tense with the verb *to have*

If to bark is *nalbar* and to have is *tulbar*, then *tulot nalto* is the present perfect for the singular (the dog has barked) and *tulet nalto* is the present perfect for the plural (the dogs have barked). Similarly, *tulremot nalto* is the past perfect for the singular (the dog had barked) and *tulremet nalto* is the past perfect for the plural (the dogs had barked).

Example of use as a predicate with the verb *to be*

If to adopt is *rapbar* and to be is *synbar*, then a boy was adopted is a *ekaplek synremot rapto* and many girls were adopted is *ekaplekzofax synremet raptozofax*.

Example of use as an adjective

If to delight is *kasbar*, then a delighted boy is a *kasto ekaplek* and many delighted girls are *kastozofax ekaplekzofax*.

Rule 9

To form a noun from a verb, add the suffix *-lek* to the stem of the verb.

Example

If *longbar* is to write, then a writer is a *longlek*.

Rule 10

To form an adjective from a noun, substitute the suffix *-le* for the suffix *-lek*.

Example

If *pellek* is beauty, then a beautiful male eagle is a *pelle verlek*, and a beautiful female eagle is a *pellezof verlekzof*. (Note the feminine ending *-zof*.)

Rule 11

To form an adverb from an adjective, add the suffix *-de* to the masculine form of the adjective. (Note that adverbs do not change their form to agree in number or gender with the word they modify.)

Example

If *pelle* is beautiful, then beautifully is *pellede*.

Rule 12

To form the possessive of a noun or pronoun, add the suffix *-oe* to the noun or pronoun after any plural or feminine suffixes.

Examples

If a *boglek* is a dog, then a dog's collar is a *boglekoe* collar.

If he is *yev*, then his book is *yevoe* book.

If she is *yevzof*, then her book is *yevzofoe* book.

Rule 13

To make a word negative, add the prefix *poh-* to the correct affirmative form.

Examples

If an active male eagle is a *sojle verlek*, then an inactive male eagle is a *pohsojle verlek*.

If the dog barks is *boglek nalot*, then the dog does not bark is *boglek pohnalot*.

▶ Artificial Language

Use the Artificial Language Supplemental Booklet on pages 122–125 to help you answer these questions. You may refer to the vocabulary and grammatical rules throughout this test section.

For each sentence, decide which words have been translated correctly. Use scratch paper to list each numbered word that is correctly translated into the Artificial Language. When you have finished listing the words that are correctly translated in sentences 1 through 20, select your answer according to the following instructions:

Mark:

    a. if *only* the word numbered 1 is correctly translated.

    b. if *only* the word numbered 2 is correctly translated.

    c. if *only* the word numbered 3 is correctly translated.

    d. if *two or more* of the numbered words are correctly translated.

    e. if *none* of the numbered words is correctly translated.

    Be sure to list only the *numbered* words that are *correctly* translated.

    Study the sample question before going on to the test questions.

Sample Sentence	**Sample Translation**
This woman crossed the river.	Bex kaplekzof chonremet ric browlek.
	1 2 3

The word numbered 1, *bex*, is incorrect because the translation of *bex* is *a*. The word *vollezof* should have been used. The word numbered 2 is correct. *Kaplekzof* has been correctly formed by adding the feminine ending to the masculine noun, applying Rule 1. The word numbered 3, *chonremet*, is incorrect because the singular form, *chonremot*, should have been used. Because the word numbered 2 is correct, the answer to the sample question is **b**.

    Now go on with questions 1 through 20 and answer them in the manner indicated. Be sure to record your answers on the separate answer sheet found at the beginning of the test.

Sentence	**Translation**
1. He identifies the driver.	**1.** Volle kalenet ric arlek.
	1 2 3
2. She is an alien.	**2.** Yev synot bexzof huslek.
	1 2 3
3. The guard is a friend.	**3.** Ric bonlek synot bex kometlek.
	1 2 3
4. The women drove the jeep.	**4.** Riczofax kaplekzofax arremet ric cublek.
	1 2 3

Sentence	**Translation**

5. That government is legal.

5. Velle almanlek synremet collede.
           1   2   3

6. The men and the women escaped.

6. Ricax kaplek cre riczofax kaplekzof pirbar.
        1   2   3

7. The alien's friend injured him.

7. Ric huslekoe kometlek liaremet yevoe.
       1   2   3

8. This boy is from that country.

8. Volle ekaplek synot mor volle failek.
    1   2   3

9. Those were difficult inspections.

9. Velle synremet brale zelbarax.
    1   2   3

10. Spies are disloyal.

10. Tatlekzof synremot inlepoh.
    1   2   3

11. She was a skillful inspector.

11. Yevzof synremot bex autilezof zelzof.
               1 2   3

12. Those aliens are not enemies of the government.

12. Velle huslekax synetpoh avelekax quea ric almanlek.
   1   2   3

13. Guards have to identify illegal workers.

13. Bonlekax tulet kalenbar pohcolle friglekax.
   1   2 3

14. The government identified these girls.

14. Ric almanlek kalenremot volle ekaplekzofax.
    1   2   3

15. She crossed the river to work illegally.

15. Yevoe chonremot ric browlek frigbar pohcolle.
   1   2   3

16. The boys' escape was difficult.

16. Ricax ekaplekax piret synbar brale.
       1   2   3

17. The shooter worked illegally.

17. Ric deglek zelremot collede.
    1   2   3

18. Those guards have loyal friends from the country.

18. Velleax bonlekax tulet inle kometlekax mor bex failek.
   1   2   3

19. The inspectors injured her.

19. Ricax zelek liaremot yevzof.
    1   2   3

20. Illegal papers are difficult to identify.

20. Pohcolle trenedlekax synret brale kalenbar.
    1   2   3

For each question in this group, select the one of the five suggested choices that correctly translates the italicized word or group of words into the Artificial Language.

> **Sample Question**
> Where are *the papers*?
> **a.** bex trenedlek
> **b.** ric trenedlek
> **c.** ricax trenedlekax
> **d.** ric trenedlekax
> **e.** bex trenedlekax

Choice **c** is the correct translation of the italicized words, *the papers*, because the definite article, *ric*, must change its ending to agree with the noun (see Rule 3), and the noun *trenedlekax* has the proper plural suffix (Rule 2).

> The men and women who *guard the country's border* have *difficult work*. Unlike
>   **21**   **22**
>
> guards who work only in *a border station*, they patrol difficult country on foot or in
>   **23**
>
> *their jeeps*. They *have to identify* aliens who attempt *to cross rivers* and desolate
>   **24**   **25**   **26**
>
> terrain. The danger of their job often tests how *loyally they guard* the country.
>   **27**
>
> *The shooting of spies* can occur, and guards risk *injury from this work*. In addition
>   **28**   **29**
>
> to the bravery needed to patrol, the border guard has to be very intelligent.
>
> He or she has to be skilled in the *identification of illegal papers*.
>   **30**

21. a. bonlek ric failek regbar
    b. bonet ric failek reglek
    c. bonet ric failekoe reglek
    d. bonot ric failekoe reglek
    e. bonlek ric failekoe reglek

22. a. brale friglekax
    b. brale friglek
    c. brale frigbar
    d. braleax friglekax
    e. bralek friglek

23. **a.** bex reglek lexlek
   b. cre regle lexlek
   c. cre reglek lexlek
   d. bex reglek lexbar
   e. bex regle lexlek

24. **a.** yevaxoe cublekax
   b. yevax cublek
   c. yevaxoe cublek
   d. yev cublekax
   e. yevoe cublekoe

25. **a.** tulet kalenet
   b. tulot kalenot
   c. tulot kalenbar
   d. tulet kalenbar
   e. tulremet kalenbar

26. **a.** chonet browlekax
   b. chonbar browlekax
   c. chonbarax browlekax
   d. chonbar browlek
   e. chonet browlek

27. **a.** inle yevax bonet
   b. inle yevzof bonet
   c. inlede yevax bonot
   d. inlede yevax bonet
   e. inle yev bonot

28. **a.** ric deget quea tatlekax
   b. ric deglek mor tatlekax
   c. ric degbar quea tatlekax
   d. ric deglek mor tatlekax
   e. ric deglek quea tatlekax

29. **a.** liale mor volleoe friglek
   b. lialek mor volle friget
   c. lialek mor volle frigot
   d. liale mor volle friget
   e. lialek mor volle friglek

30. **a.** kalenlekax quea colleax trenedlekax
   b. kalenlek quea pohcolle trenedlekax
   c. kalenlek quea pohcolleax trenedlekax
   d. kalenet quea pohcolleax trenedlekax
   e. kalenlek quea colleax trenedlekax

For this group of questions, select the one response option that is the correct translation of the English word or words in parentheses. You should translate the entire sentence in order to determine what form should be used.

Sample Question

Ricax almanlekoe tatlekax (crossed the border).
   a. chonremet bex reglek
   b. chonremot ric reglek
   c. chonremet ric reglek
   d. chonremet ric regbar
   e. chonremot bex reglek

Ricax almanlekoe tatlekax chonremet ric reglek means *The government's spies crossed the border.*

Because *chonremet ric reglek* is the only one of these expressions that means *they* (plural) *crossed the border*, choice **c** is the correct answer to the sample question.

31. Ric bonlek zelremot (his friends' papers).
   a. yevoe kometlekaxoe trenedlek
   b. yevzofoe kometlekaxoe trenedlekax
   c. yevoe kometlekoe trenedlek
   d. yev kometlekax trenedlekax
   e. yevoe kometlekaxoe trenedlekax

32. Ric kaplekzof (drove the jeep skillfully).
   a. arremot ric cublek autilede
   b. aret ric cublek autile
   c. arremet ric cublekzof autilek
   d. arremet mor cublek autilede
   e. arremet ric cublekzof autilede

33. (The governments of those countries) tulet tatlekax.
   a. Ricax almanlekax quea velleax failekax
   b. Ric almanlekax quea velleax failekax
   c. Ric almanlekax mor velleax failekax
   d. Ric almanlekax quea velle failekax
   e. Ricax almanlekax queax velleax failekax

34. (Those girls crossed) ric browlek pohcollede.
   a. Velleax ekaplekax chonremet
   b. Vollezofax kaplekzofax chonremet
   c. Vellezofax ekaplekzofax chonremet
   d. Vellezofax kaplekzofax chonremet
   e. Vellezof ekaplekzof chonremot

35. Ricax regleax bonlekax friget (loyally from their government) lexlek.
   a. inle mor yevoe almanle
   b. inlede mor yevaxoe almanlek
   c. inle mor yevaxoe almanlek
   d. inlede mor yevaxoe almanle
   e. inlede mor yevoe almanle

36. (The identification of illegal aliens) synot brale friglek.
   a. Ric kalenbar quea pohcolleax huslekax
   b. Ric kalenlek quea pohcolleax pohuslekax
   c. Ric kalenle quea colleax huslekax
   d. Ric kalenlek quea pohcolleax huslekax
   e. Ric kalenlek quea pohcolle huslekax

37. (Those border guards) tulet brale friglek.
   a. Vellekax regleax bonlekax
   b. Velleax regle bonlekax
   c. Velleax regleax bonlekax
   d. Volleax regleax bonlekax
   e. Volleax regle bonlekax

38. Ricax huslekax (shot the inspectors).
   a. degremet ricax zellekax
   b. degremet ric zellek
   c. deget ricax zellekax
   d. degremot ricax zellekax
   e. degremet ric zellekax

39. (The injured guard) tulremot frigbar.
   a. Ric liaremot bonlek
   b. Ricax liato bonlekax
   c. Bex liato bonlek
   d. Ric liato bonek
   e. Ric liato bonlek

40. (The boy and the girls) chonremet ric browlek.
   a. Ricax ekaplek cre ekaplekzofax
   b. Ricax ekaplekax cre ricaxzofax ekaplekzofax
   c. Ric kaplek cre riczofax ekaplekzofax
   d. Ric ekaplek cre riczof ekaplekzof
   e. Ric ekaplek cre riczofax ekaplekzofax

41. Riczofax avelezofax tatlekzofax (escaped from the guards).
   a. pirremet quea ricax bonlekax
   b. pirremet mor ricax bonlekax
   c. pirremet mor ric bonlekax
   d. pirbarremet mor ricax bonlekax
   e. piremet mor ricax bonlekax

42. Yevoe cublek cre (her papers were inspected).
   a. yevzofoe trenedlekax synremet zeltoax
   b. yevzofaxoe trenedlekax synremet zeltoax
   c. yevzofoe trenedlekzofax synremet zeltozofax
   d. yevzofoe trenedlek synremot zelto
   e. yevzofaxoe trenedlekax synremet zelto

For the last group of questions, select the one of the five suggested choices that is the correct form of the italicized expression as it is used in the sentence. At the end of the sentence, you will find instructions in parentheses telling you which form to use. In some sentences you will be asked to supply the correct forms of two or more expressions. In this case, the instructions for these expressions are presented consecutively in the parentheses and are separated by a dash (for example, past tense—adverb). Be sure to translate the entire sentence before selecting your answer.

   Sample Question
   Yev *bonbar* ric browlek. (present tense)
   a. bonremot
   b. bonremet
   c. boneet
   d. bonet
   e. bonot

Choices **a** and **b** are incorrect because they are in the past tense. Choice **c** is misspelled. Choice **d** is in the present tense, but it too is incorrect because the subject of the sentence is singular and therefore takes a verb with a singular rather than a plural ending. Choice **e** is the answer to the sample question.

43. Vellezofax kaplekzofax *autile* pirremet ricax bonlekax. (adverb)
   a. autilezofaxde
   b. autilekzofax
   c. autilede
   d. autile
   e. autiledezofax

44. Ricax kaplekax quea velle failek *synbar kometlek.* (past tense—plural adjective)
   a. synremot—kometleax
   b. synremet—kometlekax
   c. synremot—kometlek
   d. synremet—kometlek
   e. synremet—kometleax

45. Bonlekax tulet zelbar *colle* trenedlekax. (negative plural adjective)
   a. colleax
   b. pohcollezofax
   c. colle
   d. pohcolleax
   e. pohcolle

46. Ric ekaplekzof *piret* mor ric *degbar.* (singular past tense—singular noun)
   a. pirremot—deglek
   b. piremet—deglek
   c. pirremot—degle
   d. piremot—deglek
   e. pirremet—deglek

47. Riczofax *frigbar* synremet zeltozofax *colle.* (feminine plural noun—negative adverb)
   a. friglekax, pohcolledeax
   b. frigleax, pohcolledezofax
   c. friglekzofax, pohcollede
   d. friglekzofax, colledepoh
   e. frigbarzofax, pohcollede

48. Riczof *arbar* quea ric cublek *synbar* bex *regbar* bonlekzof. (feminine singular noun—negative singular present tense verb—feminine singular adjective)

a. arlekzof, pohsynot, reglezof

b. arlekzofax, pohsynot, reglezof

c. arlekzof, pohsynet, reglezof

d. arlekzof, pohsynot, reglekzof

e. arlekzof, pohsynot, reglezofax

49. *Yev* trenedlekax synet *brale* zelbar. (feminine singular possessive—masculine plural adjective)

a. Yevzofaxoe, braleax

b. Yevzofoe, bralekax

c. Yevoe, braleax

d. Yevzofoe, bralezofax

e. Yevzofoe, braleax

50. *Volle inle* zellekzof *synbar* mor velle failek. (feminine singular article—negative feminine singular adjective—negative singular past tense verb)

a. Vollezof, pohinlezof, pohsynremet

b. Vollezof, pohinlezof, pohsynremot

c. Vollezof, pohinleax, pohsynremot

d. Vollezofax, pohinlezof, pohsynremot

e. Vellezof, pohinlezof, pohsynremot

▶ Answers

Logical Reasoning

1. **d.** Sentence 2 in the passage lists several additional beliefs that fall under *attachment to the Constitution* (supporting choice **d**). Choice **a** is ruled out by the final sentence of the passage, which says that an applicant cannot be excluded simply because he or she believes *it might be desirable to make a change in our form of government.* However, it does not say that a person *must* have a desire to change the government, ruling out choices **b** and **c**. Choice **e** is ruled out by the final sentence of the passage.

2. **e.** Choice **e** is correct because the passage states in sentence 3 that *some people believe that too much immigration may compromise the standard of living in the United States.* Choice **a** is illogical because its two parts have nothing to do with one another. Choice **b** is illogical, because the chances are good that citizens would not want the United States' standard of living lowered (because it would affect them adversely); therefore, they would tend not to want an open immigration policy. Choice **c** is illogical because what the citizens want has nothing to do with immigration's compromising the United States' standard of living. Choice **d** is incorrect because the historical fact cannot be changed; in addition, the U.S. immigration policy is unrelated to past treatment of people who already lived here.

3. **c.** This question lists conditions under which visa requests must be refused. Choices **a**, **b**, and **d** are refuted by the third sentence. Choice **e** is incorrect because of the use of the word *among* at the start of the third sentence of the passage.

4. **e.** Choice **e** is correct because, if the child is considered to have dual nationality, then he must have met the criteria for citizenship in the state in which he was born *and* in his parents' home state—the situation described in choice **e**. Choice **a** is incorrect because in this instance the child cannot be a citizen of the parents' home state and have dual nationality. Choice **b** is incorrect because in this instance, the child cannot be a citizen of the state where he was born. Choice **c** is incorrect because in this instance, the child will be a citizen of the parents' home state and, therefore, will not be stateless. Choice **d** is incorrect because in this instance, the child will be a citizen of his parents' home state.

5. **c.** Choices **a** and **b** are incorrect because the language in the amendment says that states cannot abridge the privileges of their citizens without due process. Choice **d** is incorrect because the amendment does differentiate between *citizens* and *any person.* Choice **e** is refuted by the last part of the passage.

6. **b.** Choice **b** includes the following premises: People are accountable for their own behavior, and people are not accountable for behavior they cannot control. The logical conclusion based on these premises is that people can control their own behavior. Choice **a** would require that criminals never have control over the behavior of other people, which the argument does not prove. Choice **c** requires that people should not be held accountable for the behavior of other people. Choice **d** is not a conclusion, as it simply reiterates a premise of the argument. Choice **e** provides for the possibility that a criminal might not have control over another person's behavior, which is subject to harsh criminal sentencing.

7. b. Choice **b** is supported by the fact that, in *Matter of Kohama*, the relatives submitted evidence that they were willing and able to support the couple, and the court accepted the evidence as sufficient. The example in the passage is of relatives who lived in the United States; the passage does not discuss people with relatives in their home country (ruling out choice **a**). Choice **c** is illogical because of the word *must*—the relatives cannot force the person to immigrate. The passage simply states that aliens will be excluded if they are likely to become a public charge—there are obviously other ways to avoid becoming a public charge (such as employment), ruling out choice **e**.

8. e. Each of the other choices draws conclusions about the relative importance of activities either at the border or away from the border that cannot be validly concluded from the paragraph.

9. c. Choices **a**, **b**, and **e** are incorrect because they make assumptions about the relationship between terrorists and illegal aliens not supported by the passage. Choices **a** and **b** make assumptions possible for *some* incorrect by stating them for *all*. Choices **d** and **e** might sometimes be true, but are unsupported by the passage.

10. d. Choice **d** focuses on the combination of solutions outlined in the passage. All of the other choices make assumptions about individual solutions that are not supported by the passage.

11. e. Choice **e** is correct because it is directly supported by the second sentence and the last sentence in the paragraph. The information in choice **a** is specifically contradicted by the first sentence. Choices **b** and **c** are incorrect because there are no supporting statements in the paragraph. Choice **d** is incorrect because the passage clearly states that agency regulations and directives provide field-level guidance to agents and that the judicial branch of government interprets statutory law.

12. e. In choice **a**, the word *always* is not supported by the paragraph. Choices **b**, **c**, and **d** draw conclusions about the value of technology that are not supported from the information in the paragraph.

13. c. Choice **c** is the only statement that can be validly concluded directly from the information in the question. The statements made in answers **a**, **b**, **d**, and **e** use the words *never* and *always* to make assertions that are not supported by the paragraph.

14. b. Choice **b** accurately reflects the third sentence of the passage. The small word *unless* rules out choice **a**. Choices **c**, **d**, and **e** all erroneously apply the criteria for *becoming exempt* from the literacy requirements to *meeting* the literacy requirements.

15. a. The question asks that you identify what is NOT in the passage. Because the search-and-rescue dogs are labeled disobedient, and only *some* (not all) of the precincts have search-and-rescue dogs, it is *not* true that all precincts have disobedient dogs (supporting choice **a**). The other choices can be found in the passage and are therefore incorrect answers to this *CANNOT* question.

16. b. The second sentence says that a child is an orphan if her parents have disappeared or abandoned her, suggesting that the parents may still be alive. Choice **a** is wrong, because one of the conditions specified in the second sentence is that, in order to be considered an orphan, the parents must have *irrevocably released the child for emigration and adoption.* Choices **c** and **d** are irrelevant to the matter of who is an orphan, because both answers, instead, explain how an orphan can be *adopted.* Choice **e** is ruled out by the second sentence, which lists ways a child can become an orphan, even if the parents are still alive.

Spanish Language

1. a. *Fácil* (easy) is the closest match for *sencillo* (easy to use).

2. c. *Entender* (to understand) is the closest to *oír* (to hear).

3. d. *Custodia* (custody) is the choice that best matches *detención* (arrest).

4. a. *frente a* and *ante* both mean "before" as in "before the judge."

5. e. The only appropriate match for *al lado de* (next to) is *cerca de* (near).

6. b. *Sitúense* (place yourselves) most nearly means *siéntense* (sit down).

7. a. The best choice for *por la mañana* (in the morning) is *hasta mediodía* (until noon).

8. d. *Mala* (bad, ill) most nearly means *enferma* (sick).

9. a. The correct choice to match the meaning of *buscamos* (we are searching for) is *necesitamos* (we need).

10. d. The nearest match for *alcoba* (bedroom) is *dormitorio* (sleeping room).

11. e. *Yanquis* (Yankees) most nearly matches the meaning of *norteamericanos* (North Americans).

12. a. The best match for *Quiero* (I want) is *Deseo* (I wish).

13. e. The nearest match for *águila* (eagle) is *pájaro* (bird).

14. b. The appropriate choice to match *donaciones* (donations) is *contribuciones* (contributions).

15. c. The correct choice for *de la Patria* (of the native land) is *del País* (of the country).

16. b. The choice that most nearly matches *bastante* (enough) is *harto* (quite a lot).

17. d. The best match for *vámonos* (let's go) is *salguemos* (let's leave).

18. c. The correct choice for *después* (later) is *más tarde*, which also means later.

19. b. For *se parece* (resembles), the nearest match is *es similar* (is similar).

20. a. The correct match for *la gente* (the people) is *el pueblo* (the people).

21. e. Choices **a**, **b**, **c**, and **d** all use incorrect prepositions.

22. a. Both verbs in choice **a** represent the correct past tense in the indicative mood. In choices **b**, **c**, **d**, and **e**, the wrong verb or wrong forms of the verb have been used.

23. c. *Normalmente* correctly modifies the verb *usan*, and *diversos* is correct also.

24. a. In this choice, the two verbs are in agreement.

25. c. This choice is the one that uses the correct verb and noun combinations.

26. e. Here there is agreement of number and verb form.

27. b. This is the correct choice because of agreement of gender and of verb usage.

28. a. This is the only match because it is the only one that makes sense.

29. c. This is the right choice because it has both correct verb usage and gender agreement.

30. e. This is the only combination that correctly matches the second person plural verb form *van* (are you going) and has an appropriate preposition, *con* (with).

31. c. The other possibilities contain various errors, including incorrect prepositions, illogical structures, and incorrect verb forms.

32. a. The other possibilities contain various errors, including incorrect terms, illogical structure, and incorrect verb forms.

33. b. The other possibilities contain various errors, including incorrect terms, misplaced clauses, and disagreement of verb tenses.

34. d. This is the only choice that uses the correct verb form, number, and gender.

35. b. All the other forms have incorrect word order or agreement.

36. c. None of the other sentences have correct gender agreement.

37. d. All the other sentences misuse the subjunctive mood.

38. b. This is the only sentence that shows correct subject-verb agreement.

39. b. This is the only choice that correctly uses the construction *estar + de + acuerdo* (to be in agreement).

40. d. The other sentences display problems of verb or number agreement.

41. a. *Creer* means believe, whereas *crear* means create, which does not make much sense in this context.

42. c. *Habló* is the past tense of to speak in the third person singular. Other options do not agree in number, or are simply the wrong verb for the situation.

43. e. The subjunctive mood is appropriate here, and no available option supplies that in the present tense.

44. d. *Hay* does not mean have in the sense required here. *Tenga* is subjunctive, which is incorrect here, but *tienen* is indicative and correct.

45. c. This is the only plural verb to agree with *frijoles*.

46. e. *Vecino* is the word for neighbor.

47. d. Sickness is a temporary condition here, not an essential one, so it should be designated with a form of *estar*, not *ser*.

48. b. *Hace* is part of an idiomatic construction used to ask/state how long ago an event occurred.

49. e. When referring to events, such as parties or concerts, forms of *ser*, not *estar*, are used to designate location.

50. c. *Asistir* is the word for attend in the sense of go to a certain school.

Artificial Language

1. c. Word 1, *volle*, is incorrect because the translation of *volle* is *this*. The word numbered 2, *kalenet*, is also incorrect because the singular form, *kalenot*, should have been used. Word 3 is correct. *Arlek* has been correctly formed from the infinitive *arbar* (to drive) by applying Rules 4 and 9. Because the word numbered 3 has been identified as the only word translated correctly, the answer is **c**.

2. b. Word 1, *yev*, is incorrect because it means he, not she. Word 2, *synot*, is correct. According to Rules 4 and 6, to form the present tense of a verb, you should add the suffix *-ot* to the stem of the verb when the verb has a singular subject. Word 3, *huslek*, is incorrect. According to Rule 1, a feminine noun must take the ending *-zof*. Accordingly, the word numbered 3 should have been *huslekzof*.

3. d. Word 1, *ric*, is correct. The vocabulary lists state that *ric* is the translation for *the*. Word 2, *bonlek*, is correct. According to Rule 9, to form a noun from a verb, the suffix *-lek* should be added to the stem of the infinitive. The infinitive (as it appears in the vocabulary lists) is *bonbar*, and its stem is *bon* (note that all infinitives in the vocabulary list have the suffix *-bar* and are distinguished only by their respective stems). The word numbered 3, *kometlek*, is correct. This is the word for *friend* as it appears in the vocabulary lists. The feminine gender is not specified in the sentence, so *kometlek* does not take a feminine ending.

4. d. The word numbered 1, *kaplekzofax*, is correct. According to Rule 1, the feminine singular of a noun is formed by adding the suffix *-zof* to the masculine singular. Then, to form the plural, the suffix *-ax* should be added to the word *kaplekzof*. The word numbered 2, *arremet*, is correct. According to Rule 4, the stem of the infinitive *to drive* is *-ar* (as the infinitive form is *arbar* in the vocabulary lists). According to Rule 7, the past tense is formed by adding the suffix *-rem* to the stem of the verb and then adding the suffix *-et* when the verb is plural, so the correct translation of *drove* is *arremet*. Word 3, *cublek*, is the correct translation for *jeep* in the vocabulary lists.

5. a. Word 1, *almanlek*, is the correct translation for the word *government* in the vocabulary lists. The word numbered 2, *synremet*, is incorrect. The correct way to form the present tense singular according to Rule 6 is to add the suffix *-ot* to the stem of the verb. Accordingly, the correct translation for the word *is* would be *synot*. The erroneous word *synremet* is actually the past tense in the plural form, *were* (see Rule 7). The word numbered 3, *collede*, is incorrect. The correct translation for the word *legal*, an adjective, is *colle* (see vocabulary lists). The erroneous word *collede* is actually the word *legally*, which is formed by adding the suffix *-de* to the adjectival form (see Rule 11).

6. e. Because none of the numbered words is correct, the answer is **e**. The word numbered 1, *kaplek*, is incorrect. *Kaplek* is the word for the singular noun *man*. Since the word *men* is a plural noun, the correct translation according to Rule 2 would have been *kaplekax*. As Rule 2 states, in the Artificial Language the plural of nouns is formed by adding the suffix *-ax* to the correct singular form. The word numbered 2, *kaplekzof*, is incorrect. *Kaplekzof* is the word for the singular noun *woman*. Consequently, the word *kaplekzof* correctly includes the suffix *-zof* for the feminine form (Rule 1), but incorrectly neglects the suffix *-ax* for the plural form (Rule 2). The correct translation of *women* is *kaplekzofax*. The word numbered 3, *pirbar*, is incorrect. *Pirbar* (to escape) is the infinitive form of the verb, whereas the sentence calls for the past tense, escaped. To form the past tense (Rule 7), the suffix *-rem* should be added to the stem of the verb, and then the suffix *-et* should be added when the verb refers to a plural subject (the men and the women). Accordingly, the correct translation is *pirremet*.

7. a. Because only the word numbered 1 is correct, the answer is **a**. The word numbered 1, *huslekoe*, is correct. Because *alien's* is a possessive form, the word *huslek* (alien) must take the possessive suffix -*oe* (Rule 12). The word numbered 2, *liaremet*, is incorrect. *Liaremet* correctly applies Rule 4 to form the stem of the verb and correctly applies the suffix for the past tense, -*rem*, but it incorrectly applies the plural suffix -*et*. The correct translation for *injured* in this sentence would be *liaremot* since the verb refers to a singular subject and, therefore, takes the suffix -*ot* (see Rule 7). The word numbered 3, *yevoe*, is incorrect. The possessive ending -*oe* would apply to the possessive pronoun *his*, whereas the pronoun used in the sentence is *him*. According to the vocabulary list, the translation for *him* is *yev*. Accordingly, *yev* should have been used in the sentence.

8. d. Because two of the numbered words are correct, the answer is **d**. The word numbered 1, *volle*, is correct. According to the vocabulary lists, the correct translation for *this* is *volle*. The word numbered 2, *mor*, is correct. According to the vocabulary lists, the correct translation for *from* is *mor*. You should note that it is not always necessary to apply the grammatical rules, as is the case with these two words. In the case of these words, it is sufficient to consult the vocabulary lists. It is necessary to apply the grammatical rules only when the word in question cannot be used exactly as it appears in the vocabulary lists. The word numbered 3, *volle*, is incorrect. According to the vocabulary lists, the correct translation for *that* is *velle* (*volle* means this, as seen in the case of the word numbered 1).

9. e. Because none of the numbered words is correct, the answer is **e**. The word numbered 1, *velle*, is incorrect. The correct translation of *those* would be *velleax*, because *those* is the plural of *that*, and according to Rule 2, the plural form for pronouns must take the suffix -*ax*. The word numbered 2, *brale*, is incorrect. *Brale* means difficult (as can be seen in the vocabulary lists), but according to Rule 2, adjectives take the ending -*ax* when they are modifying a plural noun. Because the adjective *difficult* in the sentence is modifying the plural noun *inspections*, it must take the suffix -*ax*. Accordingly, the correct form to use is *braleax*. The word numbered 3, *zelbarax*, is incorrect. According to Rule 9, to form a noun from a verb, the suffix -*lek* should be added to the stem of the verb (in this case *zel*, which according to Rule 4 is the stem of the infinitive *zelbar*, to inspect). Thus, the noun *inspection* (singular) is *zellek*, but in the sentence, this noun appears in the plural (*inspections*). Consequently, according to Rule 2, *zellek* must take the ending -*ax*, thus making it the plural *zellekax*.

10. e. Because none of the numbered words is correct, the answer is **e**. The word numbered 1, *tatlekzof*, is incorrect. *Tatlekzof* is the correct word for a female spy (Rules 1, 4, and 9), whereas the word numbered 1 in the sentence refers to *spies*, in the plural and with no specification as to gender. Therefore, the correct translation would be *tatlekax*, which first forms a noun (*tatlek*) from the infinitive verb (*tatbar*) according to Rules 4 and 9, and then forms the plural *tatlekax* according to Rule 2. The word numbered 2, *synremot*, is incorrect. The verb in the English sentence is in the present tense and plural form (*are*). The correct translation in this case must be *synet*, according to Rule 6, which states that to form the present tense in the plural form you should add the suffix *-et* to the stem of the infinitive (which is itself formed by applying Rule 4). The word numbered 3, *inlepoh*, is incorrect. According to Rule 13, the adjective *disloyal* must be formed by adding the negative prefix *poh-* to the adjective *inle* (loyal). The word numbered 3, *inlepoh*, erroneously uses *poh* as a negative suffix rather than as a negative prefix. In addition, the adjective must have a plural ending according to Rule 2, since it refers to the plural noun *spies*. Consequently, the correct translation must be *pohinleax*.

11. b. Because only the word numbered 2 is correct, the answer is **b**. The word numbered 1, *bex*, is incorrect. In the Artificial Language the article *bex* (in English a, an) takes a feminine ending (see Rules 1 and 3). The correct word is *bexzof*. The word numbered 2, *autilezof*, is correct. *Autile* (skillful) is an adjective, and as such must take a feminine ending when referring to a feminine subject (see Rules 1 and 3). The word numbered 3, *zelzof*, is incorrect. Because it is a noun (inspector in English), it must first take the ending *-lek*—this is required by Rules 4 and 9, which state that to form a noun from a verb the suffix *-lek* should replace the infinitive suffix *-bar* (note that the infinitive form appears in the vocabulary lists: *zelbar*). Once the noun (*zellek*) has been formed, then the feminine suffix *-zof* must be added because the sentence has a feminine subject. Accordingly, the correct word would be *zellekzof*.

12. c. Because only the word numbered 3 is correct, the answer is **c**. The word numbered 1, *velle*, is incorrect. *Velle* means *that*, whereas the word in the sentence is the plural *those*. Accordingly, *velle* must appear in the plural, which would be *velleax* (see Rule 2, which states that the plural of an adjective must be formed by adding the suffix *-ax* to the singular form). The word numbered 2, *synetpoh*, is incorrect. The first portion of the word *synet* is the correct form of *are* in the plural (see Rules 4 and 6), but the negative form *poh* must be used as a prefix rather than as a suffix (see Rule 13). Accordingly, the correct form for *are not* in the plural must be *pohsynet*. The word numbered 3, *avelekax*, is correct. According to the vocabulary lists, the correct translation of the noun enemy is *avelek*, and according to Rule 2, the plural of a noun is formed by adding the suffix *-ax* to the singular.

13. d. Because two of the numbered words are correct, the answer is **d**. The word numbered 1, *bonlekax*, is correct. *Bonlekax* (which means guards) is formed by first changing the infinitive verb *to guard* (*bonbar*) into the singular noun *bonlek* (see Rules 4 and 10, which state that to form a noun from a verb, you should add the suffix *-lek* to the stem of the verb). Next, to make the noun plural (guards), the suffix *-ax* should be added to the singular form. The word numbered 2, *pohcolle*, is incorrect. According to Rule 13, the adjective *illegal* must be formed by adding the prefix *poh-* to the adjective *colle* (legal). According to Rules 2 and 3, the ending *-ax* must be added to make the adjective plural because it is modifying a plural noun (workers). Accordingly, the correct word would be *pohcolleax*. The word numbered 3, *friglekax*, is correct. The first portion of the noun, *friglek*, means worker; you form this noun (according to Rules 4 and 10) by adding the suffix *-lek* to the stem of the infinitive *frigbar* (to work). Next, according to Rule 2, to make the noun plural, you add the suffix *-ax* to the singular.

14. d. Because two of the numbered words are correct, the answer is **d**. Word 1, *almanlek*, is correct. According to the vocabulary lists, the correct translation for *government* is *almanlek*. Word 2, *volle* (this), is incorrect because it is an adjective and must have the feminine (*-zof*) and plural (*-ax*) endings to agree with the noun *girls*. Word 3, *ekaplekzofax*, is the correct feminine plural form.

15. b. Word 1, *yevoe*, is incorrect because it is the masculine possessive pronoun *his*; the correct translation is the feminine singular pronoun, *yevzof* (she), formed by adding the feminine singular ending to the pronoun *yev* (he), following Rule 1. Word 2, *chonremot* (crossed), is the correct past singular conjugation of the verb *chonbar* (Rules 4, 5, and 7). Word 3, *pohcolle*, is incorrect because it is the adjectival form of the word; the correct translation is the adverbial form, *pohcollede* (illegally), following Rule 11.

16. e. Word 1, *ekaplekax*, is incorrect because although it is the masculine plural noun, it lacks the required possessive ending to be translated properly; the correct translation is the possessive noun, *ekaplekaxoe* (boys'), formed according to Rules 2 and 12. Word 2, *piret*, is incorrect because it is translated as a verb; the word *escape* in the sentence is a noun, and should be translated *pirlek* (escape) from the verb, *pirbar* (Rule 9). Word 3, *synbar*, is incorrect because the verb is in the unconjugated infinitive; the verb should be in the past singular conjugation, *synremot* (was), to agree with the subject of the sentence, *escape* (Rules 4, 5, and 7).

17. a. The word numbered 1, *deglek*, is correct. The noun is formed by adding the suffix *-lek* to the stem of the verb *degbar* (Rules 4 and 9). Word 2, *zelremot*, is incorrect. Although it is in the correct singular past conjugation, it is the wrong verb. The sentence says *worked* (*frigremot*), not *inspected* (*zelremot*). The word numbered 3, *collede*, is incorrect. This is the translation for *legally*. The sentence says *illegally*, so the correct word should be *pohcollede* (Rule 13).

18. a. Word 1, *velleax* (those), is correct because it is an adjective that has the plural suffix to agree with the noun *guards* (Rule 2). Word 2, *inle* (loyal), is incorrect because it is an adjective that should have the plural suffix to agree with the noun *friends*; the correct translation is *inleax* (Rule 2). Word 3, *bex* (a, an), is an incorrect translation of the word *the* (*ric*).

19. c. Word 1, *zelek* (guard), is incorrect because it lacks the plural ending required to translate the plural noun, *inspectors* (Rule 2); the correct translation is *zelekax*. Word 2, *liaremot*, is incorrect because it is the past singular conjugation of the verb; it should be the past plural conjugation of the verb to agree with the plural subject, *inspectors* (Rules 4, 5, and 7); the correct translation is *liaremet*. Word 3, *yevzof* (her), is the correctly translated feminine form of the pronoun *yev* (him), because it has the feminine ending (Rule 1).

20. b. Word 1, *pohcolle*, is incorrect because it is an adjective that requires the plural ending to agree with the noun *papers* (Rules 2 and 3); the correct translation is *pohcolleax*. Word 2, *trenedlekax* (papers), is correct because it has the plural ending on the noun (Rule 2). Word 3, *brale*, is incorrect because it is an adjective modifying the plural noun *papers*. It should, therefore, take the plural ending (Rule 2); the correct translation is *braleax*.

21. c. The verb, *guard* (*bonet*), is in the present tense plural (Rules 4 and 6). The possessive noun, *country's* (*failekoe*), is correctly formed with the possessive suffix added to the noun (Rule 12), and the noun, *border* (*reglek*), has been correctly formed from the infinitive *regbar* according to Rule 9.

22. b. The adjective, *difficult*, is correctly translated as *brale*, and the noun, *work* (*friglek*), is correctly formed from the infinitive (Rule 9).

23. e. The article, *a*, is correctly translated *bex*; the adjective, *border* (*regle*), is correctly formed from the infinitive *regbar*, according to Rules 9 and 10; and the noun, *station* (*lexlek*), is correctly formed from the infinitive *lexbar* (Rule 9).

24. a. The plural possessive pronoun, *their* (*yevaxoe*), has been correctly formed from the singular pronoun, *he* (*yev*), by adding the plural and possessive endings (Rules 2 and 12); and the plural noun, *jeeps* (*cublekax*), has been correctly formed following Rule 2.

25. d. The verb, *have* (*tulet*), is in the correct plural present form to agree with the subject of the sentence, *they* (Rules 4, 5, and 6). The infinitive, *to identify*, is correctly translated *kalenbar*.

26. b. The infinitive, *to cross* (*chonbar*), is correctly translated, and the plural noun, *rivers* (*browlekax*), is correctly formed according to Rule 2.

27. d. The adverb, *loyally* (*inlede*), is correctly formed according to Rule 11. The plural pronoun, *they* (*yevax*), is correctly formed from the singular pronoun *he* (*yev*) by adding the plural suffix (Rule 2). The verb, *guard* (*bonet*), is in the correct plural present form to agree with the subject, *they* (Rules 4, 5, and 6).

28. e. The word *the* is correctly translated *ric*; the noun, *shooting* (*deglek*), is correctly formed from the infinitive (Rule 9). The word *of* is correctly translated *quea*, and the plural noun, *spies* (*tatlekax*) is correctly formed according to Rules 2 and 9.

29. e. The noun, *injury* (*lialek*), is correctly formed from the infinitive, *liabar*, according to Rule 9. The word *from* is correctly translated *mor*. The pronoun *this* is correctly translated *volle*. The noun, *work* (*friglek*), is correctly formed from the infinitive, *frigbar* (Rule 9).

30. c. The noun, *identification* (*kalenlek*), is correctly formed from the infinitive, *kalenbar*, according to Rule 9. The word *of* is correctly translated *quea*. The adjective, *illegal* (*pohcolleax*), is correctly formed by adding the negative prefix to the word for legal, and it is in the plural form to agree with the noun, *papers* (Rules 2 and 13). The plural noun, *papers* (*trenedlekax*), is correctly formed with the plural suffix according to Rule 2.

31. e. *Ric bonlek zelremot yevoe kometlekaxoe trenedlekax* means *The guard inspected his friends' papers*, employing the possessive ending on the possessive pronoun and noun, *yevoe* and *kometlekaxoe* (Rule 12), and attaching the plural ending to the noun, *trenedlekax* (Rule 2).

32. a. *Ric kaplekzof arremot ric cublek autilede* means *The woman drove the jeep skillfully*. *Arremot ric cublek autilede* is the only one of these expressions that means *drove the jeep skillfully*, employing the past singular conjugation of the verb, *arremot* (Rules 4, 5, and 7) and the adverbial suffix to form the adverb, *autilede* (Rule 11).

33. a. *Ricax almanlekax quea velleax failekax tulet tatlekax* means *The governments of those countries have spies*. *Ricax almanlekax quea velleax failekax* is the only one of these expressions that properly translates *the governments of those countries*, using the correct plural endings on the nouns, *almanlekax* and *failekax* (Rule 2),

and the plural ending on the adjective, *velleax* (Rules 2 and 3), and on the article, *ric*.

34. c. *Vellezofax ekaplekzofax chonremet ric browlek pohcollede* means *Those girls crossed the river illegally*. *Vellezofax ekaplekzofax chonremet* is the only one of these expressions that properly translates *those girls crossed*, using the correct feminine plural endings for the adjective, *vellezofax*, and noun, *ekaplekzofax* (Rule 2), as well as the past plural conjugation of the verb, *chonremet* (Rules 4, 5, and 7).

35. d. *Ricax regleax bonlekax friget inlede mor yevaxoe almanle lexlek* means *The border guards work loyally from their government station*. *Inlede mor yevaxoe almanle* is the only one of these expressions that properly translates *loyally from their government*. The adverb, *inlede*, is correctly formed using the adverbial ending (Rule 11); the possessive pronoun, *yevaxoe*, is correctly formed by adding the plural ending and the possessive suffix (Rules 2 and 12); and the adjective, *almanle*, is correctly formed from the noun, *almanlek*, using Rule 10.

36. d. *Ric kalenlek quea pohcolleax huslekax synot brale friglek* means *The identification of illegal aliens is difficult work*. *Ric kalenlek quea pohcolleax huslekax* is the only one of these expressions that properly translates *the identification of illegal aliens*. The noun, *kalenlek*, is formed correctly from the infinitive, *kalenbar* (Rule 9); the adjective, *pohcolleax*, is correctly formed, agreeing in number and gender with the noun and using the negative prefix (Rules 2, 3, and 13); the noun, *huslekax*, has the necessary plural ending (Rule 2).

37. **c.** *Velleax regleax bonlekax tulet brale friglek* means *Those border guards have difficult work.* Only choice **c** correctly translates these words. Choice **a** is incorrect because *vellekax* is misspelled. It should be *velleax*. Choice **b** is incorrect because the adjective *regle* needs to agree in number with the plural word *bonlekax* (guards). Choices **d** and **e** are incorrect because *volleax* means *these*, not *those*.

38. **a.** *Ricax huslekax degremet ricax zellekax* means *The aliens shot the inspectors.* Only choice **a** correctly translates these words. Choice **b** is incorrect because it means *shot the inspector*; however, the plural is required. Choice **c** is incorrect because *deget* means *shoot*, not *shot*. Choice **d** is incorrect because *degremot* is singular and the subject is plural and requires a plural verb. Finally, choice **e** is incorrect because according to Rule 3 the article *ric* requires the plural ending *-ax* to agree with the plural *zellekax* (inspectors).

39. **e.** *Ric liato bonlek tulremot frigbar* means *The injured guard had to work.* Only choice **e** correctly translates these words. Choice **a** is incorrect because *injured* is translated as a past tense verb, when it should be the past participle used as an adjective (see Rule 8). Choice **b** is incorrect because it adds the plural suffix *-ax* to *bonlek* for no reason. Choice **c** is incorrect because *bex* means *a* or *an*, not *the*. Choice **d** is incorrect because *bonek* is misspelled; it should be *bonlek*.

40. **e.** *Ric ekaplek cre riczofax ekaplekzofax chonremet ric browlek* means *The boy and the girls crossed the river.* Only choice **e** correctly translates these words. Choice **a** is incorrect because the first *the* should not be plural (there is only one boy) and because the second *the* is missing from the translation. Choice **b** is incorrect because it means *the boys*, but it should be *the boy*. Choice **c** is incorrect because it means *the man and the girls*. Choice **d** is incorrect because it means *the boy and the girl*, but it should be *the boy and the girls*.

41. **b.** *Riczofax avelezofax tatlekzofax pirremet mor ricax bonlekax* means *The [female] enemy spies escaped from the guards.* Only choice **b** correctly translates these words. Choice **a** is incorrect because *quea* means *of*, not *from*. Choice **c** is incorrect because the article *the* is missing the plural suffix *-ax* as required by Rule 3. Choice **d** is incorrect because to form the past tense, you must remove the suffix *-bar* before adding *-remet* (see Rules 4 and 7). Finally, choice **e** is incorrect because *piremet* is misspelled. It should be the stem *pir-* followed by the suffix *-remet* (thus *pirremet*, not *piremet*).

42. **a.** *Yevoe cublek cre yevzofoe trenedlekax synremet zeltoax* means *His jeep and her papers were inspected.* Only choice **a** correctly translates these words. Choice **b** is incorrect because *yevzofaxoe* means *their* (feminine plural possessive), when it should be *her* (feminine singular possessive). Choice **c** is incorrect because the feminine suffixes are added to *papers* and *inspected.* In this sentence, these words do not require a feminine suffix. Choice **d** is incorrect because *paper* and *inspected* are singular, but should have the plural suffix *-ax* according to Rule 2. In addition, the verb *synremot* is singular but should be plural, *synremet.* Choice **e** is incorrect because *yevzofaxoe* means *their* (feminine plural possessive), when it should be *her* (feminine singular possessive) and because *zelto* is missing the plural ending *-ax* as required by Rules 2 and 8.

43. **c.** *Vellezofax kaplekzofax autilede pirremet ricax bonlekax* means *Those women skillfully escaped the guards.* Choices **a**, **b**, and **e** are incorrect because they all include feminine plural endings; however, adverbs do not take gendered or numbered suffixes. Choice **d** is incorrect because it lacks the adverbial ending, *-de*, required for the formation of adverbs (Rule 11).

44. **e.** *Ricax kaplekax quea velle failek synremet kometleax* means *The men of that country were friendly.* Choices **a** and **c** are incorrect because the verb, *synremot*, is in the past singular conjugation; it should be in the past plural, *synremet*, to agree in number with the subject of the verb, *kaplekax* (Rules 4, 5, and 7). In addition, choice **c** is incorrect because the word *kometlek* is a singular noun, not an adjective. While choice **b** has the correct verb form, the word *kometlekax* is a plural noun, not an adjective. Choice **d** also has the correct verb form, but the word *kometlek* is a singular noun, not an adjective. Choice **e** has the correct verb form, and the correct form of the adjective, *kometleax* (Rule 10).

45. **d.** *Bonlekax tulet zelbar pohcolleax trenedlekax* means *Guards have to inspect illegal papers.* Choices **a** and **c** are incorrect because they are both lacking the negative prefix (Rule 13). Choice **b** is incorrect because it includes the feminine suffix when the noun that the adjective modifies is masculine plural (Rule 3). Choice **e** is incorrect because it is in the singular form, but it should be in the plural form to agree with the noun, *trenedlekax* (Rules 2 and 3).

46. **a.** *Ric ekaplekzof pirremot mor ric deglek* means *The girl escaped from the shooter.* In choices **b** and **d**, the verb form is misspelled. In choice **c**, the verb is in the correct past singular form, *pirremot* (Rules 4, 5, and 7), to agree with the singular subject, *ekaplekzof.* However, the word *degle* is the adjectival form, not a noun. In choice **e**, the verb is in the incorrect past plural form.

47. **c.** *Riczofax friglekzofax synremet zeltozofax pohcollede* means *The [female] workers were inspected illegally*. Choice **a** is incorrect because *friglekax* is the singular masculine noun and adverbs such as *pohcollede* do not require plural suffixes (see Rules 2 and 11). Choice **b** is incorrect because *fregleax* should be *freglekzofax* (see Rules 2 and 9) and adverbs do not require plural or feminine suffixes (see Rule 11). Choice **d** is incorrect because the prefix *poh-* is added as a suffix. Choice **e** is incorrect because *frigbarzofax* still has the suffix *-bar*. This should have been replaced with *-lek* according to Rules 4 and 9.

48. **a.** *Riczof arlekzof quea ric cublek pohsynot bex reglezof bonlekzof* means *The [female] driver of the jeep is not a border guard*. Choice **b** is incorrect because *arlekzofax* is plural and it should be singular. Choice **c** is incorrect because the verb *pohsynet* is plural and it should be singular. Choice **d** is incorrect because *border* is in the noun form, not the adjectival form. Finally, choice **e** is incorrect because the adjective *reglezofax* is plural and it should be singular.

49. **e.** *Yevzofoe trenedlekax synet braleax zelbar* means *Her papers are difficult to inspect*. Choice **a** is incorrect because *yevzofaxoe* means *their* (feminine plural possessive), not *her*. Choice **b** is incorrect because *bralekax* is misspelled; there is no *k* in the adjective *braleax*. Choice **c** is incorrect because *yevoe* means *his*, not *her*. According to Rule 1, the suffix *-zof* must be added. Choice **d** is incorrect because the adjective *brale* is not feminine, so it is unnecessary to add the suffix *-zof*.

50. **b.** *Vollezof pohinlezof zellekzof pohsynremot mor velle failek* means *This disloyal [female] inspector was not from that country*. Choice **a** is incorrect because the verb *pohsynremet* is plural and should be singular. Choice **c** is incorrect because the adjective *pohinleax* has the plural suffix; it should have only the feminine suffix *-zof*. Choice **d** is incorrect because the article *vollezofax* has the plural suffix *-ax*, but should be singular. Choice **e** is incorrect because *vellezof* means *that* (feminine), not *this*. It does not match the word given in the sentence.

► Scoring

To evaluate how you did on this practice exam, start by totaling the number of correct responses on the two sections of the exam—Logical Reasoning and Spanish or Artificial Language (whichever you chose to take). First, find the number of questions you got right in each part. Questions you skipped or got wrong don't count; just add up the number of correct answers.

If at least 70% of your responses on the two parts are correct, you will most likely pass the Border Patrol Exam.

Keep in mind that what's much more important than your scores, for now, is how you did on each of the basic skills tested by the exam. Diagnose your strengths and weaknesses so that you can concentrate your efforts as you prepare for the exam. Turn again to the instructional chapters that cover each of the skills tested on the Border Patrol Exam, and review the areas that gave you the most trouble.

If you didn't score as well as you would like, ask yourself the following: Did I run out of time before I could answer all the questions? Did I go back and change my answers from right to wrong? Did I get flustered and sit staring at a difficult question for what seemed like hours? If you had any of these problems, once again, be sure to go over the LearningExpress Test Preparation System in Chapter 3 again to learn how to avoid them.

After working more on the instructional chapters, take the second practice exam in Chapter 11 to see how much you've improved.

11 ▶ Border Patrol Practice Exam 2

CHAPTER SUMMARY

This is the second of the two practice tests in this book based on the Border Patrol Exam. Use this test for more practice with Logical Reasoning and Spanish or Artificial Language questions, and see how much your score has improved over the first practice test.

FOR THIS EXAM, once again simulate the actual test-taking experience as closely as possible. Work in a quiet place, away from interruptions. Tear out the answer sheet on the next page if you own this book, or xerox it if not, and use your number two pencil to fill in the circles. Use a timer or stopwatch and allow yourself three hours to complete both sections of the exam.

After the exam, use the answer explanations to see your progress on each section and to find out why the correct answers are correct and the incorrect ones are incorrect. Then use the scoring section at the end of the exam to see how you did overall.

▶ Logical Reasoning

1. ⓐ ⓑ ⓒ ⓓ ⓔ
2. ⓐ ⓑ ⓒ ⓓ ⓔ
3. ⓐ ⓑ ⓒ ⓓ ⓔ
4. ⓐ ⓑ ⓒ ⓓ ⓔ
5. ⓐ ⓑ ⓒ ⓓ ⓔ
6. ⓐ ⓑ ⓒ ⓓ ⓔ
7. ⓐ ⓑ ⓒ ⓓ ⓔ
8. ⓐ ⓑ ⓒ ⓓ ⓔ
9. ⓐ ⓑ ⓒ ⓓ ⓔ
10. ⓐ ⓑ ⓒ ⓓ ⓔ
11. ⓐ ⓑ ⓒ ⓓ ⓔ
12. ⓐ ⓑ ⓒ ⓓ ⓔ
13. ⓐ ⓑ ⓒ ⓓ ⓔ
14. ⓐ ⓑ ⓒ ⓓ ⓔ
15. ⓐ ⓑ ⓒ ⓓ ⓔ
16. ⓐ ⓑ ⓒ ⓓ ⓔ

▶ Spanish Language

1. ⓐ ⓑ ⓒ ⓓ ⓔ
2. ⓐ ⓑ ⓒ ⓓ ⓔ
3. ⓐ ⓑ ⓒ ⓓ ⓔ
4. ⓐ ⓑ ⓒ ⓓ ⓔ
5. ⓐ ⓑ ⓒ ⓓ ⓔ
6. ⓐ ⓑ ⓒ ⓓ ⓔ
7. ⓐ ⓑ ⓒ ⓓ ⓔ
8. ⓐ ⓑ ⓒ ⓓ ⓔ
9. ⓐ ⓑ ⓒ ⓓ ⓔ
10. ⓐ ⓑ ⓒ ⓓ ⓔ
11. ⓐ ⓑ ⓒ ⓓ ⓔ
12. ⓐ ⓑ ⓒ ⓓ ⓔ
13. ⓐ ⓑ ⓒ ⓓ ⓔ
14. ⓐ ⓑ ⓒ ⓓ ⓔ
15. ⓐ ⓑ ⓒ ⓓ ⓔ
16. ⓐ ⓑ ⓒ ⓓ ⓔ
17. ⓐ ⓑ ⓒ ⓓ ⓔ
18. ⓐ ⓑ ⓒ ⓓ ⓔ
19. ⓐ ⓑ ⓒ ⓓ ⓔ
20. ⓐ ⓑ ⓒ ⓓ ⓔ
21. ⓐ ⓑ ⓒ ⓓ ⓔ
22. ⓐ ⓑ ⓒ ⓓ ⓔ
23. ⓐ ⓑ ⓒ ⓓ ⓔ
24. ⓐ ⓑ ⓒ ⓓ ⓔ
25. ⓐ ⓑ ⓒ ⓓ ⓔ
26. ⓐ ⓑ ⓒ ⓓ ⓔ
27. ⓐ ⓑ ⓒ ⓓ ⓔ
28. ⓐ ⓑ ⓒ ⓓ ⓔ
29. ⓐ ⓑ ⓒ ⓓ ⓔ
30. ⓐ ⓑ ⓒ ⓓ ⓔ
31. ⓐ ⓑ ⓒ ⓓ ⓔ
32. ⓐ ⓑ ⓒ ⓓ ⓔ
33. ⓐ ⓑ ⓒ ⓓ ⓔ
34. ⓐ ⓑ ⓒ ⓓ ⓔ
35. ⓐ ⓑ ⓒ ⓓ ⓔ
36. ⓐ ⓑ ⓒ ⓓ ⓔ
37. ⓐ ⓑ ⓒ ⓓ ⓔ
38. ⓐ ⓑ ⓒ ⓓ ⓔ
39. ⓐ ⓑ ⓒ ⓓ ⓔ
40. ⓐ ⓑ ⓒ ⓓ ⓔ
41. ⓐ ⓑ ⓒ ⓓ ⓔ
42. ⓐ ⓑ ⓒ ⓓ ⓔ
43. ⓐ ⓑ ⓒ ⓓ ⓔ
44. ⓐ ⓑ ⓒ ⓓ ⓔ
45. ⓐ ⓑ ⓒ ⓓ ⓔ
46. ⓐ ⓑ ⓒ ⓓ ⓔ
47. ⓐ ⓑ ⓒ ⓓ ⓔ
48. ⓐ ⓑ ⓒ ⓓ ⓔ
49. ⓐ ⓑ ⓒ ⓓ ⓔ
50. ⓐ ⓑ ⓒ ⓓ ⓔ

▶ Artificial Language

1. ⓐ ⓑ ⓒ ⓓ ⓔ
2. ⓐ ⓑ ⓒ ⓓ ⓔ
3. ⓐ ⓑ ⓒ ⓓ ⓔ
4. ⓐ ⓑ ⓒ ⓓ ⓔ
5. ⓐ ⓑ ⓒ ⓓ ⓔ
6. ⓐ ⓑ ⓒ ⓓ ⓔ
7. ⓐ ⓑ ⓒ ⓓ ⓔ
8. ⓐ ⓑ ⓒ ⓓ ⓔ
9. ⓐ ⓑ ⓒ ⓓ ⓔ
10. ⓐ ⓑ ⓒ ⓓ ⓔ
11. ⓐ ⓑ ⓒ ⓓ ⓔ
12. ⓐ ⓑ ⓒ ⓓ ⓔ
13. ⓐ ⓑ ⓒ ⓓ ⓔ
14. ⓐ ⓑ ⓒ ⓓ ⓔ
15. ⓐ ⓑ ⓒ ⓓ ⓔ
16. ⓐ ⓑ ⓒ ⓓ ⓔ
17. ⓐ ⓑ ⓒ ⓓ ⓔ
18. ⓐ ⓑ ⓒ ⓓ ⓔ
19. ⓐ ⓑ ⓒ ⓓ ⓔ
20. ⓐ ⓑ ⓒ ⓓ ⓔ
21. ⓐ ⓑ ⓒ ⓓ ⓔ
22. ⓐ ⓑ ⓒ ⓓ ⓔ
23. ⓐ ⓑ ⓒ ⓓ ⓔ
24. ⓐ ⓑ ⓒ ⓓ ⓔ
25. ⓐ ⓑ ⓒ ⓓ ⓔ
26. ⓐ ⓑ ⓒ ⓓ ⓔ
27. ⓐ ⓑ ⓒ ⓓ ⓔ
28. ⓐ ⓑ ⓒ ⓓ ⓔ
29. ⓐ ⓑ ⓒ ⓓ ⓔ
30. ⓐ ⓑ ⓒ ⓓ ⓔ
31. ⓐ ⓑ ⓒ ⓓ ⓔ
32. ⓐ ⓑ ⓒ ⓓ ⓔ
33. ⓐ ⓑ ⓒ ⓓ ⓔ
34. ⓐ ⓑ ⓒ ⓓ ⓔ
35. ⓐ ⓑ ⓒ ⓓ ⓔ
36. ⓐ ⓑ ⓒ ⓓ ⓔ
37. ⓐ ⓑ ⓒ ⓓ ⓔ
38. ⓐ ⓑ ⓒ ⓓ ⓔ
39. ⓐ ⓑ ⓒ ⓓ ⓔ
40. ⓐ ⓑ ⓒ ⓓ ⓔ
41. ⓐ ⓑ ⓒ ⓓ ⓔ
42. ⓐ ⓑ ⓒ ⓓ ⓔ
43. ⓐ ⓑ ⓒ ⓓ ⓔ
44. ⓐ ⓑ ⓒ ⓓ ⓔ
45. ⓐ ⓑ ⓒ ⓓ ⓔ
46. ⓐ ⓑ ⓒ ⓓ ⓔ
47. ⓐ ⓑ ⓒ ⓓ ⓔ
48. ⓐ ⓑ ⓒ ⓓ ⓔ
49. ⓐ ⓑ ⓒ ⓓ ⓔ
50. ⓐ ⓑ ⓒ ⓓ ⓔ

▶ Logical Reasoning

1. Law enforcement agencies use scientific techniques to identify suspects or to establish guilt. One obvious application of such techniques is the examination of a crime scene. Some substances found at a crime scene yield valuable clues under microscopic examination. Clothing fibers, dirt particles, and even pollen grains may reveal important information to the careful investigator. Nothing can be overlooked, because all substances found at a crime scene are potential sources of evidence.

   From the information given above, it can be validly concluded that

   a. all substances that yield valuable clues under microscopic examination are substances found at a crime scene.

   b. some potential sources of evidence are substances that yield valuable clues under microscopic examination.

   c. some substances found at a crime scene are not potential sources of evidence.

   d. no potential sources of evidence are substances found at a crime scene.

   e. some substances that yield valuable clues under microscopic examination are not substances found at a crime scene.

2. Immigrants may try to enter the United States illegally for a variety of reasons. Among these reasons are to get jobs they hope will improve their financial situation, to reunite with family members in the United States, and to find political freedom. There's ongoing debate in the United States about how many immigrants should be admitted and under what conditions. Meanwhile, smugglers known as coyotes take advantage of the situation by collecting thousands of dollars from those wishing to cross the border illegally. For their money, immigrants often endure days or even weeks of unpleasant conditions and no guarantees of success or even survival.

   From the information given above, it can be validly concluded that

   a. smugglers charge too much money for the services they provide.

   b. illegal immigrants sometimes risk their lives to enter the United States with no guarantees.

   c. illegal immigrants are never successfully integrated into U.S. society.

   d. illegal immigrants always improve their financial situation in the United States.

   e. debating about immigration levels will eventually result in protecting more illegal immigrants from coyotes.

3. Border Patrol Agents are sometimes required to testify in court about their activities leading up to and during an arrest. Therefore, agents must have excellent communication skills. They need to be able to express themselves clearly in court and elsewhere so they are understood without confusion or misinterpretation. By their choice of words and how they speak, they must demonstrate to a judge or jury that they are confident and capable. A public speaking course would be an excellent way for agents to ensure that they're making the best possible impression in court.

From the information given above, it can be validly concluded that

a. excellent communication skills are important only when an agent is in court.

b. excellent communication skills are essential for all Border Patrol Agents.

c. no agents would benefit from a public speaking course.

d. trained public speakers would make excellent Border Patrol Agents.

e. an agent's choice of words and confidence have little effect on a judge or jury.

4. The printed output of some computer-driven printers can be recognized by forensic analysts. The Acme Model 200 printer was manufactured using two different inking mechanisms, one of which yields a Type A micro pattern of ink spray around its characters. Of all Acme Model 200 printers, 70% produce this Type A micro pattern, which is also characteristic of some models of other printers. Forensic analysts at a crime lab have been examining a falsified document that clearly exhibits the Type A micro pattern.

From the information given above, it can be validly concluded that this document

a. was printed on an Acme Model 200 printer, with a probability of 70%.

b. was printed on an Acme Model 200 printer, with a probability of 30%.

c. was not printed on an Acme Model 200 printer, with a probability of 70%.

d. was not printed on an Acme Model 200 printer, with a probability of 30%.

e. may have been printed on an Acme Model 200 printer, but the probability cannot be estimated.

5. Quite often, a Border Patrol Agent is required to give assistance to an injured person. Upon responding to a call to assist an injured person, an agent should be guided by the following procedure:

- Administer first aid.
- Call for medical assistance.
- Call the ambulance again if it fails to arrive within 20 minutes.
- Accompany the injured person to the hospital if he or she is unidentified or unconscious.
- Witness a search of unidentified or unconscious person.
- Attempt to identify unconscious person by searching belongings.

While on patrol, Agent Maguire observes a man lying ten yards from the international boundary in Imperial Beach, CA. Upon questioning, the man reveals he fell while scaling the border fence. He claims he is in a great deal of pain and is unable to move. Agent Maguire requests an ambulance and provides immediate first aid. He then asks the man his name. However, the man refuses to answer. The ambulance arrives in 15 minutes when a Supervisory Border Patrol Agent guides it to the remote area. Agent Maguire resumes his normal patrol duties immediately east of the area.

From the information given, it can be validly concluded that Agent Maguire failed to fulfill his obligations in this incident because he

a. did not make a second call for the ambulance when the man was in great pain.

b. failed to accompany the man to the hospital.

c. did not attempt to locate a doctor while waiting for the ambulance.

d. failed to relieve the injured man's pain through proper first aid.

e. failed to notify a Supervisory Border Patrol Agent.

6. Visa regulations allow employers in certain industries to hire foreign nationals for seasonal positions. These employers must first try to hire U.S. workers for these positions. Eligible industries include landscaping, seasonal hospitality and seasonal construction, and certain jobs in manufacturing, food packaging and processing, fisheries, and retail. Agriculture is not an eligible industry. Workers must return to their home countries at the end of the season. The program benefits both employers who need workers and foreigners who need the income.

From the information given above, it can be validly concluded that

a. foreign workers in all industries are eligible for seasonal position visas.

b. no U.S. workers are eligible for any seasonal positions.

c. a foreign worker wanting to work on a farm would not be eligible for a seasonal visa.

d. only seasonal position visas are available to foreign workers in agriculture.

e. all manufacturing jobs are available to foreigners with seasonal visas.

7. One way that a foreign national is eligible to become a lawful permanent resident of the United States is by being sponsored by a relative. The relative must be able to prove that he or she is a citizen of the United States and must demonstrate that he or she can support the foreign national at 125% above the mandated poverty line. In addition, if the relative is a U.S. citizen, then he or she may sponsor a husband or wife, unmarried children under 21, married son or daughter of any age, brother or sister (if the sponsor is at least 21), or parent (if the sponsor is at least 21).

From the information given above, it can be validly concluded that

a. if a sponsoring relative is a U.S. citizen, he or she may sponsor a husband or wife regardless of age.

b. there is no financial requirement for a U.S. citizen to sponsor a son or daughter under 21.

c. the only way that a foreign national is eligible to become a lawful permanent resident of the United States is by being sponsored by a relative.

d. the best way that a foreign national is eligible to become a lawful permanent resident of the United States is by being sponsored by a relative.

e. a U.S. citizen may sponsor a brother or sister only if the foreign national meets the age requirements.

8. The Immigration and Nationality Act (INA) provides for naturalization, the process by which a foreign citizen or national can become a U.S. citizen. Some of the requirements are continuous residence and physical presence in the United States; an ability to read, write, and speak English; a knowledge and understanding of U.S. history and government; and favorable disposition toward the United States.

From the information given above, it can be validly concluded that

a. a foreign national who speaks only French might be eligible for naturalization.

b. a foreign national with very limited understanding of U.S. history might be eligible for naturalization.

c. without a favorable disposition toward the United States, a foreign national cannot be naturalized.

d. a foreign national who cannot read English can be naturalized under certain circumstances.

e. a foreign national arriving in the United States today can become naturalized next week under certain circumstances.

9. Grounds for deportation of aliens fall into two broad categories. The first covers prohibited acts committed at or prior to entry into the United States (which includes having entered the country illegally—for example, by falsifying documents or evading inspection at the border). The second covers prohibited acts committed since entry into the United States (for example, committing a criminal offense or engaging in activity whose purpose is the overthrow of the U.S. government by force). In regard to the former category, the Immigration and Nationality Act permits the Department of Homeland Security (DHS) to look back and deport aliens who should not have been admitted in the first place, had their prohibited acts been known.

From the information given above, it can be validly concluded that

a. only aliens who have committed a deportable offense prior to entering the United States may be deported.

b. some aliens who have not committed a deportable offense prior to entering the United States may be deported.

c. aliens may be deported only if they commit prohibited acts both before and after entering the United States.

d. only aliens who have falsified documents or evaded inspection of the border may be deported.

e. only aliens who have committed criminal acts or advocated the overthrow of the U.S. government by force may be deported.

10. The U.S. Supreme Court has consistently held that the decision to admit an alien to the United States or to exclude an alien from the United States lies entirely with Congress and that Congress can set whatever terms it chooses. Congress has the authority to discriminate on the basis of nationality, race, political belief, moral character, or mental or physical disability. In addition, Congress can grant special preference to relatives of U.S. residents, and to persons possessing work skills that would tend to boost the U.S. economy. However, once admitted to the United States, aliens can claim most of the protections guaranteed by the Constitution—for example, freedom of speech and religion, freedom from unreasonable search and seizure—but not the right to hold federal elective office. Persons who are undergoing proceedings to expel them from the United States are likewise granted the safeguards of due process under the Fifth Amendment and cannot be compelled to incriminate themselves.

From the information given above, it CANNOT be validly concluded that

a. a person seeking to enter the United States has virtually no legal rights.

b. a person, once admitted to the United States, cannot hold any elected office.

c. some noncitizens are guaranteed certain constitutional rights, even if they engage in criminal activities.

d. persons pending deportation have a right to due process without regard to the opinion Congress may hold of that person.

e. a person seeking to enter the United States can be excluded on the basis of nationality or race.

Border Patrol Practice Exam 2

11. In recent years, as few as 5,200 Border Patrol Agents have apprehended a million or more illegal aliens per year. Agents routinely work alone, often arresting 20 or more aliens at one time without assistance. They often work in riot conditions, and encounter terrorists and violent gang members. The job often requires physical exertion under difficult environmental conditions.

From the information given above, it can be validly concluded that

a. working closely and well with a partner is a key element of being a Border Patrol Agent.

b. being able to think fast while working alone is important to being a successful Border Patrol Agent.

c. being a Border Patrol Agent involves apprehending illegal aliens exclusively.

d. border patrol activities are generally suspended during bad weather.

e. being in good physical condition is of little importance for Border Patrol Agents.

12. The Border Patrol sets out to protect U.S. borders by simultaneously focusing on five key strategies: apprehending terrorists and terrorist weapons illegally entering the United States; deterring illegal entries through improved enforcement; detecting, apprehending, and deterring smugglers of humans, drugs, and other contraband; using "smart border" technology; and reducing crime in border communities, thereby improving quality of life. Agents are trained to understand each of these areas, and need to be ready on short notice to implement any or all of these strategies.

From the information given above, it can be validly concluded that Border Patrol Agents

a. never prevent illegal aliens from entering the country, but focus on apprehending them after they arrive.

b. always give priority to apprehending terrorists, not smugglers.

c. always give priority to apprehending smugglers, not terrorists.

d. must focus on several strategies simultaneously to secure U.S. borders.

e. always reduce crime in border communities as a first step toward securing our borders.

13. In August 2008, U.S. and Mexican officials spoke of increased cooperation between their countries to try to reduce drug smuggling across the border.

"We are destroying the crime organizations' structure, and that has spurred more violence . . . as the drug organizations spread out to kidnapping and extortion to make money," said Manuel Suárez-Mier, legal attaché for the Mexican attorney general. "What we need is the full commitment of the United States, particularly in helping integrate technology we don't have access to. . . .

"We are seeing the benefits of greater cooperation between the United States and Mexico, but the price has been high for us," he said. "More than 2,500 people have been killed in the drug wars, and people want immediate results."

Michael Sullivan, director of the U.S. Bureau of Alcohol, Tobacco, Firearms and Explosives, said, "We have asked Mexico to assist in stopping the flow of drugs across our borders, and they have done so extraordinarily well—and at great cost to civilians and law enforcement officers targeted for execution and assassinations by the drug cartels. What Mexico asks us to do is something similar, to halt the flow of guns into Mexico."

From the information given above, it can validly be concluded that

a. U.S. and Mexican governments are frustrated by the lack of cooperation between the two countries.

b. progress is slow, and drug dealers are more successful than ever in bringing drugs across the border.

c. Mexico's efforts to limit drug traffic have been stalled.

d. Mexico has paid a price for trying to reduce drug traffic, but continued cooperation between the countries is expected to yield results over time.

e. Mexico is completely responsible for increased drug traffic and lack of technology that could improve the situation.

14. A-1 and A-2 visas to the United States are valid for as long as the Secretary of State extends recognition to the holder. A-3 visas are valid for not more than three years but may be extended in increments of not more than two years. In 2008, A-1 visas are given to Adara Janus, her husband, and their two children, because Adara is an ambassador from her country. At the same time, an A-3 visa is given to Oden Wolf, Adara's personal assistant. Also in 2008, an A-2 visa is given to Hedrick Yuli, an employee of his country's government, and an A-3 visa is given to Ron Tripp, Hedrick's personal secretary.

From the information given above, it can be validly concluded that, if Hedrick asks Ron Tripp to remain in the United States for nine years, until the year 2017, Ron

a. could not do this because his visa is valid for only three years.

b. could not do this because his visa is valid for only five years (three years plus an extension of two years).

c. could do this as long as the Secretary of State extended recognition to him.

d. could do this if he were granted three more two-year extensions.

e. could do this because of a request by his employer.

15. Although undercover work by the police or by government officials is allowed, it has limitations. For example, if an officer or agent of the government induces a person to commit a crime that the person has not contemplated committing, for the purpose of instituting criminal prosecution against that person, this is called entrapment and is illegal. Entrapment can occur in two ways: (1) by knowingly representing the crime in a false light, so that it will not be seen by the person as illegal; and (2) by employing persuasive tactics that will induce the person to commit the illegal act when that person originally had no intention of committing it.

From the information given above, it can be validly concluded that, if an undercover officer named Ron arrests a suspect named Sheryl for an act they have discussed beforehand,

- **a.** Ron is not guilty of entrapment unless Sheryl was not intending to commit the crime until Ron suggested it.
- **b.** Ron is guilty of entrapment if he suggested that the crime was not illegal, and Sheryl was already intending to commit it.
- **c.** Sheryl is not the victim of entrapment if she was not intending to commit the crime until Ron suggested it.
- **d.** Sheryl is not the victim of entrapment if she committed the crime suggested by Ron because he said it was not illegal.
- **e.** Ron is not guilty of entrapment if he suggested committing a crime and Sheryl did it without contemplating it beforehand.

16. A U.S. citizen can lose his or her citizenship in one of two ways, by denaturalization (which applies to naturalized citizens only) or by expatriation (which can apply to both naturalized citizens and citizens by birth). Denaturalization takes place when a court revokes the naturalization order because it is found to have been illegally or fraudulently obtained. Expatriation takes place when any citizen voluntarily abandons his or her country and becomes a citizen or subject of another. The Supreme Court has said, however, that the expatriate must have voluntarily performed an expatriating act in order for loss of citizenship to occur (examples are becoming a citizen of another country, serving in the military of a hostile country, or formally renunouncing nationality before a diplomatic officer of the United States).

From the information given above, it can be validly concluded that

- **a.** no denaturalization takes place if the naturalization order is found not to have been obtained legally.
- **b.** expatriation takes place only if the act of expatriating is not involuntary.
- **c.** no expatriation takes place if the act of expatriating is voluntary.
- **d.** no denaturalization takes place unless the naturalization order is found to have been obtained legally.
- **e.** expatriation takes place unless the act of expatriating is not involuntary.

► Spanish Language

If you are taking the Artificial Language Test, turn to page 165.

Part I
Read the sentence and then choose the most appropriate synonym for the italicized word.

1. Los hombres *laboraban* la tierra durante el verano.
   a. escuchaban
   b. lloraban
   c. cansaban
   d. se lavaban
   e. cultivaban

2. El sospechoso no *entregó* la arma al agente.
   a. entregaron
   b. comprobar
   c. dio
   d. llevó
   e. desentender

3. *Comienzo* a trabajar a las cinco de la mañana todos los días.
   a. Conozco
   b. Empiezo
   c. Como
   d. Enojo
   e. Traduzco

4. ¿Hay *alguna persona* aquí que entienda el español?
   a. algodón
   b. una nieta
   c. alguien
   d. un perico
   e. una pesadilla

5. Los nacionales extranjeros no *entraron* a través del puerto de la entrada.
   a. venido
   b. vinieron adentro
   c. ir
   d. cortesías
   e. llegar

6. *El señor* tiene un perro.
   a. La ventana
   b. El helado
   c. La señora
   d. El hombre
   e. La mesa

7. Yo *mercaré* algunas cosas hoy en la tienda.
   a. hablaré
   b. daré
   c. enojaré
   d. leeré
   e. compraré

8. Ud. no tiene *el derecho* de entrar ilegalmente.
   a. la capacidad
   b. el honor
   c. el privilegio
   d. la cierta
   e. la posible

9. El domingo voy a llevar mi *vestido nuevo*.
   a. perro nuevo
   b. piel nueva
   c. ropa nueva
   d. vestigo nuevo
   e. vía nueva

10. No *comprendo* la organización de nuestro gobierno.
a. deseo
b. devuelvo
c. muero
d. entiendo
e. envuelvo

11. ¿Es necesario tener pasaportes para *visitar* México?
a. viajar a
b. vigilar
c. zurcir
d. casar
e. ayudar

12. *¿Qué tal?*
a. ¿Por qué?
b. ¿Cómo estás?
c. ¿Qué lástima?
d. ¿Qué sorpresa?
e. ¿Qué baste?

13. Ellos desaparecen en *aquella ciudad*.
a. por allí
b. los de abajo
c. aquel cuervo
d. por allá
e. aquel pueblo

14. ¿Quiénes *preparaban* la comida ayer cuando Ud. llegó?
a. tiraban
b. se bañaban
c. habían
d. cocinaban
e. les gustaba

15. Todos los *agentes* observaron a los sospechosos cuando entraron por la puerta.
a. agentos
b. senores
c. policias
d. extranjeros
e. jefes

16. *El ferrocarril* es un medio principal de transporte.
a. El automóvil
b. La ferretería
c. El hipódromo
d. El funicular
e. El tren

17. *Caminamos* con los pies.
a. Andamos
b. Nadamos
c. Jugamos
d. Cantamos
e. Votamos

18. Yo tengo un *arma*.
a. instrumento
b. cuchillo
c. cuchara
d. brazo
e. dentaduras

19. Siempre se prohibe *hablar* inglés aquí.
a. tocar
b. ver
c. oír
d. pensar
e. usar

20. Ellos son gigantes, y si tienes miedo *quítate* de ahí, que yo voy a entrar con ellos en desigual batalla.

   a. vete

   b. descansa

   c. implora

   d. lastímate

   e. límpiate

Part II, Section I

Read each sentence carefully. Select the appropriate word or phrase to fill each blank space.

21. Mi coche tiene _____ motor grande y _____ rápido.

   a. una, era

   b. una, fue

   c. un, es

   d. un, carro

   e. un, my

22. Muchas veces, cuando hace mucho _____, hace mucho _____ también.

   a. tiempo, valor

   b. sol, calor

   c. nieve, frijol

   d. sol, comer

   e. viento, calma

23. _____ prefiero que _____ vengas por la tarde.

   a. Yo, tú

   b. Uds., tú

   c. Tú, Ud.

   d. Yo, nosotros

   e. Tú, Uds.

24. El agente _____ procesado al contrabandista, _____ no pudo y el detenido se escapó.

   a. hubiera, era

   b. ha, eso

   c. he, para

   d. habría, pero

   e. habremos, por

25. Las _____ no le dijeron la _____ al agente.

   a. pájaros, comida

   b. pasajero, corrección

   c. farmacia, factura

   d. familias, verdad

   e. árboles, piensamiento

26. ¿Hay _____ pulgas aquí en _____?

   a. muchas, la playa

   b. muy, la ropa

   c. los mejores, este hotel

   d. pulcras, el casa

   e. delicioso, la ventana

27. Siempre lávese _____ las manos antes de _____.

   a. tú, comiendo

   b. Ud., comer

   c. Ud., comiendo

   d. tus, comiendo

   e. Uds., comer

28. Ramón acaba de _____ para tu _____.

   a. hablar, jamón

   b. quieran, dulces

   c. salir, casa

   d. sale, casar

   e. saliré, casa

29. _____ agua no está _____.
   a. La, correcto
   b. La, terminado
   c. El, feliz
   d. La, fresca
   e. El, fría

30. En 1808 España _____ invadida por los ejércitos de Napoleón y las colonias aprovecharon _____ momento para declarar su independencia.
   a. sería, este
   b. será, este
   c. fue, este
   d. fueron, esta
   e. fuma, sera

Part II, Section II

Read each sentence carefully. Select the one sentence that is correct.

31. a. Yo sé la día México de independencia.
   b. Un escritorio mexicano se dice Carlos Fuentes.
   c. La mejor universidad de México está en la capital.
   d. Tienen presidentes Felipe Calderón.

32. a. En Brasil es hablan la idioma portuguesa.
   b. Han grupos de étnico diferentes en Brasil.
   c. Rio de Janeiro es no el capital de Brasil.
   d. Brasil es el país más grande del América del Sur.

33. a. ¿Cuál es tu nombre?
   b. Es mi llama Antonio.
   c. ¿Cómo es que me lo llamo?
   d. Soy bien vestido Antonio.

34. a. Es precise que tu pone el abrigo.
   b. No puedo decidir cuál candidato es el mejor.
   c. No temenos su libre.
   d. ¿Me pueda repetir la tercera oración?

35. a. Oy dilla ya no sabemos escuchar.
   b. Alejandro es el nombre del ombre que mirava nuestro partido.
   c. Ahora mismo tengo prisa y no puedo quedarme.
   d. Será difícil bolver antes de las onze horas.

36. a. Tráigame el bolígrafo para que puedi escribir una carta.
   b. No haz problemas que no puedas resolver.
   c. No me mires durante la presentación.
   d. Escribis el ensayo y no me diga nada.

37. a. ¿A qué hora debo traer las flores al hospital?
   b. Son los tres y medio.
   c. Mañana he dicho todo lo que tengo que decir.
   d. En este momento fui a la tienda para comprar leche y huevos.

38. a. Quiero que yo como mucha comida esta noche.
   b. La cocina esté llena de platos que nunca se usan.
   c. ¡Mi plato favorito tenga que saber como preparar!
   d. Les pregunté a los camareros que nos dieran una mesa bien ubicada.

39. **a.** Yo estudiaste física e historia en la universidad.

   b. Mi amigo no entiende por qué se estudian literatura e historia en vez de filosofía.

   c. Mis clases están a las dos y las cuatro.

   d. No he visto ninguno profesor en esto edificio.

40. **a.** Ud. ha sido muy gracioso durante toda mi visita.

   b. No sé Uds. saber tanto esta ciudad.

   c. Tu y tu eres mis amigos más fieles.

   d. Creo que ello va a prestar suyo mochila para que yo mueva mis libros.

Part II, Section III

Read each sentence carefully. Select the correct word or phrase to replace the italicized portion of the sentence. In those cases in which the sentence needs no correction, select choice **e**.

41. El jefe no quiere dejar que el detenido *devuelva* a Guatemala.

   a. enterar

   b. cruza

   c. vuelva

   d. devuelve

   e. No es necesario hacer ninguna corrección.

42. Te requieren *tener* todos los documentos necesarios.

   a. tienes

   b. tengo

   c. tenéis

   d. tienen

   e. No es necesario hacer ninguna corrección.

43. *Hemos abarcado* un sinnúmero de posibilidades y *abreviado* el tiempo que se necesita para completar los trámites.

   a. abarcando, abreviando

   b. abarcados, abreviados

   c. abarcó, abrevio

   d. abarcan, abrevian

   e. No es necesario hacer ninguna corrección.

44. Los que *abastecen* las cocinas de las unidades de rescate anoche trajeron magníficas provisiones.

   a. habían abastecido

   b. abasteciendo

   c. abastecieran

   d. abastezco

   e. No es necesario hacer ninguna corrección.

45. Mi esposa y yo *viajaría* a España el verano pasado.

   a. viajaron

   b. viajamos

   c. viajaremos

   d. ven

   e. No es necesario hacer ninguna corrección.

46. Es bastante difícil que algunos inmigrantes de países centroamericanos *se acostumbren* a la clima norteña.

   a. aclimatizan

   b. se adjusta

   c. adjustamos

   d. se usen

   e. No es necesario hacer ninguna corrección.

47. La cocaína es *un* droga peligrosa.

   a. unos

   b. una

   c. el

   d. aquel

   e. No es necesario hacer ninguna corrección.

48. *Usted* no fumas tanto como antes.

   a. Ti

   b. Ustedes

   c. Nosotros

   d. Tú

   e. No es necesario hacer ninguna corrección.

49. Durante el verano es *imprescindible* que todo el mundo asista a la escuela.

   a. sinfín

   b. precise

   c. innecesario

   d. pesadumbre

   e. No es necesario hacer ninguna corrección.

50. Hoy día pienso en *abriendo* una tienda en el centro de la ciudad.

   a. abro

   b. abrir

   c. abierto

   d. abertura

   e. No es necesario hacer ninguna corrección.

▶ Artificial Language Supplemental Booklet

To answer the Artificial Language questions, refer to the sections in this Supplemental Booklet: Vocabulary Lists and Grammatical Rules. (See Chapters 7 and 8 of this book for additional information.)

Some of the words given in the following Vocabulary Lists are not the same as those that will be given in the actual Border Patrol Exam. Therefore, it is best not to memorize them before taking the actual test. The Grammatical Rules are the same as those used in the actual test, except that some of the prefixes (word beginnings) and suffixes (word endings) used in the real test differ from those used in this Supplemental Booklet. You may also need to refer to the glossary of grammatical terms in Chapter 7 as you take the practice exams.

▶ Vocabulary Lists for the Artificial Language

Arranged Alphabetically by the English Word

ENGLISH	ARTIFICIAL LANGUAGE	ENGLISH	ARTIFICIAL LANGUAGE
a, an	bex	skillful	autile
alien	huslek	that	velle
and	cre	the	ric
boy	ekaplek	this	volle
country	failek	to be	synbar
difficult	brale	to border	regbar
enemy	avelek	to cross	chonbar
friend	kometlek	to drive	arbar
from	mor	to escape	pirbar
government	almanlek	to guard	bonbar
he, him	yev	to have	tulbar
jeep	cublek	to identify	kalenbar
legal	colle	to injure	liabar
loyal	inle	to inspect	zelbar
man	kaplek	to shoot	degbar
of	quea	to spy	tatbar
paper	trenedlek	to station	lexbar
river	browlek	to work	frigbar

Arranged Alphabetically by the Artificial Language Word

ARTIFICIAL LANGUAGE	ENGLISH	ARTIFICIAL LANGUAGE	ENGLISH
almanlek	government	kalenbar	to identify
arbar	to drive	kaplek	man
autile	skillful	kometlek	friend
avelek	enemy	lexbar	to station
bex	a, an	liabar	to injure
bonbar	to guard	mor	from
brale	difficult	pirbar	to escape
browlek	river	quea	of
chonbar	to cross	regbar	to border
colle	legal	ric	the
cre	and	synbar	to be
cublek	jeep	tatbar	to spy
degbar	to shoot	trenedlek	paper
ekaplek	boy	tulbar	to have
failek	country	velle	that
frigbar	to work	volle	this
huslek	alien	yev	he, him
inle	loyal	zelbar	to inspect

► Grammatical Rules for the Artificial Language

The grammatical rules given here are the same as those used in the Border Patrol Exam, except that the prefixes (word beginnings) and suffixes (word endings) used in the exam differ from those used here.

During the exam, you will have access to the rules at all times. Consequently, it is important that you understand these rules, but it is not necessary that you memorize them. In fact, memorizing them will hinder rather than help you, because the beginnings and endings of words are different in the version of the Artificial Language that appears in this manual than the one that appears in the actual test.

You should note that Part Three of the official Artificial Language Manual contains a glossary of grammatical terms to assist you if you are not thoroughly familiar with the meanings of these grammatical terms. You can review these now by referring back to Chapter 7.

Rule 1

To form the feminine singular of a noun, a pronoun, an adjective, or an article, add the suffix *-zof* to the masculine singular form. Only nouns, pronouns, adjectives, and articles take feminine endings in the Artificial Language. When gender is not specified, the masculine form is used.

Examples

If a male eagle is a *verlek*, then a female eagle is a *verlekzof*.

If an ambitious man is a *tosle* man, an ambitious woman is a *toslezof* woman.

Rule 2

To form the plural of nouns, pronouns, and adjectives, add the suffix *-ax* to the correct singular form.

Examples

If one male eagle is a *verlek*, the several male eagles are *verlekax*.

If an ambitious woman is a *toslezof* woman, several ambitious women are *toslezofax* women.

Rule 3

Adjectives modifying nouns and pronouns with feminine and/or plural endings must have endings that agree with the words they modify. In addition, an article (*a*, *an*, and *the*) preceding a noun must also agree with the noun in gender and number.

Examples

If an active male eagle is a *sojle verlek*, then an active female eagle is a *sojlezof verlekzof* and several active female eagles are *sojlezofax verlekzofax*.

If this male eagle is *volle verlek*, these female eagles are *vollezofax verlekzofax*.

If the male eagle is *ric verlek*, the female eagle is *riczof verlekzof* and the female eagles are *riczofax verlekzofax*.

If a male eagle is *bex verlek*, several male eagles are *bexax verlekax*.

Rule 4

The stem of the verb is obtained by omitting the suffix *-bar* from the infinitive form of the verb.

Example

The stem of the verb *tirbar* is *tir*.

Rule 5

All subjects and their verbs must agree in number; that is, singular subjects require singular verbs and plural subjects require plural verbs. (See Rules 6 and 7.)

Rule 6

To form the present tense of a verb, add the suffix *-ot* to the stem for the singular form or the suffix *-et* to the stem for the plural.

Example

If to bark is *nalbar*, then *nalot* is the present tense for the singular (the dog barks) and *nalet* is the present tense for the plural (the dogs bark).

Rule 7

To form the past tense of a verb, first add the suffix *-rem* to the stem, and then add the suffix *-ot* if the verb is singular or the suffix *-et* if it is plural.

Example

If to bark is *nalbar*, then *nalremot* is the past tense for the singular (the dog barked), and *nalremet* is the past tense for the plural (the dogs barked).

Rule 8

To form the past participle of a verb, add to the stem of the verb the suffix *-to*. It can be used to form compound tenses with the verb *to have*, as a predicate with the verb *to be*, or as an adjective. In the last two cases, it takes masculine, feminine, singular, and plural forms in agreement with the noun to which it refers.

Example of use in a compound tense with the verb *to have*

If to bark is *nalbar* and to have is *tulbar*, then *tulot nalto* is the present perfect for the singular (the dog has barked) and *tulet nalto* is the present perfect for the plural (the dogs have barked). Similarly, *tulremot nalto* is the past perfect for the singular (the dog had barked) and *tulremet nalto* is the past perfect for the plural (the dogs had barked).

Example of use as a predicate with the verb *to be*

If to adopt is *rapbar* and to be is *synbar*, then a boy was adopted is a *ekaplek synremot rapto* and many girls were adopted is *ekaplekzofax synremet raptozofax*.

Example of use as an adjective

If to delight is *kasbar*, then a delighted boy is a *kasto ekaplek* and many delighted girls are *kastozofax ekaplekzofax*.

Rule 9

To form a noun from a verb, add the suffix *-lek* to the stem of the verb.

Example

If *longbar* is to write, then a writer is a *longlek*.

Rule 10

To form an adjective from a noun, substitute the suffix *-le* for the suffix *-lek*.

Example

If *pellek* is beauty, then a beautiful male eagle is a *pelle verlek*, and a beautiful female eagle is a *pellezof verlekzof*. (Note the feminine ending *-zof*.)

Rule 11

To form an adverb from an adjective, add the suffix *-de* to the masculine form of the adjective. (Note that adverbs do not change their form to agree in number or gender with the word they modify.)

Example

If *pelle* is beautiful, then beautifully is *pellede*.

Rule 12

To form the possessive of a noun or pronoun, add the suffix *-oe* to the noun or pronoun after any plural or feminine suffixes.

Examples

If a *boglek* is a dog, then a dog's collar is a *boglekoe* collar.

If he is *yev*, then his book is *yevoe* book.

If she is *yevzof*, then her book is *yevzofoe* book.

Rule 13

To make a word negative, add the prefix *poh-* to the correct affirmative form.

Examples

If an active male eagle is a *sojle verlek*, then an inactive male eagle is a *pohsojle verlek*.

If the dog barks is *boglek nalot*, then the dog does not bark is *boglek pohnalot*.

► Artificial Language

Use the Artificial Language Supplemental Booklet on pages 165–169 to help you answer these questions. You may refer to the vocabulary and grammatical rules throughout this test section.

For each sentence, decide which words have been translated correctly. Use scratch paper to list each numbered word that is correctly translated into the Artificial Language. When you have finished listing the words that are correctly translated in sentences 1 through 20, select your answer according to the following instructions:

Mark:
- **a.** if *only* the word numbered 1 is correctly translated.
- **b.** if *only* the word numbered 2 is correctly translated.
- **c.** if *only* the word numbered 3 is correctly translated.
- **d.** if *two or more* of the numbered words are correctly translated.
- **e.** if *none* of the numbered words is correctly translated.

Be sure to list only the *numbered* words that are *correctly* translated.
Study the sample question before going on to the test questions.

Sample Sentence

This woman crossed the river.

Sample Translation

Bex kaplekzof chonremet ric browlek.
  1   2   3

The word numbered 1, *bex*, is incorrect because the translation of *bex* is *a*. The word *vollezof* should have been used. The word numbered 2 is correct. *Kaplekzof* has been correctly formed by adding the feminine ending to the masculine noun, applying Rule 1. The word numbered 3, *chonremet*, is incorrect because the singular form, *chonremot*, should have been used. Because the word numbered 2 is correct, the answer to the sample question is **b**.

Now go on with questions 1 through 20 and answer them in the manner indicated. Be sure to record your answers on the separate answer sheet found at the beginning of the test.

Sentence

1. The guard inspects identification papers.

2. Those drivers are not illegal aliens.

3. She is a loyal friend of the government.

Translation

1. Ric bonlek zelremot kalenleax trenedlekax.
              1   2   3

2. Velle arlekax pohsynet pohcolleax huslek.
          1   2   3

3. Yevzof synet bex inlezof kometlekzof quea ric almanlek.
          1   2   3

Sentence	Translation

4. The skillful inspector identifies those papers.

4. Ric autileax zellekax kalenot vellezof trenedlekax.
          1   2   3

5. This friendly girl is an enemy spy.

5. Volle kometlezof ekaplekzof synremot bexzof avelezof
   1   2
tatlekzof.
  3

6. The driver of the jeep was from this country.

6. Bex arlek quea ric cublek synremet mor volle failek.
   1   2   3

7. Those boys crossed the river.

7. Velleax ekaplekax regremet ricax browlek.
         1   2   3

8. The man shot him from the jeep.

8. Ric ekaplek degremot yev mor ric cublek.
       1   2   3

9. These women worked illegally.

9. Vollezof kaplekzof frigremet pohcolle.
    1   2   3

10. She is disloyal to spy.

10. Kaplekzof synot pohinlezof tatlekzof.
    1   2   3

11. The enemies shot the driver.

11. Ricax avelekax degremet ric arle.
       1   2   3

12. She is from the border station.

12. Yevzof synot mor ric reglek lexot.
       1   2 3

13. He has to guard the river.

13. Yev tulremot bonot ric browlekoe.
      1   2   3

14. The government inspected his papers.

14. Ric almanlek zelbremot yevaxoe trenedlek.
          1   2   3

15. These aliens escaped from his station.

15. Velleax huslekax piret mor yevoe lexlek.
   1   2   3

16. This man and boy have illegal papers.

16. Volle kaplek cre ekaplek tulet pohcolleax trenedlekax.
         1   2   3

17. The men are friends of the disloyal guard.

17. Ricax kaplekax synet kometlekax quea ric inle bonlek.
         1   2   3

18. These women work illegally.

18. Volleax kaplekzofax friget pohcolledezof.
   1   2   3

19. The illegal aliens were not injured.

19. Ricax pohcolle huslekax synet fer liatoax.
               1   2   3

20. Those women are not aliens from that country.

20. Vellezofax kaplekzofax pohsynot huslekax mor velle
                        1   2

failek.
3

For each question in this group, select the one of the five suggested choices that correctly translates the italicized word or group of words into the Artificial Language.

    Sample Question
    There is *the boy*.
    a. bex kaplek
    b. ric kaplek
    c. ric ekaplek
    d. velle ekaplek
    e. bex ekaplek

Choice **c** is the correct translation of the italicized words, *the boy*.

The *men and women* who patrol and *guard the border* have a complex and difficult
         21   **22**

job. They have to deal with both friendly and *unfriendly aliens*, as well as with well-
                                23

trained and *skillful spies*, who are often dangerous. *They have to inspect* and identify
          24   **25**

complex *governmental papers* that are written in various foreign languages, and
         26

they have to make difficult decisions, frequently alone and away from their *stations*.
                                         27

This country's borders are *skillfully guarded* and kept secure by *these loyal women*
    28   **29**   **30**

and these loyal men.

21. **a.** kaplekax cre kaplekpohax
 b. kaplekax cre kaplekzofax
 c. kaplekoe cre kaplekzofoe
 d. kaplekoe cre kaplekpohoe
 e. kaplekax bex kaplekpohax

22. **a.** bonetax ric reglek
 b. bonetax ric reglekax
 c. bonot ric reglek
 d. bonbar ric reglek
 e. bonet ric reglek

23. **a.** pohkometlekdeax huslekax
 b. pohkometlekde huslekde
 c. pohkometleax huslekax
 d. pohkometlekax huslekax
 e. pohkometlekdeax huslekdeax

24. **a.** autile tatlekax
 b. autile tatlek
 c. autileax tatlekax
 d. autileax tatbarax
 e. autile takbarax

25. **a.** yevax tulet zelbaret
 b. yevax tulot zelbar
 c. yevax tulremet zelbar
 d. yevax tulremet zelbaret
 e. yevax tulet zelbar

26. **a.** almanleax trenedlekax
 b. almanlek trenedlek
 c. almanlek trenedlekax
 d. almanlekax trenedlekax
 e. almanle trenedlekax

27. **a.** lexbarax
 b. lexlekoe
 c. lexbaroe
 d. lexlekax
 e. lexleax

28. **a.** volle failekoe
 b. volleoe failekoe
 c. volle failek
 d. volleoe failek
 e. volle faileoe

29. **a.** autiledeax bonremet
 b. autilede bontoax
 c. autilede bonto
 d. autiledeax bonremot
 e. autilede bonlekde

30. **a.** volleax inlezof kaplekzofax
 b. vollezofax inlezofax kaplekzofax
 c. volleax inle kaplekzofax
 d. vollezofax inlezof kaplekzofax
 e. vollezofax inle kaplekzofax

For this group of questions, select the one response option that is the correct translation of the English word or words in parentheses. You should translate the entire sentence in order to determine what form should be used.

Sample Question

Ricax almanlekoe tatlekax (crossed the border).
 a. chonremet bex reglek
 b. chonremot ric reglek
 c. chonremet ric reglek
 d. chonremet ric regbar
 e. chonremot bex reglek

Ricax almanlekoe tatlekax chonremet ric reglek means *The goverment's spies crossed the border.*

Because *chonremet ric reglek* is the only one of these expressions that means *they* (plural) *crossed the border*, choice **c** is the correct answer to the sample question.

31. (This boy did not have) bralekax.
- **a.** Volle ekaplek pohtulremot
- **b.** Velle ekaplek pohtulremot
- **c.** Volle kaplek pohtulremot
- **d.** Volle ekaplek tulremot
- **e.** Velle kaplek pohtulremot

32. Yevzof synot bexzof tatlekzof quea (that unfriendly government).
- **a.** vollezof pohkometlek almanlekzof
- **b.** velle pohkometle almanlek
- **c.** volle pohkometlek almanlek
- **d.** vellezof pohkometlezof almanlekzof
- **e.** velle pohkometlek almanlek

33. Yev degremot (an escaped girl).
- **a.** bexzof pirtozof ekaplekzof
- **b.** bexzof piremot ekaplekzof
- **c.** bex pirto ekaplekzof
- **d.** bexzofax pirtozofax ekaplekzofax
- **e.** bex piremot ekaplekzof

34. Kaplekax pirremet (from a border station).
- **a.** quea bex regle lexlek
- **b.** mor bex reglek lexlek
- **c.** mor ric regle lexlek
- **d.** mor bex reglekoe lexlek
- **e.** mor bex regle lexlek

35. (The enemy spy) tulremot liabar ric inle bonlek.
- **a.** Bex avelek tatbar
- **b.** Ric avele tatlek
- **c.** Ric avele tatbar
- **d.** Bex avelek tatlek
- **e.** Ric avelek tatot

36. (The river crossing) synremot brale.
- **a.** Bex browlek chonlek
- **b.** Ric browlek chonlek
- **c.** Bex browle chonlek
- **d.** Ric browlekoe chonlek
- **e.** Ric browle chonlek

37. (That driver escaped) mor ric cublek.
- **a.** Volle arlek piremot
- **b.** Velle arbar pirremot
- **c.** Velle arlek pirremot
- **d.** Vellezof arlekzof pirremot
- **e.** Velle arlek pirremet

38. Volleax pohcolleax (aliens do not have papers).
- **a.** huslekzofax pohtulet trenedlekax
- **b.** huslekax pohtulremet trenedlekax
- **c.** huslekax pohtulet trenedlekax
- **d.** huslekax pohtulot trenedlekax
- **e.** huslek pohtulet trenedlekax

39. (The station guards) tulet degbar aveleax tatlekax.
- **a.** Ricax lexleax bonlekax
- **b.** Ricax lexlekax bonlekax
- **c.** Ric lexleax bonlekax
- **d.** Ricax lexleax bonlek
- **e.** Bexax lexleax bonlekax

40. (Those skillful women were) bralezofax kalenbar.
  a. Vollezofax autilezofax kaplekzofax synremet
  b. Vellezofax autilezofax kaplekzofax synremet
  c. Vellezofax autilezofax kaplekzofax synremot
  d. Vellezof autilezof kaplekzof synremet
  e. Velle autilezofax kaplekzofax synremet

41. Vellezof (girl from the country) synot pohinlezof.
  a. kaplekzof mor ric failek
  b. ekaplekzof quea ric failek
  c. ekaplekzof mor riczof failekzof
  d. ekaplekzofax mor ric failek
  e. ekaplekzof mor ric failek

42. (His skillful guards) friget mor bex regle lexlek.
  a. Yevzofoe autilezofax bonlekzofax
  b. Yevoeax autileax bonlekax
  c. Yevoe autile bonlekax
  d. Yevoe autileax bonlekax
  e. Yevaxoe autileax bonlekax

For the last group of questions, select the one of the five suggested choices that is the correct form of the italicized expression as it is used in the sentence. At the end of the sentence, you will find instructions in parentheses telling you which form to use. In some sentences, you will be asked to supply the correct forms of two or more expressions. In this case, the instructions for these expressions are presented consecutively in the parentheses and are separated by a dash (for example, past tense—adverb). Be sure to translate the entire sentence before selecting your answer.

Sample Question
Yev *bonbar* ric browlek. (present tense)
  a. bonremot
  b. bonremet
  c. boneet
  d. bonet
  e. bonot

Choices **a** and **b** are incorrect because they are in the past tense. Choice **c** is misspelled. Choice **d** is in the present tense, but it too is incorrect because the subject of the sentence is singular and therefore takes a verb with a singular rather than a plural ending. Choice **e** is the answer to the sample question.

43. Riczofax bonlekzofax synret *inle*; *yev* synret tatlekzofax. (negative plural feminine adjective—plural feminine pronoun)
  a. inlezofax—yevzofax
  b. pohinleax—yevax
  c. pohinlezofax—yevax
  d. pohinlezofax—yevzofax
  e. inleax—yevax

44. Velle avele tatlek *tulbar* chonbar bex browlek. (past singular verb)
  a. tulet
  b. tulbaret
  c. tulremot
  d. tulremet
  e. tulot

45. Ricax *ekaplek* trenedlekax synret *colle*. (masculine plural possessive noun—negative plural adjective)
  a. kaplekaxoe—pohcolleax
  b. ekaplekaxoe—pohcolleax
  c. ekaplekax—pohcolle
  d. kaplekax—pohcolleax
  e. ekaplekaxoe—pohcolle

46. Ric *zelbar* frigot *inle*. (masculine singular noun—adverb)
  a. zelot—inlede
  b. zellek—inle
  c. zellek—inlede
  d. zellekax—inlede
  e. zelot—inle

47. *Velle* pohcollezofax huslekzofax synremet *liabar* (feminine plural article—feminine plural past participle)
   a. Vellezof, liatozof
   b. Velleaxzof, liatoaxzof
   c. Vellezofax, liatozofax
   d. Vellezofax, liazofaxto
   e. Velleax, liatoax

48. Riczofax huslekzofax *synbar* kometlekzofax quea ricax *huslek*. (negative plural present tense verb—masculine plural noun)
   a. pohsynet, huslekax
   b. synetpoh, huslekax
   c. pohsynet, huslekzofax
   d. pohsynot, huslekax
   e. pohsynremet, huslekax

49. Riczofax *regbar* bonlekzofax *arbar* ricax cublekax. (feminine plural adjective—negative plural past tense verb)
   a. reglezofax, poharemet
   b. reglezofax, poharremet
   c. reglekzofax, poharremet
   d. regleax, poharremet
   e. reglezofax, poharremot

50. Vollezofax *avelek* tatlekzofax synet autilezofax cre *inle*. (feminine plural adjective—negative feminine plural adjective)
   a. avelekzofax, pohinlezofax
   b. avelezofax, pohinlekzofax
   c. avelezof, pohinlezof
   d. avelede, pohinlezofax
   e. avelezofax, pohinlezofax

▶ Answers

Logical Reasoning

1. b. The essential information from which the answer can be derived is contained in the third and fifth sentences. The third sentence tells us, *Some substances found at a crime scene yield valuable clues under microscopic examination.* The fifth sentence explains that *all substances found at a crime scene are potential sources of evidence.* Therefore, choice **b** can be validly concluded. Choices **a, c, d,** and **e** are incorrect because they are not supported by the passage.

2. b. Choices **a, c, d,** and **e**, while they relate to issues discussed in the paragraph, draw conclusions that are not supported by the information given.

3. b. The paragraph makes it clear that communication skills are important for all Border Patrol Agents. The word *only* makes choice **a** incorrect. Choices **c** and **e** are refuted by the paragraph. Choice **d** is not supported by the paragraph.

4. e. We know from the third sentence that the Type A micro pattern exists in 70% of all Acme Model 200 printers and in some other models of printers. However, we know neither how many other models nor what percentage of other models produce the Type A micro pattern. Accordingly, the probability that the note was printed on the Acme Model 200 printer cannot be determined. Consequently, choices **a, b, c,** and **d** are incorrect.

5. b. A specific rule contained in the procedures requires Agent Maguire to accompany the man to the hospital because the man refused to identify himself and was therefore unidentified.

6. c. Choice **c** is correct because the paragraph states that agricultural jobs are excluded from the seasonal visa program. The statements made in answers **a, b, d,** and **e** are refuted by the paragraph.

7. a. Choice **a** is supported by the information in the paragraph. Choice **b** is refuted by the paragraph. Choice **c** is refuted by the phrase *One way* in the first sentence. Choice **d** is not supported; no judgment is made in the paragraph about which way is best. Choice **e** is refuted by the facts in the paragraph.

8. c. The conclusions drawn by choices **a, b, d,** and **e** are refuted by the qualifications for naturalization outlined in the paragraph. Only choice **c** is a valid conclusion.

9. b. The passage speaks of two categories of deportable aliens, those who can be deported for committing prohibited acts before coming to the United States and those who can be deported for committing them since; therefore, logically, the alien need not have committed deportable offenses before entering the United States in order to be deported (supporting choice **b** and ruling out choices **a** and **c**). Choices **d** and **e** are examples—the word *only* at the beginning of each choice rules them out.

10. b. The passage states that an alien does not have *the right to hold federal elective office*; it does not speak about other types of office (supporting choice **b**). The other choices are affirmed in the passage and are therefore the wrong answers to this question.

11. b. Choice **b** is correct because the ability to work alone is stated in the paragraph, and the ability to think fast is implied by the complications of the job listed throughout the paragraph. The conclusions drawn by answers **a, c, d,** and **e** are refuted by the paragraph.

12. d. This conclusion is correct because the paragraph implies the importance of implementing several strategies at once. Each of the other choices incorrectly focuses on using one strategy at a time.

13. d. The conclusion drawn by choice **d** is supported by the content and tone of the quotes in the passage. Each of the conclusions offered in the other answers is refuted by the passage.

14. d. The passage says that A-3 visas *may be extended in increments* [regular additions] *of not more than two years.* Since the plural word (*increments*) is used, it is reasonable to assume more than one increment can be added (supporting choice **d** and ruling out choices **a** and **b**). Choice **c** applies to A-1 and A-2 visa holders. Choice **e** is not mentioned in the passage.

15. a. Choice **a** is a convoluted way of saying, in the negative, that Ron is guilty of entrapment if Sheryl were not intending to commit the crime until he suggested it. Choice **b** is incorrect because it says that Sheryl was already contemplating committing the crime. Choices **c**, **d**, and **e** contradict the passage by saying that (1) there was no entrapment, and (2) Sheryl would not have committed the crime unless Ron suggested it or led her to think it was legal.

16. b. If choice **b** is reworded to clear out unnecessary negatives, it will read *expatriation takes place only if the act of expatriating is voluntary;* therefore, choice **b** is correct. Choice **a** says denaturalization does not take place if the naturalization order was obtained illegally, which is incorrect. Choice **c** is fairly clear and is incorrect, since expatriation must be a voluntary act. Choices **d** and **e** are incorrect—little words like *unless* are very important.

Spanish Language

1. e. *Cultivaban* (cultivated) most nearly matches *laboraban* (worked).

2. c. The choice that most nearly matches *entregó* (surrender) in the proper person is *dio* (give).

3. b. The best choice to match *comienzo* (I start) is *empiezo* (I begin).

4. c. *Alguien* (someone) means nearly the same thing as *alguna persona* (some person).

5. b. The best choice to match *entraron* (enter) is *vinieron adentro* (come in).

6. d. The best match for *el señor* (the gentleman) is *el hombre* (the man).

7. e. The only choice that matches *mercaré* (I shall buy) is *compraré* (I shall buy).

8. a. *La capacidad* (the ability) is the nearest to meaning *el derecho* (the right).

9. c. *Ropa nueva* (new clothing) is nearest in meaning to *vestido nuevo* (new dress).

10. d. *entiendo* (understood) has the same meaning as *comprendo* (understand).

11. a. The choice that most nearly matches *visitar* (to visit) is *viajar a* (to travel to).

12. b. The best choice for *¿Qué tal?* (How is it going?) is *¿Cómo estás?* (How are you?).

13. e. The best match for *aquella ciudad* (that city) is *aquel pueblo* (that town).

14. d. *Cocinaban* (were cooking) most nearly matches *preparaban* (were preparing).

15. c. *Policias* (police) most nearly means the same as *agentes* (agents).

16. e. *El tren* (the train) is the best match for *el ferrocarril* (the railroad) in this context. Choice **d**, *El funicular* (the funicular, or cable car, railroad), although close in meaning, could not be considered a principal means of transport.

17. a. The best match for *caminamos* (we go about) is *andamos* (we walk).

18. b. The best choice to match *arma* (weapon) is *cuchillo* (knife).

19. e. In this context, the choice that most nearly matches the meaning of *hablar* (to speak) is *usar* (to use).

20. a. The correct choice is *vete* (go away) because it most nearly matches the meaning of *quítate* (withdraw).

21. c. In this choice, there is agreement of tense, and the sentence makes sense.

22. b. In this choice, there is correct agreement of number and gender, and the sentence makes sense with respect to the weather.

23. a. This is the right choice because of agreement of person and correct verb form.

24. d. This is the only choice that provides the correct verb form (conditional perfect) and the correct conjunction (*pero* means *but*).

25. d. This is the only choice that makes sense.

26. a. The other choices use an incorrect word, gender, or number.

27. b. In this choice, there is agreement in person, and the correct verb form is used.

28. c. Here, there is agreement of verb form and proper word usage.

29. e. Here, there is agreement of gender (*agua* takes *el* even though it is feminine).

30. c. The choice of verb and number and gender agreement are correct.

31. c. This is the only coherent sentence about Mexico. All the others lack conjunctions or various forms of agreement.

32. d. All the other sentences contain important errors: **a** has a wrong conjugation, **b** has agreement problems, and **c** has the wrong word order.

33. a. This is the only clearly expressed thought: "What is your name?" The others are basically confused combinations of words.

34. b. This is the only sentence without a spelling error. The errors are slight but significant (e.g., *pueda/puede*).

35. c. All the other sentences contain spelling errors and therefore nonexistent words (even though they might sound alike when read aloud).

36. c. This is the only sentence that has correct use of the imperative and no other grammatical or spelling issues.

37. a. This is the only sentence that refers to time in a conventional or logical way. The others show disagreement between tense and time frame: choice **c**, for example, uses the perfect tense in reference to something happening *mañana* (tomorrow).

38. d. The other three sentences misuse subjunctive verbs.

39. b. This is the only grammatically correct sentence.

40. a. This is the only sentence without problems of agreement, accents, or case.

41. c. This is the only choice that is in the subjunctive, correctly conjugated, and grammatically accurate. *Volver* is the word for a person returning somewhere, whereas *devolver* refers to returning or replacing an object.

42. e. The sentence is correct as is.

43. d. This is the correct choice because the two verbs in the third person plural, *abarcan* (cover) and *abrevian* (shorten), agree with the masculine plural subject *manuales* (manuals).

44. e. The sentence is correct as is.

45. b. *Viajamos* (we traveled) is correct because the other verb forms use an incorrect tense or word.

46. e. Some of the other options are based on possible synonyms for the italicized verb, but none is in the correct form.

47. b. The correct choice is *una* (a, an). The others do not agree in gender.

48. d. The appropriate choice to correctly complete the sentence is *tú* (you) because it matches the verb form.

49. c. *Imprescindible*, although it may appear to be a negative term, means important or fundamental. We are looking for the opposite meaning here: It is *innecesario*, or unnecessary, during the summer for people to go to school.

50. b. Phrases such as *pensar en _____* must involve an infinitive after the preposition, not any sort of conjugated form.

Artificial Language

1. d. The word numbered 1, *bonlek*, is the correct translation of the noun *guard*, formed according to Rule 9. The word numbered 2, *zelremot*, is incorrect because it is the past tense, inspected. It should be *zelot*, which is the present singular form of the verb formed according to Rule 6. The word numbered 3, *trenedlekax*, is the correct plural form of the noun *trenedlek* (paper), formed according to Rule 2.

2. b. The word numbered 1, *velle*, is incorrect; it is an adjective that must agree in number and gender with the noun it modifies, according to Rule 3. It should be translated as *velleax*. The word numbered 2, *arlekax*, is correctly translated; it is the plural noun formed from the infinitive *arbar* (to drive), following Rules 2 and 9. The word numbered 3, *huslek*, is an incorrect translation because it is a singular noun that should be a plural formed according to Rule 2.

3. d. The word numbered 1, *yevzof*, is correctly formed; it is the feminine *she* formed from the masculine *he* by attaching the feminine singular suffix according to Rule 1. The word numbered 2, *synet*, is, according to Rule 6, incorrectly translated; it is the plural form of the verb, but the singular form, *synot*, is required here. The word numbered 3, *almanlek*, is correct.

4. e. The word numbered 1, *autileax*, is incorrect because it should be the singular, *autile*, to agree with the noun it modifies, *inspector*, according to Rule 3. The word numbered 2, *zellekax*, is an incorrect translation of *inspector* because it is in the plural form in the Artificial Language; it should be translated *zellek*. The word numbered 3, *vellezof*, is incorrect because it has a feminine singular ending, but it should be in the plural form (following Rule 3) to agree in number and gender with *trenedlekax*.

5. c. The word numbered 1, *volle*, is incorrect. It is an adjective that must agree in gender and number with the noun (Rules 1 and 3); the correct translation is *vollezof*. The word numbered 2, *synremot*, is incorrect because it is translated in the past tense; it should be *synot*, the present tense formed according to Rule 6. The word numbered 3, *tatlekzof*, is correctly translated taking the feminine ending to agree with the female subject of the sentence, *ekaplezof* (girl) (Rule 1).

6. c. The word numbered 1, *bex*, is an incorrect translation of the word *the*; it should be *ric*. The word numbered 2, *synremet*, is incorrect because it is in the plural past tense, and the verb ending should be singular (*synremot*) following Rules 4, 5, and 7. The word numbered 3, *failek*, is a correct translation of the word *country*.

7. a. The word numbered 1, *ekaplekax*, is a correctly formed masculine plural noun (Rule 2). The word numbered 2, *regremet*, is incorrect; although it has the correctly formed past plural verb ending, it is the wrong verb (bordered). It should be *chonremet* (crossed). The word numbered 3, *ricax*, is incorrect; it is the definite article, *the*, with a masculine plural suffix attached; *river* is not plural.

8. d. The word numbered 1, *ekaplek* (boy), is an incorrect translation of the word *man* (*kaplek*). The word numbered 2, *degremot*, is correct; it is the singular past tense form of the verb *degbar* (to shoot), formed according to Rules 4, 5, and 7. The word numbered 3, *yev*, is a correct translation of the word *him*.

9. e. The word numbered 1, *vollezof*, is incorrect; it is a feminine singular adjective, but should be the feminine plural, *vollezofax*, to agree with the noun it modifies, *women* (Rules 2 and 3). The word numbered 2, *kaplekzof*, is incorrect because the noun is in feminine singular form, whereas it should be the feminine plural, *kaplekzofax*, to translate the noun *women* (Rule 2). The word numbered 3, *pohcolle*, is incorrect because it is used as an adverb in the sentence, and it is missing the adverbial ending (Rule 11); it should be *pohcollede*.

10. b. The word numbered 1, *kaplekzof*, while using the appropriate feminine ending, is an incorrect translation of the word *she*. It should be the word for *he*, *yev*, in its feminine form, *yevzof* (Rule 1). The word numbered 2, *synot*, is the correct present singular form of the verb *to be*, *synbar* (Rules 4, 5, and 6). The word numbered 3, *tatlekzof*, is incorrect. *Tatlekzof* is a feminine noun formed from the verb *tatbar* according to Rules 1 and 9; however, the phrase *to spy* should be translated as the unconjugated infinitive *tatbar*.

11. d. The word numbered 1, *avelekax*, is correct; it is the plural noun formed according to Rule 2. The word numbered 2, *degremet*, is the correct past plural of the verb *degbar*, formed according to Rules, 4, 5, and 7. The word numbered 3, *arle*, is incorrect. It has the adjectival suffix *-le* (Rule 10); however, the word is used as a noun in the sentence, so it should take the noun suffix *-lek* (Rule 9).

12. a. The word numbered 1, *mor*, is a correct translation of the word *from*. Because it is a preposition, it requires no special endings. The word numbered 2, *reglek*, is incorrect. The word *border* in the original sentence is an adjective modifying the noun *station*; therefore, the correct translation requires the adjectival ending (Rule 10), and the correct translation would be *regle*. The word numbered 3, *lexot*, is incorrect because the word is a singular noun formed from the verb *lexbar* (to station), but the translation incorrectly adds the singular verb ending; the correct translation is *lexlek* (Rule 9).

13. e. The word numbered 1, *tulremot*, is incorrect because it is conjugated in the past tense; the correct translation is *tulot*, present tense singular (Rules 4 and 6). The word numbered 2, *bonot*, is incorrect because the verb is conjugated in the present tense; the phrase it translates, *to guard*, requires the unconjugated infinitive, *bonbar*, for correct translation. The word numbered 3, *browlekoe*, is incorrect because the noun has the possessive suffix, *-oe* (Rule 12); the word it translates is not a possessive noun, so the correct translation is *browlek*.

14. b. The word numbered 1, *zelbremot*, is an incorrectly formed conjugation of the verb *zelbar*. To conjugate the verb, the verb stem *bar* must be removed from the infinitive (Rule 4); the incorrect *zelbremot* retains the *b* from the stem. The correct form of the verb is *zelremot*. The word numbered 2, *yevaxoe*, is correct; it is the possessive form (*his*) of the pronoun *he*, formed correctly by adding the possessive ending (Rule 12) to the plural form. The word numbered 3, *trenedlek*, is incorrectly formed; it requires the plural ending *-ax* to correctly translate the word *papers* (Rule 2).

15. c. The word numbered 1, *velleax* (those), is an incorrect translation of the word *these*. The word numbered 2, *piret*, is incorrectly translated; it is the plural present conjugation of the verb *pirbar* (to escape). The correct translation is the plural past tense, *piremet* (Rules 4, 5, and 7). The word numbered 3, *lexlek*, is the correct form of a noun formed from a verb (Rule 9).

16. d. The word numbered 1, *cre*, is a correct translation of the word *and*. The word numbered 2, *pohcolleax*, is correctly formed, attaching the negative prefix *poh-* to the word for *legal*, *colle*, to form the adjective *illegal* (*pohcolle*), and adding *ax* to make it plural (Rule 12). The word numbered 3, *trenedlekax*, is the correctly formed plural of the noun *trenedlek*, taking the plural ending *-ax* according to Rule 2.

17. d. The word numbered 1, *synet*, is the correct present plural form of the verb *synbar* (Rules 4, 5, and 6). The word numbered 2, *quea*, is a correct translation of the word *of*. The word numbered 3, *inle*, is an incorrect translation of the adjective *disloyal*; it is lacking the negative prefix *poh-* to form the word meaning disloyal (*pohinle*), from the adjective *inle* (loyal; see Rule 13).

18. b. The word numbered 1, *volleax*, is incorrect. *Volleax* (these) is in the masculine form. Since the sentence is about a feminine subject (women), you must apply Rules 1 and 3, according to which adjectives (such as *these*) modifying a feminine noun (such as *women*) must take the ending *-zof* before taking the plural ending *-ax* (see Rule 2). Accordingly, the correct form for *these* in this sentence would be *vollezofax*.

The word numbered 2, *friget*, is correct. According to Rules 4 and 6, the present tense of a verb is formed by adding the suffix *-et* to the stem of the infinitive when the verb has a plural subject (as is the case in this sentence: *women work*). The word numbered 3, *pohcolledezof*, is incorrect. According to Rule 12, in order to form an adverb from an adjective, you should add the suffix *-de* to the adjectival form. Thus, the adverb *collede* (legally) is formed by adding the suffix *-de* to the adjective *colle* (legal). Next, when the word is negative, it takes the prefix *poh-* (see Rule 13); accordingly, the adverb *collede* takes the prefix *poh-*, thus becoming the negative adverb *pohcollede* (illegally). Finally, the word *pohcollede*, being an adverb, must never take the feminine ending *-zof*. As stated in Rule 11, adverbs do not change their form according to gender. The reason is that adverbs, by definition, modify verbs, which are, also by definition, genderless (see the discussion on verbs and adverbs in the glossary of grammatical terms in Chapter 7).

19. c. The word numbered 1, *pohcolle*, is incorrect. According to the vocabulary lists, *colle* means legal. According to Rule 13, the negative form *pohcolle* (illegal) is formed by adding the negative prefix *poh* to the affirmative. However, the adjective *illegal* is modifying a plural noun (*aliens*) in the sentence. Consequently, the adjective *pohcolle* must take the plural, ending -*ax*, thus forming the word *pohcolleax* (Rules 2 and 3). The word numbered 2, *synet*, is incorrect. *Synet* is the present tense plural, *are*, whereas the sentence has the verb in the past tense, *were*. According to Rules 4 and 7, the past tense is formed by adding the suffix -*rem* to the stem of the infinitive and then adding the suffix -*et* when the verb is in the plural form. Accordingly, the correct translation of *were* would be *synremet*. Lastly, since the sentence has this verb in the negative form, *were not*, the prefix *poh-* must be added to the verb (Rule 13), thus forming *pohsynremet*. The word numbered 3, *liatoax*, is correct. In this sentence, *liatoax* is a past participle, which is formed according to Rule 8. First, the suffix -*to* should be added to the stem of the infinitive to make the verb a past participle. Next, the suffix -*ax* should be added to the past participle because the participle is used as a predicate to modify the plural noun *aliens*.

20. c. The word numbered 1, *pohsynot*, is incorrect. The verb *are* is a plural verb and, consequently, according to Rule 6, it must take the suffix -*et*, rather than the suffix -*ot*. However, the use of the negative prefix (*poh-*) is correct, because, according to Rule 13, the prefix *poh-* should be added to the affirmative form in order to make a word negative. Accordingly, the correct word for *are not* is *pohsynet*. The word numbered 2, *huslekax*, is incorrect. According to the vocabulary lists, *huslek* means *alien*, and according to Rule 2, the plural of a noun is formed by adding the suffix -*ax*, but because the subject of the sentence is feminine (women), the suffix -*zof* must be added to the noun before making it plural (see Rules 1 and 2). Accordingly, the correct word is *huslekzofax*. The word numbered 3, *failek*, is correct. *Failek* is the word that appears in the vocabulary lists for *country*.

21. b. First, the plural noun *men* is formed, according to Rule 2, by adding the suffix -*ax* to the singular form of the noun *kaplek*. Accordingly, the correct word is *kaplekax*. Second, the word *and* (*cre*) is found in the vocabulary lists. Third, the plural noun *women* is formed, according to Rules 1 and 2, by first adding the feminine suffix -*zof* to the singular masculine form of the noun (*kaplek*) and then adding the suffix -*ax* for the plural. Accordingly, the correct word is *kaplekzofax*. Among the incorrect choices, choice **a** incorrectly uses as a suffix the negative prefix *poh-* instead of the feminine suffix -*zof*; choice **c** incorrectly uses the possessive form -*oe* instead of the plural form -*ax*; choice **d** incorrectly uses both the negative *poh-* and the possessive -*oe*; and choice **e** incorrectly uses the negative *poh-* and the article *bex* (a, an).

22. e. First, you must form the present tense of the verb *to guard* (*bonbar*). According to Rules 4 and 6, the present tense of a verb is formed by omitting the infinitive suffix *-bar* and replacing it with the suffix *-et* when the subject is plural. Because the subject of this sentence is plural (*men and women*; i.e., they), the verb should take the plural suffix. Accordingly, the correct form is *bonet*. Second, the article *the* is translated as *ric*, according to the vocabulary lists. Third, the noun *border* (*reglek*) is formed according to Rule 9 by adding the suffix *-lek* to the stem of the verb. Among the incorrect choices, choice **a** incorrectly applies Rule 2 to the verb by adding the suffix *-ax* to the plural verb *bonet*. Rule 2 is used only to form the plurals of nouns, pronouns, adjectives, and articles, not verbs. Choice **b** also incorrectly applies Rule 2 to the verb and, in addition, applies Rule 2 to the noun *reglek* (border), thus incorrectly making it the plural *reglekax* (borders). Choice **c** incorrectly uses the singular form of the verb (*bonot*), and choice **d** incorrectly uses the infinitive form of the verb (*bonbar*).

23. c. First, the word *pohkometleax* (*unfriendly* in the plural form) is formed by applying Rules 2, 3, 10, and 13. Rule 10 tells you that to form an adjective from a noun you should use the suffix *-le*, instead of the suffix *-lek*. Hence, you change the noun *kometlek* (friend), which appears in the vocabulary lists, to the adjective *kometle*. However, because the adjective is negative in the sentence and is modifying the plural noun *aliens*, you must also apply Rule 13 (thus adding the negative prefix *poh-*) and Rules 2 and 3, thus adding the plural suffix *-ax*. Second, the word *huslekax* (aliens) is formed by applying Rule 2, according to which you must add the suffix *-ax* to form the plural of a noun. Among the incorrect choices, choices **a**, **b**, and **e** erroneously apply the rule to form adverbs (Rule 11) to the noun *kometlek*. In addition, choices **b** and **e** make the same error with the noun *huslek*. Choice **d** erroneously applies the plural *-ax* to the noun form *pohkometlek* (nonfriend), rather than to the correct adjectival form (*pohkometle*).

24. c. First, the word *autileax* (*skillful* in the plural form) is formed by applying Rules 2 and 3, according to which the suffix *-ax* must be added to the adjective *autile* (skillful) because it is modifying the plural noun *spies*. Second, the word *tatlekax* (spies) is formed by applying Rules 2, 4, and 9, according to which in order to form a noun from a verb, you should add the suffix *-lek* to the stem of the infinitive, and next, you should add the suffix *-ax* to make the noun plural. Among the incorrect choices, choices **a**, **b**, and **e** incorrectly neglect Rules 2 and 3 by using the singular adjective *autile*. In addition, choice **b** fails to use the correct plural for *spies*; and choices **d** and **e** neglect Rule 9 to form a noun and instead use the infinitive *to spy* (*tatbar*) with the plural ending *-ax* (which, according to Rules 2 and 3, is only for nouns, pronouns, adjectives, and articles).

25. e. First, the pronoun *yevax* (they) is formed according to Rule 2 by adding the plural suffix to the singular pronoun *yev* (he). (Remember that all nouns and pronouns, unless referring to a specifically feminine subject, are assumed to be masculine.) Second, the verb *tulet* (*have* in the plural present tense) is formed according to Rules 4 and 6 by adding the plural suffix *-et* to the stem of the infinitive. Third, the infinitive *zelbar* (to inspect) is found in the vocabulary lists. Among the incorrect choices, choice **a** erroneously adds the plural verb form *-et* to the infinitive *zelbar*, choice **b** erroneously uses the verb in its singular form *tulot*, and choices **c** and **d** erroneously use the past tense *tulremet*; in addition, choice **d** erroneously adds the plural verb ending *-et* to the infinitive *zelbar*.

26. a. First, the adjective *almanleax* is formed by changing the suffix *-lek* in the noun *almanlek* (government) to the adjectival suffix *-le*, thus transforming the noun into the adjective *almanle* (governmental), and then adding the plural suffix *-ax* to the adjective, since adjectives modifying plural nouns must take plural endings (see Rules 2, 3, and 10). Second, the plural noun *trenedlekax* (papers) is formed, according to Rule 2, by adding the plural suffix *-ax* to the singular form of the noun. Among the incorrect choices, choices **b** and **c** erroneously use the singular noun *almanlek* (government), and in addition, choice **b** also erroneously uses the singular noun *trenedlek* (paper); choice **d** erroneously uses the plural noun *almanlekax* (governments); and choice **e** erroneously uses the singular form of the adjective *almanle* (governmental).

27. d. The plural noun *lexlekax* (stations) is formed by first applying Rule 10, according to which in order to form a noun from a verb, you should add the suffix *-lek* to the stem of the verb. Then, apply Rule 2, according to which you must add the suffix *-ax* to form the plural of a noun. Among the incorrect choices, choice **a** incorrectly applies Rule 2 and adds the suffix *-ax* to the infinitive *lexbar*, choice **b** incorrectly applies Rule 12 and adds the possessive suffix *-oe* to the noun *lexlek*, choice **c** incorrectly applies the possessive suffix *-oe* to the infinitive *lexbar*, and choice **e** incorrectly applies Rule 10 to form the adjectival form *lexle* instead of the noun *lexlek*.

28. a. First, the word *volle* means *this* and is found in the vocabulary lists. Second, the word *failekoe* is a possessive form, which is formed according to Rule 12 by adding the suffix *-oe* to the noun *failek* (country), also found in the vocabulary lists. Among the incorrect choices, choices **b** and **d** erroneously add the possessive *-oe* to the adjective *volle*, choices **c** and **d** erroneously omit the possessive in *failek*, and choice **e** erroneously uses an adjectival form (*faile*) instead of the noun *failek*.

29. b. First, the adverb *autilede* (skillfully) is formed, according to Rule 11, by adding the suffix *-de* to the masculine form of the adjective *autile* (which appears in the vocabulary lists). Second, the verb *bontoax* is in the form of a past participle (*guarded*). According to Rule 8, the past participle of a verb is formed by adding the suffix *-to* to the stem of the verb. Also, according to Rule 8, when the participle is used as a predicate with the verb *to be*, it must take the plural form if the noun it modifies is plural. Among the incorrect choices, choices **a** and **d** erroneously add the plural suffix *-ax*, which is NOT used for adverbs; in addition, choices **a** and **d** erroneously use the past tense of the verb rather than the participle. Choice **c** uses the correct adverb (*autilede*), but fails to add the plural ending to the participle. Choice **e** erroneously uses the adverbial ending *-de* to the noun *guard* (*bonlek*), rather than using the participle.

30. b. First, the adjective *vollezofax* (these) is formed, according to Rules 1, 2, and 3, by adding the feminine suffix *-zof* and then the plural suffix *-ax* to the singular form (*volle*). Second, the adjective *inlezofax* (loyal) is formed, according to the same rules, by adding the same suffixes, *-zof* and *-ax*, to the singular form (*inle*). Third, the noun *kaplekzofax* (women) is formed, according to Rules 1 and 2, by adding the suffix *-zof* to the noun *kaplek* (man) and then adding the suffix *-ax* to *kaplekzof* (woman) to make it plural. Among the incorrect choices, choices **a** and **c** incorrectly omit the feminine suffix in the adjective *volleax*; in addition, choice **a** incorrectly omits the plural suffix in the adjective *inlezof*, and choice **c** incorrectly omits both the feminine suffix and the plural suffix in the adjective *inle*. Choice **d** incorrectly omits the plural suffix in the adjective *inlezof*, and choice **e** incorrectly omits both the feminine suffix and the plural suffix in the adjective *inle*.

31. a. *Volle ekaplek pohtulremot bralekax* means *This boy did not have difficulties. Volle ekaplek pohtulremot* is the only one of these expressions that means *this boy did not have.*

32. b. *Yevzof synot bexzof tatlekzof quea velle pohkometle almanlek* means *She is a spy of that unfriendly government. Velle pohkometle almanlek* is the only one of these expressions that properly translates *that unfriendly government.* The adjectives, *velle* and *pohkometle*, are in the correct form, agreeing with the masculine noun, *almanlek* (Rule 3), and the adjective, *pohkometle*, has the correct negative prefix (Rule 13).

33. a. *Yev degremot bexzof pirtozof ekaplekzof* means *He shot an escaped girl.* Only choice **a** correctly translates these words. *Bexzof pirtozof ekaplekzof* is correct because it correctly adds the feminine ending *-zof* to *bex* and to *ekaplek*, making both words feminine. *Pirtozof* is correct because *escaped* is a past participle used as an adjective. If you review Rule 8, to form this, you must add the suffix *-to* to the stem of the verb *pirbar* and then add the suffix *-zof* because the subject is feminine and must agree. The other choices are incorrect because of incorrect translations or lack of agreement with the feminine subject.

34. e. *Kaplekax pirremet mor bex regle lexlek* means *Men escaped from a border station. Mor bex regle lexlek* is the only one of these expressions that properly translates *from a border station*, because the adjective, *regle* (border), is correctly formed from the infinitive, *regbar*, following Rules 9 and 10, and the noun, *lexlek* (station), is correctly formed from the infinitive, *lexbar*, following Rule 9.

35. b. *Ric avele tatlek tulremot liabar ric inle bonlek* means *The enemy spy had to injure the loyal guard. Ric avele tatlek* is the only one of these expressions that properly translates *the enemy spy*, where the adjective *enemy* (avele), is correctly formed from the noun *avelek* (Rule 10), and the noun *spy* (tatlek), is correctly formed from the infinitive *tatbar* using Rule 9.

36. e. *Ric browle chonlek synremot brale* means *The river crossing was difficult. Ric browle chonlek* is the only one of these expressions that properly translates *the river crossing*, because the word *the* is correctly translated; the adjective *browle* has the correct adjectival ending (Rule 10); and the noun, *chonlek*, is correctly formed from the infinitive *chonbar* (Rule 9).

37. c. *Velle arlek pirremot mor ric cublek* means *That driver escaped from the jeep.* Only choice **c** correctly translates these words. Choice **a** is incorrect because the word for *that* is *velle*, not *volle*. Also, *piremot* is misspelled; it should be *pirremot*. Choice **b** is incorrect because *arbar* is in the infinitive, but the noun *driver* (*arlek*) is required. Choice **d** is incorrect because *that* and *driver* are unnecessarily feminine. Remember, if gender is not specified, use the masculine form. Choice **e** is incorrect because the verb *pirremet* is plural but the subject of the sentence is singular.

38. c. *Volleax pohcolleax huslekax pohtulet trenedlekax* means *These illegal aliens do not have papers.* Only choice **c** correctly translates these words. Choice **a** is incorrect because the word for aliens has the feminine suffix *-zof*, although that is not required in this sentence. Choice **b** places the verb in the past tense (*pohtulremet*) but the present tense is required. Choice **d** is incorrect because the verb *pohtulot* is singular, but the subject is plural (aliens). Finally, choice **e** is incorrect because Rule 2 has not been applied to *huslek*; it should be *huslekax*.

39. a. *Ricax lexleax bonlekax tulet degbar aveleax tatlekax* means *The station guards have to shoot enemy spies.* Only choice **a** correctly translates these words. Choice **b** is incorrect because station is an adjective, so according to Rule 10, the suffix *-le* should be added. Choice **c** is incorrect because the article *the* (*ric*) has to agree with the plural subject *guards* (see Rule 3). Choice **d** is incorrect because the word *bonlek* should have the plural suffix *-ax* to agree with the sentence. Choice **e** is incorrect because *bexax* is not the correct translation of the word *the*.

40. b. *Vellezofax autilezofax kaplekzofax synremet bralezofax kalenbar* means *Those skillful women were difficult to identify.* Only choice **b** correctly translates these words. Choice **a** is incorrect because *vollezofax* means *these*, not *those*. Choice **c** is incorrect because the verb *synremot* is singular and the subject is plural (women). Choice **d** is incorrect because even though all the words have the correct feminine suffix added (see Rule 1), they are missing the plural suffix *-ax*. Choice **e** is incorrect because *velle* means *that*, not *those*; according to Rule 3, adjectives, including articles, must agree in gender and number.

41. e. *Vellezof ekaplekzof mor ric failek synot pohinlezof* means *That girl from the country is disloyal.* Only choice **e** correctly translates these words. Choice **a** is incorrect because *kaplekzof* means *woman*, not *girl*. Choice **b** is incorrect because *quea* means *of* and the sentence needs the word *from*. Choice **c** is incorrect because the words *the country* are not feminine, so they do not require the suffix *-zof* (remember, unless gender is specified, use the masculine form). Finally, choice **d** is incorrect because *ekaplekzofax* is plural and the sentence needs the word *girl*, not *girls*.

42. d. *Yevoe autileax bonlekax friget mor bex regle lexlek* means *His skillful guards work from a border station.* Only choice **d** correctly translates these words. Choice **a** is incorrect because the feminine suffix *-zof* has been added unnecessarily. Unless you are told that a word is feminine, you should not add *-zof*. Choice **b** is incorrect because *yevoeax* is not a word; the correct construction according to Rule 12 is *yevaxoe*, which is the word for *their* (masculine plural possessive); the word required here is *his*. Choice **c** is incorrect because the adjective *autile* must agree with the subject (see Rule 3) so it should be *autileax*. Choice **e** is incorrect because *yevaxoe* is the word for *their* (masculine plural possessive) but the word required is *his*.

43. d. *Riczofax bonlekzofax synret pohinlezofax; yevzofax synret tatlekzofax* means *The [female] guards are disloyal; they are spies.* Choices **a** and **e** are incorrect because the adjective is lacking the negative prefix, *poh-* (Rule 13). Choice **b** is incorrect because both the adjective and the pronoun are in the masculine form. Choice **c** is incorrect because the pronoun is in the masculine plural form. In choice **d,** the adjective has the negative prefix (Rule 13), and both the adjective and the pronoun have the feminine plural endings (Rule 2).

44. c. *Velle avele tatlek tulremot chonbar bex browlek* means *That enemy spy had to cross the river.* Choices **a** and **e** are incorrect because they are in the present tense. Choice **b** is incorrect because the singular suffix *-et* has been added to the infinitive, not to the stem. Choice **d** is incorrect because it is the past plural form. Only choice **c** is the past singular verb for *had.*

45. b. *Ricax ekaplekaxoe trenedlekax synret pohcol-leax* means *The boys' papers are illegal.* In choices **a** and **d**, the noun is misspelled. In choices **c** and **e**, the adjective is singular, but it should be plural. In choice **b**, the possessive noun *ekaplekaxoe* has the proper plural ending (Rule 2), and the correct possessive suffix; *pohcolleax* has the proper negative prefix (Rule 13).

46. c. *Ric zellek frigot inlede* means *The inspector works loyally.* Choices **a** and **e** are incorrect because the word *zelot* is a conjugation of the verb, not the noun form. Choice **b** is incorrect because *inle* is the adjectival, not the adverbial, form. Choice **d** is incorrect because *zellekax* is the plural form of the noun. In choice **c**, the noun, *zellek*, is in the correct masculine form of the noun, and is properly formed from the infinitive, *zelbar* (Rule 9); further, the adverb, *inlede*, has been formed properly with the adverbial ending according to Rule 11.

47. c. *Vellezofax pohcollezofax huslekzofax synremet liatozofax* means *Those [female] illegal aliens were injured.* Choice **a** is incorrect because both the article and the past participle should have the plural suffix *-ax*. Choice **b** is incorrect because *velleaxzof* and *liatoaxzof* are not the correct constructions. According to Rules 3 and 8, respectively, it should be *vellezofax* and *liatozofax*. Choice **d** is incorrect because Rule 8 shows that the suffix *-to* should precede any suffixes indicating gender or number. Finally, choice **e** is incorrect because both words are lacking the feminine suffix *-zof*.

48. a. *Riczofax huslekzofax pohsynet kometlekzofax quea ricax huslekax* means *The [female] aliens are not friends of the [male] aliens.* Choice **b** is incorrect because according to Rule 13, *poh-* is a prefix, not a suffix. Choice **c** is incorrect because the word *aliens* should be masculine, not feminine, so it should not have the suffix *-zof*. Choice **d** is incorrect because *pohsynot* is the negative singular present tense verb, but it should be plural. Choice **e** is incorrect because *pohsynremet* is the negative plural past tense verb.

49. b. *Riczofax reglezofax bonlekzofax poharremet ricax cublekax* means *The [female] border guards did not drive the jeeps.* Choice **a** is incorrect, because *poharemet* is an incorrect spelling of *poharremet*. According to Rules 4 and 7, you take the root of *arbar*, which is *ar-*, and add the suffix *-rem*. Thus it should be *poharremet*. Choice **c** is incorrect because *reglekzofax* is a noun, but should be an adjective, which requires the suffix *-le* (see Rule 10). Choice **d** is incorrect because the adjective *regleax* is missing the feminine suffix *-zof*. Finally, choice **e** is incorrect because *poharremot* is singular, but the sentence requires the plural *poharremet*.

50. e. *Vollezofax avelezofax tatlekzofax synet autile-zofax cre pohinlezofax* means *These [female] enemy spies are skillful and disloyal.* Choice **a** is incorrect because *avelekzofax* is the noun *enemies.* What is required is an adjective, so the suffix *-le* should have been used according to Rule 10. Choice **b** is incorrect because *pohinlekzofax* is misspelled; there should be no *k* in this word. Choice **c** is incorrect because *avelezof* is the feminine singular form, but the feminine plural is required. Choice **d** is incorrect because *avelede* is formed like an adverb, not like an adjective as required by the sentence.

► Scoring

A good score on the reasoning and language sections of the test is necessary to be considered for the oral interview. Each question on the test is weighted according to DHS standards. It is a good idea to total the number of correct answers to get a complete picture of your strengths and weaknesses.

You have probably seen improvement between your first practice exam score and this one, but if you didn't improve as much as you'd like, here are some options:

- **If 60% of your answers were incorrect**, reconsider taking the Border Patrol Exam at this time. A good idea would be to take more practice tests.
- **If 60–70% of your answers were correct**, you need to work as hard as you can to improve your skills. Check out the LearningExpress book *501 Challenging Logic and Reasoning Problems*. If your difficulty is with Spanish, try some of the books from the "Resources" part of Chapter 9, "Checking Your Spanish Proficiency." If you have trouble with the Artificial Language, review Chapter 8, "Using the Artificial Language Manual" and the Artificial Language Manual itself in Chapter 7. It might also be helpful to ask friends and family to make up mock test questions and quiz you on them.
- **If 70–85% of your answers were correct**, you could still benefit from additional work by going back to the instructional chapters.
- **If 85% of your answers were correct**, that's great! That kind of score should make you a good candidate for a Border Patrol Agent job. Don't lose your edge, though; keep studying right up to the day before the exam.

There's an old joke that goes like this: In New York City, a visitor stops someone on the street and asks, "How do I get to Carnegie Hall?" The other person answers, "Practice."

The key to success in almost any pursuit is to prepare for all you're worth. By taking the practice exams in this book, you've made yourself better prepared than other people who may be taking the exam with you. You've diagnosed where your strengths and weaknesses lie and learned how to deal with the various kinds of questions that will appear on the test. So go into the exam with confidence, knowing that you're ready and equipped to do your best.

NOTES

NOTES

NOTES

NOTES

NOTES

NOTES

NOTES